What Should Banks Do?

D0743646

What Should Banks Do?

ROBERT E. LITAN

THE BROOKINGS INSTITUTION
Washington, D.C.

Library of Congress Cataloging-in-Publication data:

Litan, Robert E., 1950–
   What should banks do?
   Includes index.
   1. Banks and banking—United States.   I. Title.
HG2491.L58   1987   332.1′0973   87-18235
ISBN 0-8157-5270-9
ISBN 0-8157-5269-5 (pbk.)

9 8 7 6 5 4 3 2 1

THE BROOKINGS INSTITUTION is an independent organization devoted to nonpartisan research, education, and publication in economics, government, foreign policy, and the social sciences generally. Its principal purposes are to aid in the development of sound public policies and to promote public understanding of issues of national importance.

The Institution was founded on December 8, 1927, to merge the activities of the Institute for Government Research, founded in 1916, the Institute of Economics, founded in 1922, and the Robert Brookings Graduate School of Economics and Government, founded in 1924.

The Board of Trustees is responsible for the general administration of the Institution, while the immediate direction of the policies, program, and staff is vested in the President, assisted by an advisory committee of the officers and staff. The by-laws of the Institution state: "It is the function of the Trustees to make possible the conduct of scientific research, and publication, under the most favorable conditions, and to safeguard the independence of the research staff in the pursuit of their studies and in the publication of the results of such studies. It is not a part of their function to determine, control, or influence the conduct of particular investigations or the conclusions reached."

The President bears final responsibility for the decision to publish a manuscript as a Brookings book. In reaching his judgment on the competence, accuracy, and objectivity of each study, the President is advised by the director of the appropriate research program and weighs the views of a panel of expert outside readers who report to him in confidence on the quality of the work. Publication of a work signifies that it is deemed a competent treatment worthy of public consideration but does not imply endorsement of conclusions or recommendations.

The Institution maintains its position of neutrality on issues of public policy in order to safeguard the intellectual freedom of the staff. Hence interpretations or conclusions in Brookings publications should be understood to be solely those of the authors and should not be attributed to the Institution, to its trustees, officers, or other staff members, or to the organizations that support its research.

Foreword

AMERICAN financial institutions and markets are undergoing revolution-
ary change. New financial instruments are being developed at a dizzying
pace, spurred on by rapid changes in technology. Markets that were
once segmented by law and by custom are breaking down. With interest
rates on deposits no longer controlled, banks and thrift institutions now
actively compete with other financial institutions for funds. Barriers to
bank and thrift expansion across state lines are gradually falling.

In *What Should Banks Do?* Robert E. Litan examines the issues
raised in the current debate over the major remaining financial market
barrier—the legal segmentation between banks and other financial and
nonfinancial enterprises. Litan argues that a number of forces, notably
continuing technological advances and deregulation at the state level,
will inevitably erode this barrier. This process will bring both benefits
and risks to American consumers and taxpayers. Accordingly, he argues
that the central challenge facing federal policymakers is to structure the
way in which financial product-line barriers are removed so that benefits
are maximized and the risks limited.

Litan discusses two broad approaches for meeting this challenge.
Both would allow banking organizations to diversify their product and
service offerings through holding companies. But in one fundamental
respect they differ. Under the first alternative, bank subsidiaries could
operate as they now do, collecting insured deposits and relending them
to customers, while operating parallel affiliates engaged in other financial
(and possibly nonfinancial) businesses. The various risks posed by these
broader bank powers would be addressed piecemeal through regulation.
The second alternative—"narrow banking"—would restrict the banking
entities of highly diversified organizations to investing insured
deposits in safe and liquid securities, notably U.S. Treasury issues and
securities guaranteed by the federal government. Lending by these
diversified institutions would be divorced from deposit taking, and

funded instead through the uninsured securities markets. Litan favors this second approach to financial product deregulation, although he argues that the first approach, too, would produce social benefits that outweigh the risks.

Robert E. Litan is a senior fellow in the Brookings Economic Studies program. He is grateful to many persons who read all or significant parts of the manuscript and provided many helpful criticisms, suggestions, and comments, including Richard C. Aspinwall, Samuel Chase, Robert W. Crandall, Anthony Downs, Robert A. Eisenbeis, Robert Eisenmenger, Tamar Frankel, Thomas F. Huertas, Richard Kopcke, Richard Levin, Merton J. Peck, Stephen A. Rhoades, Alice M. Rivlin, James Tobin, and Clifford M. Winston. In addition, he benefited from comments at seminars hosted by staff economists at the Federal Reserve Board, the Federal Reserve Bank of Boston, and the Federal Reserve Bank of New York. He further appreciates the extensive research assistance of Janet Chakarian, Theodore Correl, and Kim Orchen. Finally, he thanks Margaret Oosterman for editing the manuscript, Victor M. Alfaro and Jonathan E. Lubick for checking it for factual accuracy, and Jacquelyn G. Sanks for handling many drafts in word processing. Alice Fins prepared the index.

This study was supported by a grant from the Andrew W. Mellon Foundation. Brookings is grateful for that assistance.

The views expressed in the study are those of the author and should not be ascribed to any of the persons or organizations acknowledged above, or to the trustees, officers, or other staff members of the Brookings Institution.

BRUCE K. MAC LAURY
President

July 1987
Washington, D.C.

Contents

1. Introduction   1

2. The U.S. Financial System: A Historical Account   8

An Overview of Banks and Other Financial Institutions *8*
Banks and the Development of Financial Services *12*
Constraining Banks *25*
The Crumbling of Bank Regulation *33*

3. Benefits from Financial Product Diversification   60

Benefits from Enhanced Competition *61*
Economies of Scope *74*
Activity Diversification *81*

4. The Risks of Financial Product Deregulation   99

Financial System Risks *99*
Aggregate Concentration *118*
Specific Abuses *131*

5. Policy Alternatives   144

The Case for Structural Separation *145*
Reducing the Risks of Financial Product Diversification
   Piecemeal *148*
A Comprehensive Approach to Financial Product
   Diversification *164*
Conclusion *189*

Appendixes

A. Distinguishing Benefits of Added Competition from
Economies of Scope *190*
B. Estimating the Reduction in Risk from Financial Product
Diversification *193*

Index   199

Tables

2-1. Net Interest Margin and Loan Loss Provisions for Banks, 1980–85   48

2-2. List of Permissible Nonbank Activities for Bank Holding Companies, 1971–86   52

2-3. Powers of Banks in Foreign Countries   56

2-4. Authorized Activities of State-Chartered Banks in Selected States   57

3-1. Market Statistics for Financial Service Industries   64

3-2. Measures of Securities Underwriting Concentration in the U.S. and European Securities Markets, 1980–85   66

3-3. Sample List of Major Diversified Financial Service Firms   79

3-4. Coefficients of Variation (CV) and Correlation Coefficients (CR) for Banking of After-Tax Earnings for Selected Industries, Selected Years, 1953–82   86

3-5. Coefficients of Variation of Pair-Wise Combinations of Banks and Other Selected Financial Activities, 1962–82   88

3-6. Composition of Estimated Efficient Portfolios, 1965–82   92

3-7. Composition of Estimated Efficient Portfolios, 1973–82   93

4-1. Means and Coefficients of Variation of After-Tax Earnings for Bank Holding Companies and Their Subsidiary Banks, 1978–84   106

4-2. Coefficients of Variation of the Ten Riskiest Banks and Their Holding Companies from Table 4-1 (Excluding Continental Illinois Corporation), 1978–84   108

4-3. Entry by Nonbanking Firms into Banking, 1977–85   114

4-4. Ranking of the World's Twenty Largest Banking Organizations, 1970, 1986   126

4-5. Five-Firm Bank Concentration Ratio and GNP Growth for Six Major Industrialized Countries, 1950–85   129

Figures

2-1. Financial Intermediaries and Brokers   9

2-2. Percentage Distribution of Assets of Financial Intermediaries, Selected Years, 1835–1945   18

2-3. Transaction Media, 1970–85   36

2-4. Providers of Mortgage Credit, Selected Years, 1965–85   42

2-5. Providers of Credit to Nonfinancial Businesses, Selected Years, 1965–86   43

2-6. Providers of Consumer Credit, Selected Years, 1965–85   44

2-7. U.S. Banks' Share of Short- and Intermediate-Term Credit Extended to Domestic Nonfinancial Corporations, 1952–85   45

2-8. Percentage Distribution of Assets of Financial Institutions, Selected Years, 1946–85   46

3-1. Risk and Returns of Selected Financial Activities, 1965–82   90

4-1. Performance Measures for the Banking Industry, 1972–85   101

4-2. Price-Earnings Multiples, 1979–85   121

4-3. Percentage of Total Bank Deposits Held by the Ten Largest
U.S. Banks, 1940–85   122

4-4. Concentration of Domestic Deposits among the Fifty Largest
U.S. Banks, 1980, 1985   123

4-5. Shares of Total Deposits of the World's 500 Largest Banks Held
by the U.S. and Foreign Banks, Selected Years, 1970–85   125

5-1. Differentials between Commercial Paper and CD Interest Rates   180

A-1. Benefits of Additional Competition and Lower Cost Entry in an
Imperfectly Competitive Market   191

B-1. Hypothetical Diversification Opportunities Open to Bank
Holding Companies in a Deregulated Environment   196

CHAPTER ONE

Introduction

NOT LONG AGO the question posed by this book's title—*What Should Banks Do?*—yielded a single, straightforward answer. Most banks were primarily limited to accepting deposits and extending loans; to conducting business in their home states or even home counties; and to paying interest on deposits at rates no higher than federally authorized ceilings. Thrift institutions—financial intermediaries chartered to channel consumer savings into financing home ownership—were subject to similar restrictions. Dating largely from the Depression and strengthened by certain post–World War II legislation, the various limitations were designed to ensure the safety and soundness of depository institutions, to prevent conflicts of interest that could distort credit allocation, and to minimize aggregations of wealth and political power.

Two economic forces have eroded this tidy legal framework. *Inflation* brought down deposit interest rate limits by fueling the explosion of money market mutual funds, which by the early 1980s were severely threatening the continued viability of the bank and thrift industries. For this reason, Congress and federal regulators were forced to remove deposit interest rate controls.

Rapid advances in information and computer-related technologies have also contributed to eroding the Depression-era limitations. Restrictions against geographic expansion by banking organizations make little sense and are easily circumvented when institutions and other traders instantaneously buy and sell assets around the world. Similarly, the legal barriers preventing banks and nonbank financial organizations from competing in the same lines of business are becoming obsolete, at least in economic terms. As Walter Wriston, former chairman of Citicorp, has observed, the "business" of firms in the financial services industry is providing, storing, and communicating information.[1] Banks provide and store loan and deposit balances; insurance companies keep track of

---

1. Walter B. Wriston, *Risk and Other Four-Letter Words* (Harper and Row, 1986).

1

sums they owe to policyholders under certain contingencies (accidents, illnesses, and deaths); and securities firms arrange and record transactions involving financial instruments. As the costs of data storage and retrieval have fallen, firms in each of these "informational" businesses find it increasingly attractive and sensible to engage in the others as well.

Not surprisingly, the new economic realities are motivating different types of financial service firms—and their lawyers—to search for loopholes in a legal framework that market developments are rendering obsolete in order to expand into new markets and to offer new services. To date, however, financial product expansion has largely been one-sided: nonbanking firms have discovered ingenious ways to engage in banking, but banks and thrifts have had more difficulty diversifying into other lines of business. Over time, this disparity should disappear. States will gradually expand the authorized activities of their state-chartered depositories. Such expansion should eventually impel Congress to react by liberalizing the powers of federally chartered banks and thrifts or their holding companies.

However, it is unlikely that the federal barriers preventing banks and other organizations from competing in the same activities will be significantly relaxed any time soon. Over the past three years, Congress has considered but failed to enact legislation that would modestly expand bank holding companies' powers. The legislative deadlock has not been unexpected. To end the debate over expanded bank powers, lawmakers must choose between powerful financial interests—the banking industry on the one hand and the insurance, securities, and real estate industries on the other. No wonder that few lawmakers have been eager to enter the fray.

This study attempts to take advantage of the hiatus in federal legislative activity to address the controversial and thus far unresolved policy issues surrounding financial product deregulation. To be sure, other issues relating to financial institutions now on the public policy agenda are also important. Reforming the deposit insurance system is critical, considering the recent dramatic increases in bank and thrift failure rates. The barriers to interstate banking also continue to be removed, despite protests in various quarters.

Nevertheless, this book gives special attention to the range of permissible activities for financial organizations, particularly for depository intermediaries, because of the fundamental role that financial institutions play in the economy. As intermediaries between savers and investors, financial institutions make possible the channeling of surplus funds accumulated by individuals and businesses toward their most productive uses elsewhere in the economic system. Together, the various types of financial service firms today hold over $5 trillion in private financial assets, and their services account for approximately 15 percent of the nation's annual gross national product.[2] Clearly, with such large sums at stake, which activities these institutions are permitted to carry out and under what conditions are central issues that merit attention.

Market forces will play a central role in the resolution of these issues. As just suggested, continuing technological developments affecting the financial services industries and competition among the states, in the absence of inhibiting federal legislation, will inevitably erode over time whatever legal barriers remain between banks and nonbank organizations. The empirical evidence surveyed in subsequent chapters of this book suggests that this process should be allowed to occur, perhaps accelerated. Allowing banking organizations to enter other financial businesses from which they are barred would modestly increase competition in those businesses and therefore benefit consumers. Eliminating existing financial product-line barriers would also permit diversified financial organizations to realize "economies of scope," cost savings from jointly producing and delivering similar services and products. And perhaps most important, financial product deregulation would allow banking and thrift organizations to better diversify their risks and therefore to strengthen their financial positions and reduce their exposure to failure.

Nevertheless, if not properly guided or constrained, easing financial product-line restrictions could permit some risk-seeking organizations— particularly the larger financial firms most likely to diversify broadly in a fully deregulated environment—to expose their depositories and the federal agencies insuring them to greater financial risks. An environment permitting liberal financial product diversification could also allow financial managers to exploit conflicts of interest and could lead to excessive aggregate concentration of wealth and power. A central challenge confronting federal policymakers—which this study addresses—is to develop mechanisms that limit these risks, while allowing society to reap the gains of financial product diversification.

2. U.S. Task Group on Regulation of Financial Services, *Blueprint for Reform: The Report of the Task Group on Regulation of Financial Services* (Government Printing Office, 1984), p. 16.

What form should these ground rules take? One minimal requirement widely agreed upon is to oblige diversified financial conglomerates to wall off their banking and nonbanking activities by conducting them through separate, albeit affiliated, corporations. Most regulators prefer separating banking from nonbanking activities because it simplifies their jobs and eliminates jurisdictional overlaps. Separation may also help prevent conflicts of interest from infecting bank loan decisions. Perhaps most important, separation is designed to reduce the chances that losses in nonbank activities could impair the soundness of insured banks and thrifts.

During its first term, the Reagan administration offered Congress a financial product deregulation package that followed the separation model. Specifically, the legislation proposed that more broadly defined "financial holding companies" be allowed to engage in virtually any financial activity. In late 1984, the Senate passed a stripped-down version of the administration's proposal, but the House refused to act. The legislative stalemate continued into the 1986 congressional session and remains today, despite growing recognition among financial market participants, regulators, and many legislators that a fundamental over-haul of the nation's financial services laws is long overdue.

Nevertheless, the continuing deadlock in Congress reflects deep-seated conflicts among well-identified financial interests, as well as a certain skepticism about the sufficiency of separation requirements to address the fundamental dangers that further financial product deregula-tion is perceived to pose. Many, for example, question whether, in practice, depositories—particularly major banks—would let their trou-bled affiliates sink into bankruptcy and are therefore fearful that financial product deregulation could diminish the safety and soundness of the banking system. Others are concerned that allowing depository institu-tions to affiliate with a broad range of other business activities would erode a long-standing tradition in this country of separating banking from commerce.

A fundamental theme of this study, however, is that banks and other financial and nonfinancial institutions will continue to find ways of diversifying the financial services they offer. Unless Congress affirma-tively steps in to redraw clear distinctions between different types of financial institutions—a highly unlikely event—the only relevant policy question that remains is what legal and regulatory framework, apart from corporate separateness requirements, should best govern this diversification process.

One approach is to address each of the concerns raised by further financial product deregulation piecemeal, albeit within a holding company structure. To prevent diversified financial organizations from growing excessively large or accumulating too much economic power, aggregate size limitations may be placed on permissible mergers involving banking and nonbanking organizations. To deter conflicts of interest, banks may be prohibited from lending funds to affiliates or their customers. To contain the risks to the safety and soundness of the banking system, the government may want to require those banks that engage in activities not traditionally associated with "banking" to be more strongly capitalized than other banks or to be subject to more intensive supervision. Congress and federal regulators are already moving in this direction. Rocked by the rising numbers of bank and thrift failures, the federal bank regulatory agencies have recently increased capital requirements for insured depositories and have proposed that those requirements be tied to the amount of risk that institutions assume. Together with Congress, the regulatory agencies are studying whether also to tie deposit insurance to the risks of bank and thrift activities.

Finally, the separation requirements themselves can be significantly strengthened. Banks and their nonbank affiliates can be required to conduct business under different names, to operate out of different offices, and to be run by different managers and directors. The Federal Deposit Insurance Corporation (FDIC) recently required this "bona fide" subsidiary approach for those state-chartered banks it supervises (non-members of the Federal Reserve System) that are allowed under their state laws to deal in and underwrite corporate securities. The FDIC has also proposed that all insured banks be required to conduct insurance underwriting and real estate development activities, if the states in which they do business permit them this freedom, in strictly separated subsidiaries.

There is a second, more comprehensive and ultimately more desirable approach, however, to financial product deregulation, which could break the existing congressional deadlock by fully answering each of the concerns that opponents of expanded bank powers have raised. It lies in splitting the transactions functions from the intermediation functions that depositories belonging to highly diversified financial service firms perform.

Specifically, financial holding companies could be authorized to engage in a broad range of financial (or even nonfinancial) activities only if their depository subsidiaries invest deposit funds exclusively in low-risk and highly liquid assets, such as government securities. Financial conglomerates would extend loans through separate corporate affiliates funded, like other commercial enterprises, through combinations of uninsured equity and debt. The splitting of deposit taking and lending would be *optional*: it would apply only to those depository organizations that want to engage in a broader range of businesses than bank holding companies are currently allowed to enter. Those bank and thrift holding companies that do not seek to extend their activities would continue to be able to fund their loans with insured deposits.

Divorcing deposit-taking from risk-bearing activities performed by depositories—so-called safe or narrow banking—has much to recommend it. It would eliminate the concern that in a fully deregulated environment depositors' funds either would be used to bail out "risky" nonbank activities or unfairly channeled to customers of nonbank affiliates. The proposal would also address concerns that highly diversified financial organizations would accumulate or control excessive amounts of economic resources. Fears of both conflict of interest and undue concentration primarily stem from the fact that deposit insurance allows banks to gather large pools of funds and thereby to exercise significant control over the allocation of credit. If banks in highly diversified organizations could not fund their loans with insured deposits, these fears would not be warranted.

The following chapters explore the legal and economic underpinnings of the various policy alternatives. Chapter 2 begins with a historical overview, describing the origins and development of specialized financial institutions. This specialized structure is crumbling because of inflation, advances in technology, and growing competition among the states, forces that have already eroded interest rate controls and barriers to banks' geographic expansion.

Chapter 3 examines three potential benefits of the continuing breakdown of financial product-line restrictions. The chapter concludes that because most activities into which banks and thrifts want entry are already competitive, the least significant benefits lie in enhanced competition. Some gains may result from economies of scope that diversified financial service firms could realize by offering multiple services. However, the largest social benefits should accrue from the smoothing of earnings patterns that activity diversification will permit. Indeed, calculations based on profit data published by the Internal Revenue Service suggest that the typical bank or bank holding company could substantially cut the variability of its earnings (while keeping average earnings constant) in a fully deregulated environment.

Chapter 4 surveys the risks of financial product diversification. It finds that the risks to the safety and soundness of the banking system from financial product diversification cannot easily be dismissed. However, expansion into banking by firms outside the industry will probably pose greater safety-related risks than activity diversification by existing bank and thrift organizations. The chapter further suggests that while added financial product diversification may produce an increasing number of larger organizations, there is little evidence that this result will lead to serious social, political, or economic harm. The chapter concludes that most of the alleged potential conflicts of interest to which opponents of financial product deregulation have pointed can adequately be handled under existing law. However, supplemental measures may be required to deter certain remaining potential abuses.

Chapter 5 concludes the study by outlining two basic policy frameworks for minimizing each risk identified in chapter 4, while preserving the social benefits that financial product-line competition will eventually produce. Either approach—piecemeal reform or a comprehensive plan requiring separation of deposit-taking and lending functions in diversified financial organizations—would satisfy this objective. The challenge for policymakers will be to act decisively to maximize the benefits of financial product diversification, while limiting its risks, before the rapid changes in the financial services industries make it too late to do so.

CHAPTER TWO

The U.S. Financial System: A Historical Account

EXAMINING history is often useful in seeking solutions to controversial policy questions. Financial product deregulation raises policy issues that are well-suited to this type of exercise. Reviewing the development of financial institutions and services in the United States reveals trends and forces that overshadow the current narrow debate over the scope of bank powers. Market forces, abetted by competition among states, have consistently frustrated federal government attempts to control and compartmentalize the activities of banking organizations and their competitors. Continuing advances in technology will add to this frustration. The critical challenge facing federal policymakers, therefore, is not so much whether to constrain the activities of financial organizations, but whether to structure the process of continuing financial product diversification so that it best serves society.

This chapter gives the historical foundation for this conclusion. It outlines the various functions of financial institutions and the reasons for regulating them, banks in particular. The chapter then traces the efforts to compartmentalize the financial services sector in the United States and describes the countervailing forces that have largely defeated those efforts over three successive periods: the colonial era through 1933; 1934 through 1970; and the years since 1970.

An Overview of Banks and Other Financial Institutions

Financial services arise where saving and investing are conducted as separate activities and where savers are different from investors. In primitive societies, even those where commodities (such as gold or silver) are used as media of exchange, individuals fund their investments from their current incomes and past savings. In more developed econ-

Figure 2-1. *Financial Intermediaries and Brokers*

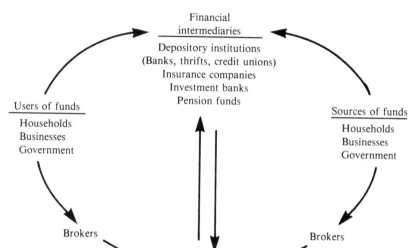

omies, however, different economic agents perform saving and investing. Savers with surplus funds lend to or join hands with (through equity
participation) investors willing to assume risks and to undertake new
productive activities. The more efficient the matching process, the faster
an economy will grow.

As shown in figure 2-1, two alternative types of financial institutions
help channel funds from surplus-spending sources of funds (savers) to
deficit-spending users of funds (investors). *Dealers* or *brokers* match
savers with investors directly or indirectly, or each with an intermediary
institution. Securities brokers and underwriters, for example, assist
corporations and governmental units in raising capital by distributing
their obligations directly to securities investors. Insurance brokers aid
this matching process indirectly by bringing insurance purchasers together with insurance underwriters, who place surplus monies not
required for payouts with ultimate deficit-spending units.

Unlike brokers, who take little or no risk in their matching activities,
financial intermediaries make it their business to assume risk. An
intermediary operates by issuing claims on itself to sources of funds and
lending the proceeds to capital users. In developed economies, a variety
of specialized intermediaries has arisen. Commercial banks and thrift
institutions (those organized primarily to finance real estate and construc-

tion), for example, use deposits placed with them by firms and individuals to make loans to consumers, firms, and homeowners. Insurance companies place funds from the sale of insurance contracts (or promises to make payments if certain events occur) in equities, bonds, and mortgages. Pension funds make similar investments with the funds entrusted to them by individuals planning their retirements (and by corporations on their behalf).

Financial intermediaries are able to perform their functions by collecting large pools of funds. This accumulation allows intermediaries to diversify the risks of their investments and to take advantage of economies of scale in collecting and assessing financial information in extending loans and purchasing financial instruments. Thanks to the "law of large numbers," intermediaries can assume that payment on only a small fraction of their liabilities—deposits for banks and thrifts, payment obligations for pension funds and insurance companies—will be required any given day or week. Accordingly, these financial institutions can invest the bulk of their funds in assets that may be illiquid, such as traditional commercial loans, which usually promise greater returns than short-term low-risk financial obligations. In this way, financial intermediaries are generally able to "transform" their demand or short-maturity liabilities to their depositors or policyholders into longer term, less liquid, and higher yielding assets, the obligations of their borrowers. This transformation promotes economic growth, stimulating investment by reducing the cost of credit and encouraging saving by widening investment opportunities for spending units with surplus funds.[1]

Historically, banks have been viewed as "special" intermediaries because they are the only type of financial institution that can *create* funds to be channeled to capital users.[2] The original "banks" were sixteenth century goldsmiths who learned to profit from the gold placed with them for safekeeping by lending a fraction of their total gold deposits for short periods to other merchants. By the eighteenth century, banks in Europe and in the American colonies discovered that they need not loan out gold itself, but instead could keep it in reserve and issue bank notes redeemable in gold (or other metal "specie"). In this fashion, early

    1. See Tim S. Campbell, *Financial Institutions, Markets, and Economic Activity* (McGraw-Hill, 1982), pp. 246–74.

    2. For a recent comprehensive statement that banks continue to be "special" today, see *Federal Reserve Bank of Minneapolis, Annual Report, 1982: Are Banks Special?*

banks were able to create money, an attractive substitute for gold or government-issued currency, and to lend it to merchants, their primary customers.[3] These bank notes circulated among third parties as money. Banks became payments processors as well, transferring notes among themselves and later—through clearinghouses and correspondent relationships—the checking account deposits of their customers.

Banks found that their dual functions of managing payments and providing intermediation were a mixed blessing. Their ability to create money enabled them to dominate financial intermediation in the United States at least until the middle of the twentieth century. But this same ability also motivated the states and federal government to subject banks to restrictive regulation.

The first and most important motivation for bank regulation has been to ensure the *safety and soundness* of the banking and monetary system. Although banks enhance the public's liquidity,[4] they also expose the economy at large to a serious risk of instability. By definition, a bank's primary liabilities (demand deposits) are due at any time, while its principal assets (loans) are not liquid. If many bank depositors suddenly and simultaneously convert their demand deposits to specie or currency, the money supply can implode. Banks would have to cease new lending and refuse to renew maturing loans. The United States experienced major financial panics in the late 1800s and early 1900s for precisely this reason.[5]

The potential instability of the banking system was vividly demonstrated by the bank runs in the midst of the Depression. President Franklin D. Roosevelt was forced to declare a "bank holiday" in March 1933 to stem a massive nationwide run. Congress responded by establishing federal deposit insurance, which removed the incentives for depositors to withdraw their funds on the slightest fear or rumor that their bank may not be safe. Deposit insurance has since worked well to preserve the stability of the banking system, even in the face of major

---

3. For excellent histories of modern banking, see Bray Hammond, *Banks and Politics in America from the Revolution to the Civil War* (Princeton University Press, 1957); and John Kenneth Galbraith, *Money: Whence It Came, Where It Went* (Penguin, 1975), pp. 28–76.

4. See Douglas W. Diamond and Philip H. Dybvig, "Banking Theory, Deposit Insurance and Bank Regulation," *Journal of Business,* vol. 59 (January 1986), pp. 55–68.

5. Financial panics also occurred in earlier periods when holders of bank notes rushed to demand specie.

economic shocks.[6] Nevertheless, deposit insurance has not eliminated the need for regulation to ensure the safety and soundness of the banking system. To the contrary, it has underscored the importance of regulation to minimize the exposure of the deposit insurance agencies, and ultimately the federal Treasury, to massive losses stemming from unwise and risky investments made by banks.[7]

The second motivation for bank regulation has been to ensure that *credit is fairly and honestly allocated*. Banks have evolved as major sources of credit, using funds deposited with them for safekeeping. Without some kind of regulatory supervision, some banks could take unfair advantage of their unique position as guardians of deposits (now federally insured) to channel credit on other than strictly neutral economic criteria—that is, the creditworthiness of borrowers and the likelihood that loans will be repaid with interest on a timely basis. As a result, an extensive system of federal and state supervision has been erected to prevent bank directors, officers, and employees from defrauding or stealing from depositors and from exploiting conflicts of interest in extending loans to favored interests, including affiliated enterprises.

The last motivation for bank regulation has been to ensure that *banking organizations do not grow too large, thus too economically or politically powerful*. This fear of aggregate concentration, among other factors, prompted many states to restrict the branching authority of banks. It has continued to restrain Congress from authorizing nationwide interstate banking.

Each of these three justifications for regulating banks has also been invoked at various times for keeping them from ranging outside their original limited activities—issuing notes (backed by specie, and later, by government securities), accepting deposits, and extending loans.

Banks and the Development of Financial Services

In the United States, many banks originally had little interest in engaging in other activities. But as the American economy grew, its

6. This fact has been recognized across a broad spectrum of economists, from John Kenneth Galbraith, in *The Great Crash, 1929,* 2d ed. (Houghton Mifflin, 1961), p. 170, to Milton Friedman and Anna Jacobson Schwartz, in their classic *A Monetary History of the United States, 1867–1960* (Princeton University Press for National Bureau of Economic Research, 1963), p. 434.

7. See, for example, Mark J. Flannery, "Deposit Insurance Creates a Need for Bank Regulation," *Federal Reserve Bank of Philadelphia Business Review,* January–February 1982, pp. 17–20.

individuals and corporations developed more sophisticated financial needs—for insurance and securities, as well as traditional banking services. Banks responded by diversifying into other financial activities in the late nineteenth and early twentieth centuries. This movement was halted in the Depression with the passage of the Glass-Steagall Act, which divorced commercial from investment banking. Three decades later, Congress broadened its separation requirements by strictly limiting the nonbank activities that bank holding companies could undertake through separately incorporated subsidiaries. But this effort to compartmentalize different types of financial institutions is doomed to fail, for the reasons elaborated in the concluding section of the chapter.

The Rise of Specialized Financial Institutions

One hallmark of a developed market economy is the relative strength and importance of private financial institutions that supply long-term financing. In less developed societies, lenders are so uncertain about the future—particularly about the stability of the currency and the government—that if they are willing to lend at all, it is only for short periods and generally at high interest rates. In contrast, in developed economies, intermediaries (and surplus-spending units) have confidence in making longer term commitments.

Specialized financial intermediaries developed because commercial banks did not meet the specific credit demands of various segments of the population. The first banks in Europe and in the United States were merchants' clubs or credit unions—that is, institutions where merchants pooled their funds (as either equity or deposits) to finance their purchases of goods, generally for no longer than ninety days.[8] Given these origins, it is not surprising that the early American banks generally restricted their activities to conducting short-term commercial transactions. But other factors also contributed to their narrow focus.

American banks and the federal and state governments that chartered them inherited their attitudes toward banking from England, specifically, from the Bank of England. Parliament chartered the Bank of England as a private corporation in 1694, but the bank eventually grew into England's central bank. Foreshadowing similar concerns that later surfaced in the United States, English merchants feared that, left unfettered, the Bank

---

8. Bray Hammond, "Long and Short Term Credit in Early American Banking," *Quarterly Journal of Economics*, vol. 4 (November 1934), pp. 79–103.

of England would not only monopolize banking but use its vast economic power to monopolize commercial activities as well. As a result, Parliament prohibited the bank from dealing or trading in merchandise.[9]

The United States copied this prohibition on the mixing of banking and commerce. The 1787 charter of the first incorporated bank in the United States, the Bank of North America, prohibited that bank from trading in goods or owning more real estate than was necessary to operate its business or to use for loan collateral.[10] Similar restrictions were placed in the charters of the First and Second National Banks of the United States, as well as in state bank charters issued by the legislatures of New York and Pennsylvania, homes of most of the largest early American banks.[11]

Early banking theory and practice also limited the range of bank activities. In particular, English banks followed the "real bills" doctrine developed by Adam Smith. Under this doctrine, prudent banks must only extend short-term, self-liquidating loans to finance the conversion of raw materials into goods and their transportation to market.[12] Proponents of the doctrine believed that bank credit would then safely expand and contract with the strength of overall economic activity.[13] Banks that made longer term loans, it was argued, would risk having insufficient funds to lend when the pace of economic activity increased, or even worse, would not be able to satisfy demands for specie when noteholders presented their bank notes for redemption. The real bills doctrine

9. For a more complete accounting of this history and its subsequent impact on banking in the United States, see Bernard Shull, "The Separation of Banking and Commerce: Origin, Development, and Implications for Antitrust," *Antitrust Bulletin,* vol. 28 (Spring 1983), pp. 255–79.

10. Edward L. Symons, Jr., and James J. White, *Banking Law* (St. Paul, Minnesota: West Publishing, 1984), p. 7.

11. Hammond, *Banks and Politics in America,* p. 63. The First National Bank of the United States was chartered in 1791 over strong objections from agrarian interests, which feared that a strong federal bank would be inimical to a democratic government. Similar objections prevented the renewal of the Second Bank of the United States charter, which was granted in 1816 but expired in 1836.

12. Adam Smith, *An Inquiry into the Nature and Causes of the Wealth of Nations,* 5th ed. (London: Methuen, 1930), p. 287.

13. As one leading nineteenth century American scholar put it: "The more the discounts of a bank are confined to business paper, the more is the institution a handmaiden to commerce, the more is its capital within its reach and consequently the more safe it is from the adverse fluctuations of trade." Professor George Tucker in *Hunt's Merchant's Magazine,* February 1858, quoted in Herman E. Krooss and Martin R. Blyn, *History of Financial Intermediaries* (Random House, 1971), p. 78.

strongly influenced American banking, although many banks in the first half of the nineteenth century eventually began to lend on a longer term basis.[14]

Finally, most early American banks specialized in the narrow activities of issuing bank notes and financing short-term commercial transactions within limited geographic areas because the stage of development of the American economy suited this narrow focus. Although, as discussed below, American businesses later developed demands for other financial services—particularly access to long-term finance and insurance—the early banks were small and their expertise relatively limited. Thus they were not in a position to provide a broad array of financial services. Moreover, the United States in its early years did not have a broad middle class with sufficient wealth to need sophisticated financial services. Indeed, commercial banks were not eager to service small individual accounts, which they believed were not profitable.[15]

To summarize, a number of factors contributed to specialization by commercial banks in the United States (and other industrialized countries) through most of the nineteenth century. Accordingly, other types of specialized financial institutions, each imported from Europe, arose to meet the financial needs that commercial banks either would not or could not satisfy.

Individuals, for example, needed a convenient and safe place in which to deposit their savings, and facilities for obtaining loans to finance major purchases, especially construction of their homes. In 1819 *mutual savings banks*—savings intermediaries owned by their depositors— arose to meet the first need by accepting small savings deposits, which these banks invested exclusively in federal and state securities. By the

14. Indeed, the Second Bank of the United States took equity positions in some ventures and also engaged in some longer-term financing. Ibid., p. 44. In addition, many private banks were originally established to fund specific capital projects—gas lighting, canal construction, fishing, and later agricultural development—creating a pattern of specialization that later led to a series of bank failures. Hammond, "Long and Short Term Credit in Early American Banking," p. 86; and Edward L. Symons, Jr., "The Business of Banking in Historical Perspective," *George Washington Law Review*, vol. 51 (August 1983), pp. 676–726. Although the vestiges of the real bills doctrine remain today, the notion that commercial bank credit should be limited to the "real" needs of business was never the self-regulating device its proponents claimed it to be. In fact, real bills lending is highly procyclical, encouraging businesses to expand in good times, but depriving them of credit when the economy turns sour.

15. Lewis J. Spellman, *The Depository Firm and Industry: Theory, History and Regulation* (Academic Press, 1982), p. 19.

1840s and 1850s, however, many savings banks were diversifying their investments to include business loans, corporate stock, and residential mortgages. Mutual savings banks were particularly popular in the major industrial cities of the North, where large numbers of wage earners lived, but the banks made little headway in the South and West, where agriculture was the predominant economic activity.

In 1831 *building and loan associations* began forming to fill individuals' needs for long-term financing for residential construction. The original building and loans grew slowly, since they were organized as limited life funds, which members joined by making monthly payments on their share subscriptions and then taking turns drawing on the funds for mortgages. The funds terminated when all members had purchased their homes. In the 1880s, however, a new organizational form was introduced in Ohio. Known as the Dayton plan, it allowed depositors to withdraw their savings after meeting certain time conditions. Thereafter, these *savings and loan associations* (S&Ls) grew rapidly. By the turn of the twentieth century, over 5,000 S&Ls were operating in the United States.

Credit unions were the last consumer-based financial intermediary to develop in the United States. Formed in the early 1900s, the first credit unions were modeled after the mutual organizations of the S&Ls, but concentrated on providing small, generally unsecured credit to their members. Credit unions filled an important unmet demand for medium-term nonresidential financing because savings institutions at that time were generally barred from extending unsecured personal loans. More-over, as late as the beginning of the twentieth century, there were almost no consumer lenders in the United States, primarily because low state-imposed usury ceilings discouraged the lending of funds to consumers.

Specialized institutions also developed to meet the nonbanking financial needs of commercial enterprises. In particular, *insurance underwriters* developed to spread the risks of certain catastrophic hazards. As with early banks, the early insurers were merchants, who required protection against the risk that their imports from overseas would be lost at sea. Rather than self-insure, merchants in pre-Revolutionary times formed underwriting pools to spread marine risks. By the middle of the eighteenth century, mutual organizations were also being formed to insure against fire hazards.[16]

16. By 1824 at least seventy-four general insurance companies had been formed in the United States, with combined capital in excess of $25 million. Kfrom and Blyn, *History of Financial Intermediaries,* p. 36.

In contrast to the growth of property-casualty insurance, life insurance developed more slowly, primarily because few individuals in the early years of the republic had sufficient discretionary income to spend on what was then considered a luxury. This situation changed radically by the late nineteenth century. Between 1890 and 1930, assets held by life insurers exploded from less than $1 billion to $107 billion.[17] Today, life insurers collectively hold three times the assets held by property-casualty insurers.

The single notable exception to the specialized focus of early American commercial banks was in securities underwriting. The early securities business in the United States revolved almost exclusively around the placement of federal and state government bonds, and somewhat later of railroad bonds, with institutional investors and wealthy individuals. Investment syndicates, or pools of wealthy merchants—forerunners of today's large investment banks—bought these bonds (often with borrowed money from commercial banks) to resell them at a profit. By the 1820s and 1830s, commercial banks were also competing in the same business. Indeed, the Second Bank of the United States was a major underwriter of government securities until Congress refused to renew its charter in 1836.[18]

The mixing of commercial and investment banking, however, attracted strong criticism following the crash of 1837, when roughly one-quarter of all chartered banks failed.[19] The United States Bank of Pennsylvania, which was among the largest of these casualties, was brought down primarily because of its heavy involvement in securities underwriting, activities that were promoted by the bank's president, Nicholas Biddle, who was also president of the Second Bank of the United States. Foreshadowing steps that Congress would take one century later, the rash of bank failures prompted a number of states, including New York, to restrict incorporated banks from securities trading and investment.[20]

17. Ibid., p. 140.
18. For historical accounts of early American investment banking activities, see Fritz Redlich, *The Molding of American Banking: Men and Ideas,* vol. 2 (New York: Hafner Publishing, 1951), pt. 2, chaps. 14, 21; and Vincent P. Carosso, *Investment Banking in America: A History* (Harvard University Press, 1970), chap. 1.
19. Benjamin J. Klebaner, *Commercial Banking in the United States: A History* (Hinsdale, Ill.: Dryden Press, 1974), pp. 32–33.
20. H. Parker Willis and Jules I. Bogen, *Investment Banking* (New York and London: Harper and Brothers, 1929), pp. 152–70; and Symons and White, *Banking Law,* p. 33.

Figure 2-2. *Percentage Distribution of Assets of Financial
Intermediaries, Selected Years, 1835–1945*

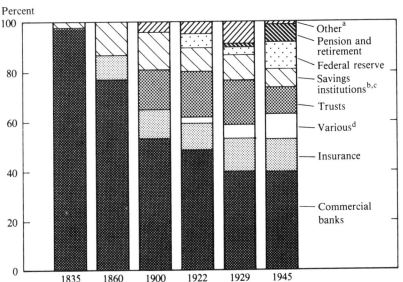

Sources: Figures for 1835 from U.S. Bureau of the Census, *Historical Statistics of the United
States, Colonial Times to 1970* (GPO, 1975), pt. 2; 1860 figures from Herman E. Krooss and Martin R.
Blyn, *A History of Financial Intermediaries* (Random House, 1971), pp. 93, 122; 1900–45 figures from
Raymond W. Goldsmith, *Financial Intermediaries in the American Economy since 1900* (Princeton
University Press for National Bureau of Economic Research, 1958), pp. 73–76.
   a. Represents difference between "standard definition" and "broad definition" totals.
   b. Derived from *Historical Statistics*, pp. 1020, 1033.
   c. Deposits.
   d. Includes fraternal insurance organizations, savings bank life insurance, credit unions, and
investment companies.

The early attempts to divorce commercial from investment banking
redirected commercial banks but did not stop them from underwriting
securities. From 1840 to the beginning of the Civil War, investment
banking came to be dominated by private banks, unincorporated enterprises that accepted deposits, made loans, and underwrote securities
without a formal banking charter. After the Civil War, some private
investment banks expanded into major financial enterprises.

   What data exist for the early American period indicate that despite
the development of the various specialized nonbank financial institutions, commercial banks dominated financial intermediation throughout
the nineteenth century. As shown in figure 2-2, commercial bank
organizations held 98 percent of assets of all financial intermediaries in
1835, or shortly after the first savings intermediaries had formed.

Although that share declined as trust companies, insurance companies, pension funds, and savings institutions rapidly grew, commercial banks continued for more than a century thereafter to be the dominant financial intermediaries in the United States.

Bank Diversification

The industrial revolution that followed the Civil War in the United States also changed the character of the financial services sector. Between 1860 and 1890, while national income grew about threefold, total assets of all financial intermediaries multiplied six times.[21] The expanding economy helped create a larger middle class that came to demand a wider range of financial services. All types of intermediaries grew faster than the economy (although, as shown in figure 2-2, not at the same rate).[22]

Banking organizations began to diversify after the Civil War into other financial activities, notably the underwriting of securities. However, this product-line expansion developed in a peculiar manner, primarily through state-chartered banks and affiliates. Because this pattern has been repeated in recent years, the dual federal-state feature of the American banking system bears further elaboration.

Except for the experiments with the First and Second Banks of the United States, all incorporated banks in the United States operating before the Civil War received their charters from the states. Until the demise of the Second Bank of the United States, the states granted bank charters only by special act of their legislatures. Beginning in 1836, this began to change as states—led by Michigan and New York—started to charter any incorporated bank that met certain minimum capital and other requirements. So-called free banking spread quickly throughout the country.[23]

21. Krooss and Blyn, *History of Financial Intermediaries*, p. 92.
22. There is a well-documented tendency for financial intermediaries in an economy to grow more rapidly than national income (or gross national product). See Raymond W. Goldsmith, *Financial Structure and Development* (Yale University Press, 1969); and John G. Gurley and Edward S. Shaw, *Money in a Theory of Finance* (Brookings, 1960).
23. The first free banking act, passed in Michigan in 1837, was subsequently ruled unconstitutional. It was also a practical failure. It and later free banking acts required groups forming a bank to deposit securities with a state official. Although the depositors would be repaid from the securities if the bank failed, the collateral requirements were poorly enforced; forty banks failed before the Michigan act was declared unconstitu-

The modern system of dual bank regulation arose accidently when Congress adopted the National Currency Act of 1863, amended in 1864 as the National Bank Act.[24] This legislation established for the first time a method of chartering national banks through the Comptroller of the Currency, created as an office within the Treasury Department. Borrowing heavily from banking legislation adopted in New York, the National Bank Act authorized national banks to engage in a series of specific activities—notably deposit taking and lending—as well as generally to "carry on the business of banking," a term not specifically defined.[25]

The primary objective of the National Bank Act was to help the federal government finance the Civil War. All national banks were required to purchase with specie federal bonds and paper currency that the Treasury issued and to hold these instruments against the issue of their own bank notes. The Civil War banking legislation also had a second and more permanent purpose: to establish a more orderly, and ultimately, exclusively federal banking system to replace the chaotic explosion of state banks. It is a remarkable fact that until Congress authorized the Treasury to issue paper currency in 1862, the United States had no national paper currency, but instead 7,000 different kinds of notes issued by 1,600 state banks.[26] Many of these notes were almost worthless. Indeed, the numerous bank failures of the free banking era were mainly due to unrestrained note issue by state-chartered banks.[27] The multiplicity of bank notes also introduced uncertainty into commercial transactions. Noteholders generally resolved this uncertainty by accepting discounts when attempting to use bank notes as a means of payment.[28]

---

tional. The free banking act adopted in 1838 in New York then became the model for similar legislation in other states, as well as for the National Bank Act. Symons and White, *Banking Law*, p. 22.

24. Kenneth E. Scott, "The Dual Banking System: A Model of Competition in Regulation," *Stanford Law Review*, vol. 30 (November 1977), pp. 1–56. Of course, a "dual" bank system, in which state banks coexisted with the First and Second National Banks of the United States, was also present in the early nineteenth century. But this early system differed dramatically from the later system since it allowed only a single bank chartered at the federal level.

25. During the 1960s Comptroller of the Currency James Saxon attempted to construe the term "business of banking" broadly to encompass a wide range of activities, but those efforts were rebuffed by the courts. Comptroller Saxon's efforts are discussed later in this chapter.

26. Galbraith, *Money*, p. 98.

27. An estimated 40 percent of all banks chartered between 1830 and 1860 failed. Krooss and Blyn, *History of Financial Intermediaries*, p. 75.

28. The dominant trade publication for the banking industry today, *American Banker*,

The leading advocate of national banking legislation, Treasury Secretary Salmon P. Chase, also wanted the nation to develop a uniform national currency. He believed that if the notes of national banks had special advantages, such as automatic conversion into specie at par, their notes would gradually develop into a uniform national currency. Equally important, state-chartered banks would be induced to convert to national charters. By the end of 1864, however, only 150 state-chartered banks had switched. In 1865 Congress decided to accelerate the conversion process by placing a 10 percent tax on all state bank notes. The tax soon had its intended effect. The number of state-chartered banks dwindled from 1,466 in 1863 to just 247 by 1868.[29]

But the demise of the state banking system was not to be. Like many subsequent federal government attempts to regulate the development of the banking system, the state bank note tax stimulated financial innovation. State-chartered banks circumvented the tax by aggressively marketing checking accounts, which were not taxed. Meanwhile, national banks were severely constrained by the requirement that their note issues be backed by federal bonds. As a result, national bank note currency expanded not with the needs of business—as the proponents of the real bills doctrine advocated—but with the demand for and supply of Treasury securities. After the Civil War, when the federal government gradually reduced its level of outstanding debt, the supply of Treasury securities fell. The low supply of Treasury securities forced a contraction in national bank note circulation, thus limiting the ability of national banks to expand.

State-chartered banks had another advantage: they could extend mortgages, or loans secured by real estate. In contrast, the National Bank Act strictly limited national banks to extending commercial credit, reflecting the strong influence of the real bills doctrine. Not surprisingly, state-chartered banks flourished in the expanding rural areas of the country, where farmers used their real estate as collateral to obtain crop loans.

In short, the National Bank Act had the unintended effects of not only creating a dual banking system but ironically of eventually thwarting the development of national banks themselves. Whereas in 1870 state-

---

started in the 1830s by regularly publishing the discounts on notes that various banks issued.

29. U.S. Department of Commerce, Bureau of the Census, *Historical Statistics of the United States: Colonial Times to 1970* (Government Printing Office, 1975), pt. 2, p. 1030.

chartered banks had come close to extinction, by 1900 they outnumbered their national counterparts 5,000 to 3,790 and held 55 percent of all bank deposits.[30]

Although it appeared duplicative, the dual system of federal and state regulation played a central role in the breakdown of specialized financial functions in the late nineteenth and early twentieth centuries. In particular, the competition between chartering authorities at the two levels of government resulted in a regulatory dialectic: certain states would give their banks broader powers, which the federal government would eventually be forced to match to preserve the national banking system. One early illustration of this process is the congressional decision in 1913 to allow national banks to engage in real estate lending and to act as trustees, powers that many states had long authorized for their state banks.[31]

More significant, state chartering played a critical role in furthering bank participation in securities underwriting, which became a lucrative business after the Civil War. State-chartered banks and then private banks had been major securities underwriters before 1860. But after the Civil War, an explosion in new securities issued to finance the construction of railroad lines across the West attracted new firms into investment banking, particularly aggressive private entrepreneurs adept at marketing railroad and government bonds to a mass market.[32] Although national banks were authorized (and indeed required) to purchase federal securities for investment, they were barred from meeting this challenge.[33] Two intermediaries stepped into the breach: trust companies, originally organized to manage estates but later active in the securities and banking

30. Ronald Paul Auerbach, *Historical Overview of Financial Institutions in the United States* (Washington: Federal Deposit Insurance Corporation, 1980), p. 9. See also Klebaner, *Commercial Banking in the United States,* pp. 56–57.

31. National bank powers were expanded by the Federal Reserve Act, whose more famous provisions created the Federal Reserve System.

32. Most of the leading investment banking firms today were organized in the decades following the Civil War, including J. P. Morgan and Co. (predecessor to Morgan Stanley and Co.); Goldman Sachs and Co.; Kuhn, Loeb and Co., and Lehman Brothers (predecessors to Shearson Lehman American Express); Kidder Peabody and Co.; and Chas. D. Barney and Co. (now part of Smith, Barney and Co.). See Ervin Miller, "Background and Structure of the Industry," in Irwin Friend and others, *Investment Banking and the New Issues Market* (Cleveland, Ohio: World Publishing, 1967), p. 88.

33. In 1902 the Comptroller of the Currency formally ruled that national banks had no legal authority to underwrite corporate securities. Similarly, a number of court rulings during this period barred national banks from engaging in commercial activities.

businesses, and banks chartered by states that permitted them to underwrite securities.[34]

Bank interest in securities underwriting intensified after World War I. During the war, many banks had acquired considerable expertise in distributing federal bonds (Liberty Bonds), whetting their appetites for securities underwriting business after the war. Their interest grew stronger during the 1920s, as businesses increasingly turned away from bank borrowing and instead used retained earnings and open-market commercial paper to finance investment projects.[35] The number of state banks engaged in the securities business, either directly or through affiliates, jumped from 205 in 1922 to 356 in 1929.[36] Many were affiliated with national banks, which used these associations to circumvent the restrictions on their own securities activities.[37]

The more liberal bank underwriting authority that the states granted eventually prompted Congress to level the playing field for national banks. In the McFadden Act of 1927—famous today primarily for its interstate branching restrictions—Congress included provisions allowing national banks to underwrite those securities that the Comptroller approved. Initially, the Comptroller construed this authority narrowly and approved bank underwriting of only corporate bonds. However, as the number of state-chartered banks in the securities business continued to grow, the Comptroller felt compelled to expand the approved list to include corporate equities as well.

The McFadden Act liberalizations accelerated the trend toward bank participation in securities underwriting, particularly of bonds. In 1927 banks and their affiliates originated just 22 percent of all bond issues; by 1930 that share had jumped to 45 percent, although only 566 of the

---

34. Symons and White, *Banking Law*, pp. 33–34.

35. Loans and discounts as a proportion of total assets of New York City banks, for example, fell from 55 percent at year-end 1920 to 44 percent by year-end 1929. Mark J. Flannery, "An Economic Evaluation of Bank Securities Activities before 1933," in Ingo Walter, ed., *Deregulating Wall Street: Commercial Bank Penetration of the Corporate Securities Market* (Wiley, 1985), p. 68.

36. W. Nelson Peach, *The Security Affiliates of National Banks*, Johns Hopkins University Studies in Historical and Political Science, vol. 58, no. 3 (Johns Hopkins Press, 1941), p. 83.

37. Ibid., pp. 66–70. National banks resorted to a variety of techniques in creating these affiliates, including direct ownership or the distribution of equity shares of the affiliates pro rata to bank shareholders. Many national banks also did not need to charter state banks, and instead engaged in securities underwriting through affiliated trust companies or nonspecialized corporations (with unrestricted state charters).

nation's 25,000 banks doing business in 1930 were engaging in securities activities.[38]

The multiple activities of certain commercial banks at the turn of the twentieth century also led to interlocking relationships among leading financial intermediaries. With the emergence of large-scale oil and manufacturing companies in the late 1800s, both investment and commercial bankers needed larger pools of capital to finance the flotation of increasingly large securities issues. Accordingly, commercial and investment bankers often joined forces with insurance companies and the new trust companies to form underwriting syndicates. In many cases, these relationships were cemented by joint ownership and interlocking directorates, combinations that led to the famous Armstrong investigation of 1905–06 and the "money trust" investigations of the Pujo committee in 1912.[39] The committee's recommendation that national banks be barred from securities underwriting was not to be adopted, however, for another two decades.[40]

Finally, with advances in transportation and communication—the railroad, the automobile, and the telephone and telegraph—banks also began to expand geographically after the Civil War. During the nineteenth century, the Comptroller had discouraged branching by national banks, as had many states, primarily because of public fears that larger banks would accumulate too much power if permitted to expand freely. In 1900 less than 2 percent of the nation's banks operated branch offices.[41] But gradually states liberalized their branching laws, impelling Congress to allow in the McFadden Act of 1927 national banks limited branching rights in the cities of their main offices if state-chartered banks had similar rights.[42] By the end of 1929, 800 banks were operating branch offices; another 2,000 banks that operated in "unit" banking states (where branching was prohibited) belonged to banking "chains" (collections of banks with common ownership) or were affiliates of bank holding

---

38. Ibid., pp. 83, 109.

39. See Douglass C. North, "Life Insurance and Investment Banking at the Time of the Armstrong Investigation of 1905–1906," *Journal of Economic History*, vol. 14 (Summer 1954), pp. 209–28.

40. The recommendations of the Pujo committee are set forth in the *Report of the Committee Appointed Pursuant to House Resolutions 429 and 504 to Investigate the Concentration of Control of Money and Credit*, H. Rept. 1593, 62 Cong., 3 sess. (GPO, 1913).

41. Auerbach, *Historical Overview of Financial Institutions*, p. 10.

42. National banks were not accorded the same branching privileges as their state-chartered counterparts, however, until 1933.

companies. In total, multi-office banks on the eve of the Depression held more than half of all assets in the American banking system.[43] Moreover, banks' geographic expansion did not stop at American borders. Such major banks as National City Bank and Transamerica (predecessor to Bank of America) had opened offices in numerous countries around the world.[44]

Constraining Banks

Although the U.S. economy embarked on a major expansion in the decade following World War I, the American banking system experienced much instability. In the 1920s about 6,000 banks closed their doors. Over 80 percent of these banks, however, were small, mostly rural institutions with capital less than $100,000,[45] a pattern that reflected the large numbers of small banks chartered during this period. The Depression made matters much worse. Between 1930 and 1933, nearly 9,000 of the nation's 25,000 commercial banks failed. The casualty list included many larger urban institutions. The environment clearly was ripe for radical revision of the legal framework governing depository institutions.

Depression-Era Legislation

Franklin Roosevelt came to office in March 1933 in the midst of an economy-wide collapse and a nationwide bank run. Roosevelt dealt with the immediate crisis first by announcing a bank holiday and then authorizing a gradual reopening of basically sound banks. Later in his first term he launched the most far-reaching program of reform and regulation of the financial services industry in American history.

First, and perhaps most important, the president signed emergency legislation in 1933 and then permanent legislation in 1934 creating federal

43. "Branch, Chain and Group Banking: December 1929," *Federal Reserve Bulletin,* vol. 16 (April 1930), p. 147.

44. Harold Van B. Cleveland, Thomas F. Huertas, and others, *Citibank, 1812–1970,* Harvard Studies in Business History 38 (Harvard University Press, 1985); and Marquis James and Bessie R. James, *Biography of a Bank: The Story of Bank of America N.T. and S.A.* (Harper and Brothers, 1954).

45. Susan Kennedy, *The Banking Crisis of 1933* (University of Kentucky Press, 1973).

insurance for bank deposits up to $2,500, a concept both Roosevelt and Congress had previously denounced or rejected.[46] Significantly, in creating the insurance program and the Federal Deposit Insurance Corporation (FDIC) to administer it, Congress brought state-chartered banks under federal supervision for the first time.[47] In 1934 Congress also authorized for the first time the chartering of federal savings and loans and created a parallel insurance program for savings accounts at eligible thrift institutions. The newly created Federal Savings and Loan Insurance Corporation (FSLIC) administered this insurance program.[48]

Second, Congress included in the Banking Act of 1933 provisions to restrict the ability of banks to compete with each other and with other financial institutions. It was widely believed at the time that excessive competition in the banking industry had been responsible for or had contributed to the rash of bank failures. For example, the commonly held view alleged that interest rate competition for bank deposits had induced banks to seek out higher yielding and hence riskier loans.[49] In the Banking Act of 1933, Congress accepted this view and prohibited banks from paying any interest on demand deposits and delegated to the Federal Reserve the authority (Regulation Q) to set ceiling rates on time and saving deposits.

Third, the 1933 banking act revised federal regulation of banks' geographic expansion, which had been introduced in the McFadden Act in 1927. On the one hand, the 1933 legislation liberalized the McFadden branching restrictions by granting national banks the same branching rights that states extended to state-chartered banks. On the other hand,

46. One hundred fifty federal deposit insurance bills were introduced in Congress but failed to pass between 1886 and 1930. The United States was not the first country to introduce deposit insurance on a nationwide basis. Czechoslovakia established a sophisticated system in 1924 to insure 80 percent of the deposits at both commercial and savings banks. Ian S. McCarthy, "Deposit Insurance: Theory and Practice," *International Monetary Fund Staff Papers*, vol. 27 (September 1980), pp. 578–600.

47. Various states tried deposit insurance programs in both the pre– and post–Civil War eras. Ineffective state supervision was the reason why many of these programs failed. See George J. Benston, "Deposit Insurance and Bank Failures," *Federal Reserve Bank of Atlanta Economic Review*, vol. 68 (March 1983), p. 8.

48. In 1933 the Federal Home Loan Bank system was established to provide a central reserve system for savings institutions to parallel the Federal Reserve System created for banks in 1913.

49. Similar arguments have recently been made in connection with the deregulation of bank deposit interest rates in the 1980s. See Albert M. Wojnilower, "The Central Role of Credit Crunches in Recent Financial History," *Brookings Papers on Economic Activity, 2:1980*, pp. 277–326.

the act imposed new requirements limiting group or chain banking, which a number of banking organizations had used to expand across state lines in the 1920s.[50]

Finally, the 1933 banking legislation incorporated provisions that have come to be known as the Glass-Steagall Act, which its sponsors designed to divorce commercial from investment banking. Four provisions of this act stood out. Sections 16 and 20 prohibited national and state banks belonging to the Federal Reserve System ("member" banks) from underwriting corporate equity and debt securities; similarly, section 21 prohibited any entity engaged in securities underwriting from engaging in deposit banking as well; and section 32 prohibited officer, director, or employee interlocks between member banks and securities underwriters.

Congress enacted the Glass-Steagall provisions mainly because of the single-minded efforts of Senator Carter Glass, a legislator respected for his financial know-how dating back to his critical role in securing passage of the Federal Reserve Act. Glass adhered strongly to the traditional real bills view of commercial banking. He believed that the intertwining of commercial and investment banking in the 1920s had contributed to the 1929 stock market crash and to the wave of bank failures that swept across the country in the early 1930s. Congress rejected these views in the early years of the Depression by consistently voting down Senator Glass' proposals to divorce commercial from investment banking. However, the political climate began to change in 1932, after hearings orchestrated by the chief counsel of the Glass subcommittee, Ferdinand Pecora, uncovered various abuses involving large banks and their securities affiliates.[51] These hearings revealed that certain banks had made loans to securities purchasers to help support artificially securities prices, dumped "bad" securities with correspondents or in trust accounts, and used securities affiliates to relieve the banks of their bad loans and to purchase stock in companies to which the banks had loaned money. The hearings also revealed that several leading bankers had evaded income taxes by failing to report substantial sums as income.[52]

---

50. Chain banking organizations consisted of a number of banks held by common owners.

51. *Stock Exchange Practices*, Hearings before a Subcommittee of the Senate Committee on Banking and Currency on S. Res. 84 and S. Res. 239, 72 Cong., 2 sess. (GPO, 1933).

52. Anthony Saunders, "Securities Activities of Commercial Banks: The Problem

Although the Pecora hearings did not establish a widespread pattern of abuses by securities affiliates of banking organizations, they did help to fan public sentiment against the banking community, which not surprisingly intensified as the bank failure rate accelerated into 1933. By the time President Roosevelt declared the bank holiday, the new chairman of the Chase Manhattan Bank, Winthrop Aldrich, endorsed the separation of commercial and investment banking in principle and announced that his bank was planning to drop its securities affiliate. National City Bank, too, said it would abandon the securities underwriting business.[53] By this time, however, Congress was ready to take formal action to require the separation of commercial from investment banking. In the emergency environment following the bank holiday, the Glass-Steagall Act was thus to become an integral component of the legislative program to "rescue" and reform the banking system.

The Glass-Steagall Act did not, however, totally divorce commercial from investment banking. The act exempted state-chartered banks that were not members of the Federal Reserve System. Most of these banks were small. It allowed all banks to underwrite debt instruments of the federal government and general obligation municipal bonds (those secured by a municipality's taxing authority), apparently because these securities were viewed to be less risky than corporate securities. It permitted bank affiliates to participate in the prohibited underwriting activities as long as the affiliates were not "principally engaged" in these activities. Significantly, the act did not prohibit banks from merely executing securities orders on behalf of customers without giving them investment advice. Finally, the separation requirements in the act did not prohibit American banks from underwriting corporate securities in foreign markets. Each of these exemptions or qualifications has since been exploited by an increasing number of banking organizations intent on expanding their securities activities.[54]

Many commentators have challenged the weight of the evidence on

---

of Conflicts of Interest," *Federal Reserve Bank of Philadelphia Business Review,* July–August 1985, pp. 17–27.

53. For summaries of events leading up to and surrounding the passage of the Glass-Steagall Act, see Edward J. Kelly, "Legislative History of the Glass-Steagall Act," and Flannery, "Economic Evaluation of Bank Securities Activities," in Walter, *Deregulating Wall Street,* pp. 41–65, 67–87.

54. Thomas G. Fischer and others, "The Securities Activities of Commercial Banks: A Legal and Economic Analysis," *Tennessee Law Review,* vol. 51 (1984), pp. 467–518. This point is also discussed later in this chapter.

which Congress finally acted in approving the Glass-Steagall provisions.[55] Securities abuses in the late 1920s were not confined to securities affiliates of banks but were widespread throughout the industry. Congress addressed these evils through the disclosure and registration requirements of the Securities Act of 1933 and the Securities Exchange Act of 1934. Chapter 5 outlines several mechanisms for preventing any remaining problems that bank affiliation with securities underwriters may cause without divorcing investment from commercial banking functions.

Holding Company Legislation

The Glass-Steagall Act set another important precedent by subjecting bank holding companies (BHCs) to regulation for the first time, by prohibiting affiliations between banks or their holding companies and securities firms. Nevertheless, the act placed no other restrictions on either the geographic or product-line activities of BHCs.[56] At the time, these omissions had little practical importance. Those banks that survived the Depression were preoccupied with staying afloat and were reluctant even to extend loans.[57] This conservative behavior was also reflected in the actual *decline* in the number of bank holding companies, from fifty-two in 1936 (when BHCs were defined as organizations controlling three or more banks) to just forty-six in the mid-1950s (when BHCs were more broadly defined as organizations owning at least 25 percent of two or more banks).[58] Equally significant, few BHCs had taken advantage of the liberal legal landscape to develop interstate banking systems or to range into other businesses.

55. See, for example, Flannery, "Economic Evaluation of Bank Securities Activities"; and Thomas F. Huertas, "An Economic Brief Against Glass-Steagall," *Journal of Bank Research,* vol. 14 (Autumn 1984), pp. 148–59.

56. The act limited its regulation of BHCs to requiring their registration with the Federal Reserve and to controlling the loans that banks made to their holding company affiliates. This subject is explored further in chapters 4 and 5.

57. Between 1929 and 1940, total loans as a fraction of bank assets fell from 58 percent to just 26 percent. Cash and government securities took up the slack, rising from 23 percent of assets to 61 percent over the same period. This situation persisted through World War II as government controls were placed on consumer and corporate borrowing. By 1945 commercial banks held 60 percent of their assets in government bonds and cash and just 16 percent in loans.

58. Donald T. Savage, "A History of the Bank Holding Company Movement, 1900–78," in Board of Governors of the Federal Reserve System, *The Bank Holding Company Movement to 1978: A Compendium* (The Board, 1978).

Nevertheless, many federal legislators continued to be concerned about the virtually unlimited freedom of BHCs. Legislation to regulate BHC expansion was repeatedly introduced in Congress. Indeed, in 1943 the Federal Reserve Board proposed such action.[59] Congress finally responded thirteen years later by enacting the Bank Holding Company Act of 1956 (BHCA), after the federal courts rejected the Federal Reserve Board's efforts to dismantle the Transamerica Corporation (predecessor to today's Bank of America), which had come to dominate banking markets in five western states.[60]

The BHCA had two principal components. One prohibited multibank holding companies—those controlling at least 25 percent of two or more banks—from engaging in any nonbanking activities that the Federal Reserve had not determined were "of a financial nature" and "so closely related to the business of banking or managing or controlling banks as to be a proper incident thereto."[61] The other provision, enacted as the Douglas Amendment to the act, constrained BHCs from interstate expansion by prohibiting interstate bank acquisitions unless specifically authorized by the state in which the acquired bank was located. This effective delegation of authority to the states paralleled the delegations of interstate branching authority in the McFadden Act and the Banking Act of 1933.[62]

Congress limited BHCs from product and geographic expansion in 1956 not so much to protect the safety and soundness of the banking system but to prevent undue concentration of banking resources and to preserve fair credit allocation.[63] The BHCA contained one important loophole, however: its restrictions did not apply to holding companies that controlled only a *single* bank. Like many such legislative omissions,

59. Board of Governors of the Federal Reserve System, *Annual Report, 1943*, p. 37.

60. See Stephen Halpert, "The Separation of Banking and Commerce Reconsidered" (University of Miami, August 1986).

61. However, the 1956 act specifically approved BHC participation in a limited set of activities directly related to banking, including owning and managing BHC property, providing services to subsidiary banks, operating a safe deposit company, and liquidating property acquired by subsidiary banks.

62. The BHCA also established for the first time competitive standards that the Board was required to apply in deciding whether to approve BHC acquisitions. At the same time, the act grandfathered a number of interstate banking networks that had been formed before 1956.

63. *Bank Holding Company Act Amendments, 1966*, S. Rept. 1179, 89 Cong. 2 sess. (GPO, 1966); Symons, "Business of Banking," p. 719; and "The Bank Holding Company Act of 1956," *Stanford Law Review*, vol. 9 (March 1957), p. 346.

the unitary BHC exception was not widely exploited for some time. This conservative behavior eventually changed. By the mid-1960s certain banks began forming holding companies to raise funds directly by selling unregulated commercial paper in order to circumvent the Regulation Q ceilings on interest rates payable on bank deposits. The number of unitary BHCs climbed rapidly toward the end of the decade, a period that saw an explosion in the formation of conglomerates throughout the economy. By 1970 over 700 unitary BHCs had been formed (many by nonbanking concerns) and had expanded outside the banking business, not only into other financial activities (insurance, securities, and real estate) but into a broad range of manufacturing and retailing activities as well.[64]

The explosion of unitary BHCs prompted Congress to amend the BHCA in 1970 to cover one-bank holding companies. The 1970 amendments also forced the unitary BHCs that had diversified to divest themselves of all enterprises that were not engaged in activities "closely related to the business of banking." Somewhat anomalously, Congress did not take parallel action in the Savings and Loan Holding Company Act, which in 1967 had subjected multithrift holding companies to restrictions on product-line expansion. These restrictions were similar to those placed on BHCs in the 1956 BHCA.

While Congress was shutting off attempts by bank holding companies to diversify their activities, the courts were stopping similar efforts by national banks. During the 1960s Comptroller of the Currency James J. Saxon aggressively interpreted the National Bank Act to authorize national banks to engage directly in the underwriting of revenue bonds, insurance agencies, courier services, travel agencies, personal property leasing, and the data processing business. Many state banks responded by converting to national charter during this period.[65] However, a series of judicial decisions eventually rebuffed each one of the Comptroller's rulings, thus limiting national banks to traditional deposit and loan activities.[66]

---

64. For an excellent description of this expansion, see "One-Bank Holding Companies before the 1970 Amendments," *Federal Reserve Bulletin,* vol. 58 (December 1972), pp. 999–1008.

65. Scott, "Dual Banking System," pp. 23–30.

66. Specifically, the rulings rested on interpretations of a provision in the National Bank Act allowing national banks to "exercise all such *incidental powers* as shall be necessary to carry on the business of banking" (emphasis added). These rulings and

Bank Innovation and Circumvention of Regulation

The end of World War II ushered in major changes in the American industry. With memories of the Depression receding, commercial banks returned to their traditional lending activities. By 1960 commercial banks had lifted their loan-to-asset ratio to 53 percent, about double the ratio immediately after the war.

Banks required added funds to finance their new investment activities. But they were constrained by the Regulation Q ceilings on deposit interest rates, which made deposits difficult to attract as interest rates on federal securities increased. Banks solved their problem by introducing a series of innovations during the 1960s. These innovations, in turn, helped to chip away at both deposit rate ceilings and restrictions on banks' interstate expansion.

The first innovation occurred in 1961, when large New York banks began aggressively to market large ($100,000) negotiable certificates of deposit (CDs), or short-term interest–bearing instruments whose interest rates were not regulated under Regulation Q. CDs also became a useful vehicle for banks to attract funds from other states. Between 1960 and 1967, CDs outstanding expanded from less than $1 billion to more than $20 billion.[67]

The second innovation was spawned by the credit crunch of 1965–66, when restrictive monetary policy pushed market interest rates above the Regulation Q ceiling. At the time, Regulation Q did not apply to savings accounts at S&Ls, so bank depositors began to switch their bank accounts to thrifts. To forestall this movement, Congress extended Regulation Q to thrift institutions in late 1966 (but, in the interest of promoting the housing industry, allowed thrifts to pay up to a half point more in interest than commercial banks).

Even though market interest rates receded thereafter, many banking organizations justifiably continued to fear that in the next credit crunch, Regulation Q would produce a "disintermediation" of funds from both banks and thrifts into open market securities. Therefore in the late 1960s, numerous banks began to organize themselves as unitary BHCs and to

---

the subsequent judicial decisions overruling them are described in detail in Jeffrey D. Dunn, "Expansion of National Bank Powers: Regulatory and Judicial Precedent under the National Bank Act, Glass-Steagall Act, and Bank Holding Company Act," *Southwestern Law Journal*, vol. 36 (June 1982), pp. 765–92.

67. Krooss and Blyn, *History of Financial Intermediaries*, p. 226.

raise funds by "downstreaming" the proceeds of commercial paper issued by their parent holding companies. The unitary BHC also proved to be an attractive vehicle for banking organizations to diversify into a wide range of nonbank activities, as already discussed.

Third, American banking organizations significantly expanded their international activities during the late 1960s. Banks opened foreign branches to raise funds in overseas markets where interest rate controls were not in effect. Between 1965 and 1972, the number of foreign branches operated by American banking organizations increased from 211 to 627; the assets held in these branches jumped eightfold.[68]

The Crumbling of Bank Regulation

Like sand castles on an ocean beach, the restrictions imposed on depository institutions in the Depression and again in the post–World War II era were doomed to be washed away by tides of economic change. As just noted, this erosion began in the 1960s as banks found new ways to raise funds by circumventing the federal limitations on deposit interest rates and interstate expansion. A number of additional developments in the 1970s and 1980s accelerated the pace of change.

Double-digit inflation in the mid-1970s and again in the early 1980s led to double-digit interest rates, which not only rendered deposit interest rate ceilings completely untenable but also indirectly helped to erode the geographic and product-line barriers to banks' expansion. Meanwhile, rapid technological advances enabled banks to collect deposits and extend loans across state lines without opening full-service banking offices. Technology also accelerated entry by nonbanking organizations into the activities long dominated by banks. As several observers recently noted: "Today, almost anyone with a large computer can provide many of the financial services previously provided only by banks."[69]

68. Donald D. Hester, "Innovations and Monetary Control," *Brookings Papers on Economic Activity, 1:1981,* p. 153. In 1969 the Federal Reserve imposed a 10 percent marginal reserve requirement on offshore, or Eurodollar, bank borrowings. The Federal Reserve also requested its member banks to confine the activities of their offshore branches to developing new international business rather than to using their branches as a way of shifting funds to avoid reserve requirements on domestic deposits.

69. Thomas G. Fischer and others, "Securities Activities of Commercial Banks," p. 470. For a comprehensive examination of the role of technology in the financial services industry, see U.S. Congress, Office of Technology Assessment, *Effects of Information Technology on Financial Services Systems* (OTA, 1984).

Significantly, the dual system of state and federal bank regulation aided the relaxation of each of the major restrictions on bank activities. State approvals of interest-bearing transactions accounts in the early 1970s foreshadowed the removal of Regulation Q at the federal level several years later. State rather than federal actions are removing interstate banking barriers. The states are also in the forefront of the movement to relax barriers to banks' product-line expansion.

To summarize, although disparate in scope, the removal or erosion of each of the pillars of the Depression-era regulatory regime that governed banks shares a common heritage. The same forces that led to the elimination of interest rate controls are now leading to the dismantling of interstate banking restrictions and will eventually bring down the walls separating banking from other types of enterprises.

The Demise of Interest Rate Controls

Although banks had begun to innovate around Regulation Q in the 1960s, federal control of bank deposit interest rates was not completely doomed until institutions other than commercial banks began to offer deposit substitutes. Two such offerings, both launched in 1972, were instrumental: negotiable order of withdrawal (NOW) accounts originally authorized for Massachusetts thrifts, and money market funds (MMFs). Of the two, NOW accounts had the lesser initial impact because they were first allowed in only a few New England states.

Money market funds started slowly, primarily because the T-bill interest rate only temporarily rose above the Regulation Q ceiling between 1972 and 1975. But when T-bill rates jumped into double digits in the late 1970s and early 1980s, funds invested in MMFs proliferated— from $3 billion in 1977 to $233 billion in 1982.[70]

Double-digit inflation was largely responsible for the huge growth in MMF assets. However, advances in computer processing were also important. With the introduction of the cash management account by Merrill Lynch in 1978, some operators of MMFs added check writing, or transactions, features to their funds by contracting with banks to process checks drawn on those funds. These contractual arrangements

---

70. For a history of the rise and fall of interest rate controls, see R. Alton Gilbert, "Requiem for Regulation Q: What It Did and Why It Passed Away," *Federal Reserve Bank of St. Louis Review*, vol. 68 (February 1986), pp. 22–37.

could not have been implemented without inexpensive data storage and processing capabilities.

The rapid increase in MMF assets led Congress to begin dismantling the deposit interest rate regulatory regime that was putting banks and thrifts at a severe competitive disadvantage. In 1980 Congress took an important first step by authorizing banks and thrifts nationwide to offer NOW accounts to individuals (but not corporations) and by directing a newly created interagency committee, the Depository Institutions Deregulation Committee (DIDC), to phase out deposit interest ceilings by 1986.

The DIDC approached its mandate cautiously, however, by concentrating its early actions on raising interest ceilings on time deposits and certificates of deposit with longer term maturities. Not surprisingly, these limited steps failed to halt the continuing growth of MMFs. Accordingly, Congress directed the DIDC in the Garn–St Germain Act of 1982 to accelerate the deregulation process by creating new categories of deposits free of interest rate ceilings and directly competitive with MMFs. The committee responded by authorizing unregulated money market deposit accounts (MMDAs), which allowed only limited check writing and required account balances of at least $2,500, and super-NOWs, which allowed unlimited check writing and $1,000 minimum balances. The new accounts successfully stopped the growth of MMFs. By the end of 1983, assets of MMFs had slipped from their 1982 peak of over $240 billion to $181 billion. Since then, MMF assets have climbed back to exceed $250 billion; funds held in MMDAs, however, have exploded beyond $500 billion (see figure 2-3).

The Evolution of Interstate Banking

Federal law has long permitted certain banking activities to be operated on an interstate basis despite the restrictions in the McFadden and Bank Holding Company acts. Banks have been able to establish offices in other states solely to extend loans (loan production offices or LPOs) and to accept deposits and extend loans to aid international trading transactions (Edge Act corporations).[71] In addition, the BHCA

71. The most recent compilation of these activities reported that as of December 1982, forty-four banking organizations controlled 202 LPOs spread across thirty-four states; as of June 30, 1982, there were 143 interstate Edge Act offices in nineteen states controlled by forty-nine banking organizations. David D. Whitehead, "Interstate Bank-

Figure 2-3. *Transaction Media, 1970–85*

Trillions of dollars

Sources: *Federal Reserve Bulletin* (monthly), various issues.

of 1956 "grandfathered" the interstate banking operations of nine BHCs, which control over one hundred banks in twenty-one states.[72] Banks have also been able to solicit deposits and to market their credit cards in other states without establishing offices there. From the outset, the

ing; Probability or Reality?'' *Federal Reserve Bank of Atlanta Economic Review,* vol. 70 (March 1985), pp. 6–17.

72. Ibid. Notably, until Congress corrected the difference in treatment between foreign and domestic banks in 1978, foreign banks were allowed to operate interstate. The International Banking Act of 1978 rectified this disparity but also grandfathered existing interstate networks that foreign banks owned. Through the end of 1983, these grandfathered institutions included seven international banking organizations controlling fifteen interstate banks in three states.

BHCA has permitted bank holding companies to conduct their authorized nonbanking operations interstate.

Nevertheless, both the McFadden Act and the BHCA for a long time had the effect of preventing banking organizations from opening *full-service* banking offices—those capable of both accepting deposits and extending loans—in other states. This effect occurred because none of the states took advantage of the "escape clauses" written into the law that permitted states, if they so desired, to open up their markets to banks or their holding companies headquartered in other states.

The banking landscape began to change in the mid-1970s. At first, two geographically remote states searching for additional capital—Alaska and Maine—opened their borders without restrictions to bank holding companies from other states. Other states, such as New York, were more protective of their local banks and permitted out-of-state bank entry only on a reciprocal basis. Perhaps most important, however, certain states—six in New England and eventually thirteen in the southeastern states—began in the early 1980s to enact so-called regional banking statutes, permitting entry only by out-of-state holding companies from specific (often neighboring) states, but excluding banking organizations headquartered in California, Texas, and New York.[73] In 1985 the Supreme Court upheld the lawfulness of these discriminatory arrangements, pointing to a long-standing federal interest in "widely dispersed control of banking" and to the fact that the BHCA permitted regional statutes because it delegated to the states the decision whether and how to open their borders to out-of-state banking organizations.[74] Through the end of 1986, thirty-seven states had enacted some type of interstate banking law; the banks in these states collectively held more than 91 percent of U.S. domestic banking assets. Significantly, eighteen states have provided for nationwide banking by 1990.[75]

73. In many cases, the reciprocity statutes have not produced neatly defined regions. For example, the New Jersey law offers reciprocity with Missouri. Maryland includes Arkansas but not its neighbor New Jersey. Georgia, North Carolina, and South Carolina allow entry by banking organizations from Kentucky; but the Kentucky statute allows entry by organizations located only in contiguous states. See Larry A. Frieder, "The Interstate Landscape: Trends and Projections," in Herbert Baer and Sue F. Gregorash, eds., *Toward Nationwide Banking: A Guide to the Issues* (Federal Reserve Bank of Chicago, 1986), pp. 1–16.

74. See *Northeast Bancorp, Inc.* v. *Board of Governors of the Federal Reserve System*, 472 U.S. 159 (1985). For a thorough discussion of this decision and the interstate banking movement generally, see Geoffrey P. Miller, "Interstate Banking in the Court," *Supreme Court Review*, 1985, pp. 179–225.

75. Victor L. Saulsbury, "Interstate Banking—An Update," Federal Deposit Insurance Corporation, *Regulatory Review*, July 1986, pp. 1–17.

The interstate banking movement gathered momentum during the period when deposit interest controls were also being lifted. Removing Regulation Q stimulated competition for funds not only among banks, which were still subject to the geographic expansion restrictions imposed by the McFadden Act and the BHCA, but also between banks and nonbank institutions, particularly securities firms and mutual funds, which were free to establish offices nationwide. Many states realized that nationwide banking was inevitable, and that without additional freedom, their own banks would operate at a growing disadvantage in the new competitive age. By discriminating against money center banks at an early stage, states enacting regional statutes could permit local institutions to grow large enough to avoid being swallowed by New York and California banking organizations when nationwide interstate banking was finally authorized. The regional arrangements have radically altered the structure of American banking by fostering the emergence of new regional "super-banks," a development whose implications are explored in chapter 4.

Ironically, the steady relaxation of geographic restrictions by the states has made Congress unwilling to amend either the McFadden Act or the BHCA to authorize nationwide interstate banking. In 1985 the House Banking Committee approved legislation that authorized regional banking compacts but required states participating in them to allow entry by BHCs from *any* state beginning in 1990. However, momentum for such "nationwide trigger" legislation died after the Supreme Court upheld the regional banking statutes.

Nevertheless, both federal and state legislators have been impelled by economic events to push along interstate banking where it promises to ease the burden of bank and thrift failures on the federal deposit insurance agencies and on local economies. In the Garn–St Germain Act of 1982, for example, Congress allowed thrifts and banks to cross state lines when purchasing failed depository institutions.[76] In early 1986, the Federal Home Loan Bank Board (FHLBB) adopted rules enabling thrifts that acquire financially troubled savings and loans to purchase healthy

76. The 1982 legislation permitted out-of-state bank holding companies to acquire failed banks with assets over $500 million. The act also permitted banking organizations and thrifts to acquire ailing and failed savings and loans without any size restraint. At the same time, however, the 1982 law placed restrictions on these interstate purchases by allowing in-state bidders on failing banks and thrifts the right to match bids by out-of-state institutions. At this writing, Congress was expected before the end of 1987 to extend and expand the Garn–St Germain provisions, which expired in December 1986.

thrifts in three additional states.[77] In addition, certain states such as Texas, which has long opposed both interstate banking and statewide branching, liberalized their banking laws in 1986 to entice out-of-state banking organizations to help rescue ailing in-state institutions.

Interstate banking has also developed through the exploitation of a loophole in the Bank Holding Company Act that, as the Supreme Court has recently held, permits both banking and nonbanking organizations to operate nationwide limited-purpose or "nonbank banks."[78] The nonbank bank loophole exists because the BHCA, which limits geographic and activity diversification of banking organizations, defines a "bank" as an entity that *both* accepts deposits and extends commercial loans. An institution that performs one but not both of these functions, therefore, is not a "bank" within the meaning of the act. Beginning in 1980, nonbanking firms began to exploit this statutory language by opening new limited-purpose banks or converting existing institutions into nonbank banks limited to servicing consumer customers.[79] Through 1985, over fifty BHCs had obtained preliminary approval from the Comptroller's office to operate a collective total of over 260 limited-purpose banks. However, a Florida federal district court has enjoined the Comptroller from granting final approvals pending that court's resolution of a challenge to the lawfulness of limited-purpose banks under the National Bank Act.[80] More significant, the nonbank bank loophole will be closed, at least for applications not approved before March 1987, if legislation approved by a House-Senate conference committee in July 1987 is signed into law by the president.

Some analysts have had difficulty in explaining why, on strictly economic grounds, many banks seek to grow larger and to expand across state lines. They point to studies of bank operating costs, which have

77. The Bank Board also announced in 1986 a new policy permitting thrifts located in states that authorized reciprocal entry by out-of-state banking organizations the same interstate expansion authority as the banking organizations in those states.

78. In *Board of Governors of the Federal Reserve System* v. *Dimension Financial Corporation et al.*, 474 U.S. 361 (1986), the Supreme Court rejected an attempt by the Federal Reserve to inhibit the growth of nonbank banks by widening the definition of "demand deposits" under the BHCA to include NOW accounts and by expanding the definition of "commercial loan" to include commercial paper.

79. The nonbank bank movement was launched when Gulf and Western acquired Fidelity National Bank of Concord, California, and then obtained approval from the Comptroller to "debank" Fidelity by divesting it of its commercial loans.

80. *Independent Bankers Association of America* v. *Comptroller of the Currency*, no. 84-1404 (D. Fla., February 15, 1985), unpublished opinion.

generally failed to demonstrate that there are economies of scale in banking above $100 million in deposits.[81]

Nevertheless, there are two compelling reasons, which most cost studies do not capture, why so many banks want to grow. First, federal and state statutes limit the amount banks can lend to any single borrower. Accordingly, as banking organizations grow larger they become able to attract the banking business of larger borrowers.[82]

Second, the cost estimates generally do not consider the benefits of portfolio diversification that banks may realize through growth, especially through geographic expansion. Smaller banks are less able than larger banks to diversify their deposit sources and loan portfolios, particularly if they are located in smaller communities and are limited by state law in their ability to expand, either through branches or multibank holding companies.[83] This fact explains why smaller banks historically have held more capital as a percentage of assets than larger banks.[84] It also explains why bank failures in the 1920s were concentrated among smaller institutions and, more recently, why most of the failed

81. For an excellent summary of the numerous studies of scale economies in banking, see B. Frank King, "Interstate Expansion and Bank Costs," *Federal Reserve Bank of Atlanta Economic Review*, May 1983, *Special Issue*, pp. 40–45. A significant shortcoming of these studies, however, is that they are based on data collected by the Federal Reserve that do not include banks with assets above $1 billion. Of two recent cost studies with larger banks in the data base, one finds only small-scale economies at banks with $1 billion in assets (Sherrill Shaffer, "Scale Economies in Multiproduct Firms," *Bulletin of Economic Research*, vol. 36 [May 1984], pp. 51–58); while the other finds significant economies of scale for banks as large as $2.5 billion in assets (Colin Lawrence and Robert P. Shay, "Technology and Financial Intermediation in Multiproduct Banking Firms: An Econometric Study of U.S. Banks, 1979–1982," in Lawrence and Shay, eds., *Technological Innovation, Regulation, and the Monetary Economy* [Cambridge, Mass.: Ballinger, 1986]). Significantly, one recent study has found substantial economies of scale in the lending activities of Japanese banks. See Masahiro Kuroda and Takashi Kaneko, "Economies of Scale and Lending Behavior in the Banking Industry," *Bank of Japan Monetary and Economic Studies*, vol. 4 (April 1986), pp. 1–40.

82. Under the 1982 Banking Act, national banks can lend no more than 15 percent of their capital to any single borrower on loans not secured by marketable securities. However, by forming lending syndicates among all its individual banks, a multibank holding company can effectively aggregate the lending limits of its participating banks.

83. One recent econometric study of diversification by bank holding companies with assets above $5 billion has found that the risk of bank failure is inversely related to bank size. John H. Boyd and Stanley L. Graham, "Risk, Regulation and Bank Holding Company Expansion into Nonbanking," *Federal Reserve Bank of Minneapolis Quarterly Review*, vol. 10 (Spring 1986), pp. 2–17.

84. Samuel H. Talley, "Bank Capital Trends and Financing," Staff Studies 122 (Board of Governors of the Federal Reserve System, February 1983).

banks in the 1980s have also been small (with deposits less than $50 million) and have been concentrated in states with branching restrictions.[85]

The Erosion of Financial Product-Line Barriers

The same combination of forces that eroded barriers to price and geographic competition among banks—inflation, technology, and innovation at the state level—has also produced gaping holes in the legal walls designed to separate banking and nonbanking enterprises. To date, however, the breakdown of financial product-line barriers has been largely one-sided: it has been far easier for nonbanking firms to offer services that compete with banks than for banks to offer services that compete with nonbanking firms. This disparity should be corrected over time, the pace depending on the speed with which the federal regulatory agencies, state legislatures, and ultimately Congress expand bank and thrift powers.

Invasion of Banking by Nonbanks. In recent years banks have faced greatly increased competition from nonbanking institutions in activities and markets that banks have traditionally dominated.[86] The intensity of the invasion has varied among the various traditional "banking" activities.

On the lending side, not all of the developments have been adverse to the banking industry. As shown in figures 2-4 and 2-5, banks have actually increased their shares of mortgage and business credit since 1965. In addition, banks' share of consumer credit in 1985 was no lower than it was twenty years earlier (figure 2-6). However, the relative position of banks in this market has deteriorated rather sharply since 1980 because thrifts are significantly expanding their consumer lending activities.

85. Between January 1, 1982, and June 30, 1985, 179 of the 221 bank failures in the United States (81 percent) involved institutions with deposits less than $50 million. John Bovenzi, "Current Trends," in Federal Deposit Insurance Corporation, *Economic Outlook,* vol. 3 (June 1985), pp. 2–3. Between 1982 and 1984, 128 of the 165 bank failures (78 percent) occurred in states with limited or unit branching. Robert E. Litan, "Evaluating and Controlling the Risks of Financial Product Deregulation," *Yale Journal on Regulation,* vol. 3 (Fall 1985), p. 25.

86. See, for example, Christine Pavel and Harvey Rosenblum, "Banks and Nonbanks: The Horse Race Continues," *Federal Reserve Bank of Chicago Economic Perspectives,* vol. 9 (May–June 1985), pp. 3–17.

Figure 2-4. *Providers of Mortgage Credit, Selected Years, 1965–85*

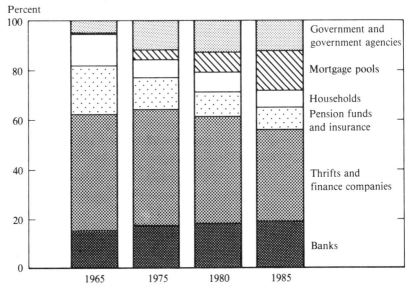

Source: "Flow of Funds Accounts, 1986" (Board of Governors of the Federal Reserve System, 1986).

The banking industry has suffered a far more serious erosion in its share of short- and intermediate-term lending (the predominant portion of total business credit) to commercial enterprises. As shown in figure 2-7, banks dominated this credit market until the late 1960s. Since then, however, corporations have increasingly turned to the commercial paper market and to branches and subsidiaries of foreign-based banks. At the end of 1960, commercial paper issued by nonfinancial corporations and finance companies totaled $4.5 billion. By the end of 1985, that figure had climbed more than fortyfold, to over $200 billion. In contrast, commercial and industrial loans extended by banks increased by only elevenfold over the same period, from $43 billion to $494 billion.[87]

The booming securities market of the 1980s has also encouraged

87. These trends are especially evident among large manufacturing corporations (those with assets above $1 billion), which in 1974 satisfied 59 percent of their short-term funding needs with bank loans and only 33 percent with commercial paper. By 1985 this borrowing pattern had reversed so that only 26 percent of their short-term borrowing was obtained through bank loans, while 52 percent was raised through commercial paper. See Testimony of Dennis Weatherstone in *The Internationalization of Capital Markets*, Hearings before the Senate Committee on Banking, Housing and Urban Affairs, 99 Cong. 2 sess. (GPO, 1986), p. 19.

Figure 2-5. *Providers of Credit to Nonfinancial Businesses, Selected Years, 1965–85*

Percent

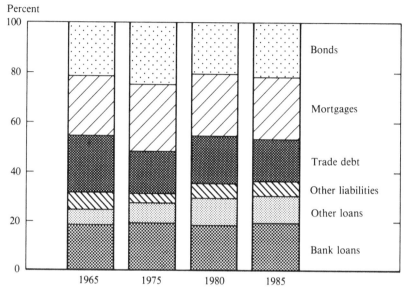

Source: See figure 2-4.

public corporations to raise funds directly through the capital markets rather than by borrowing from banks. Between 1979 and 1985 the volume of new securities (excluding commercial paper) offered by corporations increased threefold, from $50 billion to $156 billion. In contrast, commercial loans held by banks increased by only 70 percent, from $291 billion to $496 billion.

On the liability side, banks have largely been able to hold their own since late 1982, when Congress authorized banks and thrifts to offer unregulated money market accounts to compete with money market mutual funds. In 1985 banks and thrifts held over 90 percent of all interest-bearing retail deposit accounts, or the same level as they held in 1981.[88]

However, depository institutions have steadily lost market share in the hotly contested individual retirement account (IRA) market. In 1982, for example, banks and thrifts combined attracted 71 percent of all funds

88. Richard H. Mead and Kathleen A. O'Neil, "The Performance of the Banks' Competitors," in Federal Reserve Bank of New York, *Recent Trends in Commercial Bank Profitability* (The Bank, 1986), p. 317.

Figure 2-6. *Providers of Consumer Credit, Selected Years, 1965–85*

Percent

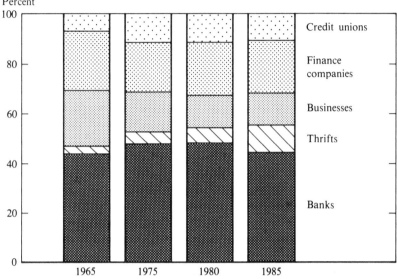

Source: See figure 2-4.

held in IRAs. But by 1984 the share held by the two depositories had declined to 65 percent; mutual funds and securities brokers had taken up the slack.[89]

In the long run, the most disturbing challenge to the banking industry is the effort by nonbanking—and even nonfinancial—firms to become modern financial supermarkets that offer the same services as banks and much more. Diversified financial conglomerates such as American Express, Merrill Lynch, and Prudential-Bache are household names, providing a wide range of depository, lending, and investment services. Less well known, but potentially even more significant, is the entry by *non*-financial giants into financial services. The finance subsidiaries of the two largest American automobile companies—Ford and General Motors—lend not only to automobile purchasers but also to home purchasers. General Electric's finance subsidiary, GE Credit is a leading business lender, and with the recent acquisition of Kidder Peabody, GE is now a major investment banker. The nation's largest retailer, Sears, Roebuck and Co., also has subsidiaries offering real estate and securities brokerage services, insurance, and bank and thrift services (discussed below).

89. Ibid., p. 319.

Figure 2-7. *U.S. Banks' Share of Short- and Intermediate-Term Credit Extended to Domestic Nonfinancial Corporations, 1952–85*

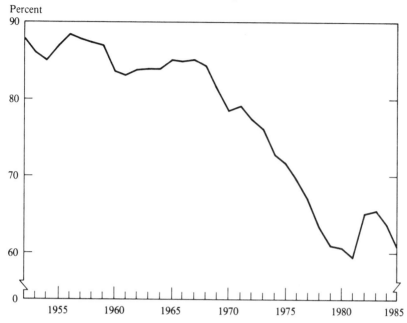

Percent

Source: *Appendices to the Statement of Paul A. Volcker, Chairman, Board of Governors of the Federal Reserve System,* before the Subcommittee on Commerce, Consumer and Monetary Affairs of the House Committee on Government Operations (Board of Governors of the Federal Reserve System, 1986), app. D, chart 2.

a. U.S. banks' holdings of nonmortgage loans and short-term paper issued by nonfinancial corporations as a share of nonfinancial corporations' total nonmortgage loans plus short-term paper outstanding.

All these trends are reflected in the declining relative importance of commercial banks as financial intermediaries in the United States. As shown in figure 2-8, commercial banks held 57 percent of all assets held by American financial institutions (excluding trusts) in 1946. By 1985 banks' share had fallen to just 33 percent.

Two anomalies—some would call them loopholes—in the legal framework governing financial institutions are aiding these invasions of nonbanking organizations into activities that banks once dominated. First, unlike the Bank Holding Company Act, the Savings and Loan Holding Company Act was never amended to include activity restrictions on those thrift holding companies (THCs) that own a single thrift institution. With legal distinctions between commercial banks and thrifts disappearing, the unitary THC device is permitting the erosion not only

Figure 2-8. *Percentage Distribution of Assets of Financial Institutions, Selected Years, 1946–85*

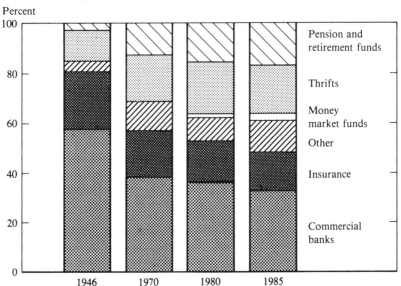

Source: Alan S. McCall and Victor L. Saulsbury, "The Changing Role of Banks and Other Private Financial Institutions," Federal Deposit Insurance Corporation, *Regulatory Review*, April 1986, p. 6.

of financial product-line barriers but also of the basic distinction between banking and commerce. An expanding number of well-known nonfinancial enterprises have been able to conduct bank activities—accepting deposits and making consumer and commercial loans—by purchasing only one savings and loan. These companies include: Ford Motor Co., J. C. Penney Financial Corp.; International Telephone and Telegraph; National Steel Corp.; Parker Pen Co.; Sears, Roebuck and Co.; and Transamerica Corp.

Second, nonbanking organizations have increasingly taken advantage of the nonbank bank loophole in the BHCA to open limited-purpose banks, to sell to their customers a wide range of banking and nonbanking services and products. Among the companies that now own nonbank banks are Aetna Life and Casualty Company; Control Data Corp.; Drexel Burnham Lambert; Dreyfus Corp.; E. F. Hutton; Gulf and Western; J. C. Penney Company; Merrill Lynch, Pierce, Fenner and Smith; Prudential-Bache Securities; and Sears, Roebuck and Co. These firms are prominent in the securities, insurance, and retailing industries. The nonbank bank owned by Sears, Greenwood Trust Company of

Delaware, was the fastest growing bank in the United States in 1986, with deposits increasing from just $27 million in 1985 to $1.05 billion by the end of 1986.

Explaining Nonbank Competition to Banks. Why are banks being assaulted from so many directions? Deposit interest rate regulation has been an important contributing factor. As already discussed, deposit rate ceilings in the inflationary environment of the 1970s and early 1980s spawned the creation of the NOW account and the MMF. The latter device in particular brought securities firms and then insurance companies into the banking business. The inflationary surge of the 1970s was also responsible for blurring the legal distinctions between banks and thrifts. By producing a mismatch between the single-digit interest rates thrifts earned on their long-term mortgages and the double-digit interest rates they were forced by market pressures to pay their depositors, inflation impelled Congress in the early 1980s to allow federally chartered thrifts to compete in consumer and commercial lending activities traditionally dominated by banks.[90] Although existing savings and loans have been hesitant about using their new asset powers, newly chartered thrifts have been more aggressive in diversifying into nonmortgage lending.[91]

The diversified financial conglomerates, which thrive on their ability to offer a wide range of financial services, see their entry into banking as a way to cross-sell all those services to the customers of each of the subsidiaries or divisions in these organizations. Sears, for example, now markets its securities and real estate brokerage services to its credit card holders. With its new, highly successful "Discover" card, Sears is also marketing its banking services (through its Delaware-chartered nonbank bank) to its retail customers.

90. In 1980 Congress authorized federally chartered thrifts, as part of the Depository Institutions Deregulation and Monetary Control Act, to invest up to 20 percent of their assets in consumer loans, to offer credit cards, and to accept NOW accounts, all in direct competition with commercial banks. Two years later when the thrift situation had deteriorated even further, Congress again expanded the powers of federal thrifts, raising the consumer loan ceiling to 30 percent of assets and authorizing those thrifts to accept demand deposits from individuals (but not businesses) and to invest up to 10 percent of assets in commercial loans. For a thorough description of the thrift industry's condition during this period, see Andrew S. Carron, *The Plight of the Thrift Institutions* (Brookings, 1982).

91. See Robert E. Goudreau, "S&L Use of New Powers: Consumer and Commercial Loan Expansion," *Federal Reserve Bank of Atlanta Economic Review*, vol. 69 (December 1984), pp. 15–35; and Robert A. Eisenbeis, "New Investment Powers for S&L's: Diversification or Specialization?" *Federal Reserve Bank of Atlanta Economic Review*, vol. 68 (July 1983), pp. 53–62.

Table 2-1. *Net Interest Margin and Loan Loss Provisions for Banks, 1980–85*

Percent of assets

Item	1980	1981	1982	1983	1984	1985
Net interest margin						
All banks	3.09	3.17	3.28	3.25	3.26	3.36
Banks with less than $100 million in assets	4.31	4.39	4.40	4.28	4.17	4.27
Banks with assets between $100 million and $1 billion	3.85	3.94	4.00	3.90	3.89	4.00
Large banks other than money center	2.81	2.94	3.06	3.02	3.13	3.31
Nine money center banks	2.06	2.10	2.34	2.40	2.38	2.36
Loan loss provisions						
All banks	0.25	0.26	0.40	0.47	0.57	0.66
Banks with less than $100 million in assets	0.27	0.29	0.42	0.51	0.63	0.86
Banks with assets between $100 million and $1 billion	0.26	0.27	0.42	0.43	0.46	0.61
Large banks other than money center	0.29	0.29	0.46	0.56	0.64	0.56
Nine money center banks	0.19	0.21	0.30	0.36	0.50	0.74

Sources: Deborah J. Danker and Mary M. McLaughlin, "Profitability of Insured Commercial Banks in 1984," *Federal Reserve Bulletin,* vol. 71 (November 1985), pp. 845–49; and Danker and McLaughlin, "Profitability of Insured Commercial Banks in 1985," *Federal Reserve Bulletin,* vol. 72 (September 1986), pp. 628–32.

To quantify precisely the effect that intensified nonbank competition has had on banks is difficult, but that effect undoubtedly has been negative. The industry's after-tax return on assets fell from its recent peak of 0.80 percent in 1979 to just 0.65 percent in 1984, although it recovered to 0.71 percent in 1985. Banks of all sizes suffered an erosion in profitability over this period, except for the large banks ($1 billion or more assets) outside money centers.[92] Somewhat surprisingly and contrary to conventional wisdom, the elimination of Regulation Q does not appear to have contributed directly to the decline in bank profitability. As shown in table 2-1, the net interest margin (spread) for all banks, except those with less than $100 million in assets, has remained stable or widened since Congress launched deposit interest rate deregulation in 1980.[93] Instead, the table highlights that banks have become less

92. Deborah J. Danker and Mary M. McLaughlin, "Profitability of Insured Commercial Banks in 1984," *Federal Reserve Bulletin,* vol. 71 (November 1985), pp. 836–49; and Larry D. Wall, "Profits in '85: Large Banks Gain while Others Continue to Lag," *Federal Reserve Bank of Atlanta Economic Review,* vol. 71 (August–September 1986), pp. 18–31.

93. For a somewhat different view, see Andrew Silver, "Impact of Deposit Rate

profitable because they have been required to raise their loan loss reserves, despite steady economic expansion.

The increase in bank loan losses in part reflects deliberate choices that bank managers are making to assume greater risk. These choices are reflected in ill-advised loans, especially in lending markets where banks have encountered stiffer competition. With prime quality borrowers turning more to open markets for commercial paper, long-term debt, and equity for funds, banks are being left to fund higher credit risks. Moreover, both the recent downturn in bank profits and the escalation in the bank failure rate appear to have exceeded what could have been expected based on cyclical factors alone, suggesting that basic structural forces are weakening the industry's profitability.[94]

Not all of the banking industry's rising loan losses, however, can be attributed to a deliberate effort to increase risk to compensate for the increased competition in traditional bank product markets. Many banks with large loan commitments to troubled developing countries have steadily added to their loan loss reserves, squeezing their profits. Moreover, forces over which banks have had no control—notably the 1981–82 recession and the deflation in the agricultural and energy sectors—have also been highly influential in depressing bank profitability.[95]

The Expansion of Bank and Thrift Powers

The banking industry in recent years has intensified its efforts to obtain broader powers to meet its added competition. The Reagan administration has been sympathetic with this campaign. In 1983 it

Deregulation and the Increased Competition for Bank Funds," in Federal Reserve Bank of New York, *Recent Trends in Commercial Bank Profitability*, pp. 193–221.

94. A study by FDIC economists found that 70 percent of the variation in the quarterly bank failure rate between 1970 and June 1984 could be accounted for by various cyclical measures (including the corporate debt burden and the unemployment rate). See John Bovenzi and Lynn Nejezchleb, "Bank Failures: Why Are There So Many?" in Federal Deposit Insurance Corporation, *Economic Outlook*, vol. 2 (August 1984), pp. 6, 11–12. The deterioration of banking industry performance since 1984 in the face of continued economic expansion, however, suggests that deeper structural forces are depressing the industry. See Federal Reserve Bank of New York, *Recent Trends in Commercial Bank Profitability*, chaps. 5–8.

95. The increasingly divergent performance of different sectors of the economy has contributed to the weakening of bank loan portfolios. See Arnold Kling, "The Banking Crisis from a Macroeconomic Perspective" (Board of Governors of the Federal Reserve System, Financial Studies Section, November 1986).

proposed legislation (S. 1609 and H.R. 3537) to authorize bank holding companies to engage, through separate corporate subsidiaries, in a broad range of financial activities, including real estate investment and broker-age, insurance underwriting and brokerage, and the underwriting and brokerage of securities (but excluding the underwriting of corporate securities). Late the following year, the Senate overwhelmingly ap-proved (by a vote of eighty-nine to five) a stripped-down version of the administration's proposal (S. 2851), sponsored by Senator Jake Garn, then chairman of the Senate Banking Committee. The Senate bill would have expanded BHC powers to include discount securities brokerage and the underwriting of revenue bonds, mortgage-backed securities, and commercial paper; it also would have permitted BHCs to acquire healthy thrift institutions. But the House did not take up this modest addition to BHC activity authority, and accordingly, the Senate bill died with the close of the 1984 congressional session.[96]

The stalemate on expanded bank powers has continued. In 1986 Senator Garn again offered a modest expansion of BHC powers, but this proposal never emerged out of the Senate Banking Committee. By 1987 the debate had shifted from expansion to a *freezing* of BHC powers. As part of a plan to bolster the resources of the beleaguered FSLIC, the Senate passed a bill that, among other things, would impose a one-year moratorium on the ability of the Federal Reserve or the Comptroller to expand the authorized nonbanking activities of BHCs and banks and that would prohibit new nonbank banks (while limiting the growth of existing limited-purpose banks). The House-passed FSLIC rescue leg-islation had no such features. At this writing, the House-Senate confer-ence committee had sided with the Senate version, but it was not certain that Congress would enact the compromise legislation and, if so, whether the president would sign it.

The outlook for passage of sweeping federal banking legislation any time soon, therefore, is not promising. But the dim prospects do not mean that the legal framework governing competition between different types of financial institutions will remain static. To the contrary, in one or more ways depository organizations are likely over time to gain additional powers without federal legislation.

First, the federal regulators are likely to broaden gradually the list of domestic nonbank activities that banks or BHCs are permitted. As

96. Chapter 5 provides a more complete description of certain aspects of S. 1609 and S. 2851.

shown in table 2-2, between 1978 and 1984, the Federal Reserve Board added seven new permissible domestic activities by regulation, largely to allow BHCs added opportunities to generate fee income in brokerage (but not risk underwriting). The Board has also allowed individual BHCs even broader powers by specific order, rendered on a case-by-case basis. Significantly, most of the orders have been issued since 1980. Although the Federal Reserve continues to be constrained by the "closely related to the business of banking" and "proper incident to banking" tests of the BHCA in defining the list of authorized domestic nonbank activities, continuing changes in the financial marketplace have driven and will continue to drive the Board to become more permissive.[97]

These market pressures are most evident in the recent testing of the outer limits of the Glass-Steagall Act by both the Federal Reserve and the Comptroller.[98] In 1983 the Federal Reserve first ruled that a BHC could own and operate a discount brokerage firm, one that executes trades but does not provide investment advice.[99] The Fed was forced to concede that discount brokerage was "closely related to the business of banking" because the Comptroller had earlier permitted joint ventures between national banks and discount brokers; indeed, by the time the Fed ruled, more than 200 banks had completed such arrangements.[100] Today, over 2,000 banking organizations offer discount brokerage services.[101]

Another blow to the spirit of Glass-Steagall came in the closing days

97. In 1986, for example, the Board proposed to allow BHCs to invest in real estate development, but not in excess of 5 percent of capital. It also expanded the authority of BHCs to sell insurance in small towns with populations less than 5,000. For a general description of the Board's policies toward nonbank activities of BHCs, see "The Federal Reserve Board's Oversight of the Domestic and International Activities of U.S. Banks and Bank Holding Companies," *Appendices to the Statement by Paul A. Volcker, Chairman, Board of Governors of the Federal Reserve System,* before the House Subcommittee on Commerce, Consumer and Monetary Affairs of the Committee on Government Operations (The Board, 1986), app. B.

98. See generally, Stephen J. Friedman and Connie M. Friesen, "A New Paradigm for Financial Regulation: Getting From Here to There," *Maryland Law Review,* vol. 43, no. 3 (1984), pp. 436–38.

99. In early 1987 the Supreme Court held that federal banking law does not prohibit banks from offering discount brokerage services wherever they are permitted to do banking business—including across state lines.

100. *Restructuring Financial Markets: The Major Policy Issues,* Committee Print, Report from the Chairman of the Subcommittee on Telecommunications, Consumer Protection, and Finance of the House Committee on Energy and Commerce, 99 Cong. 2 sess. (GPO, 1986), p. 82.

101. See Mead and O'Neil, "Performance of the Banks' Competitors," p. 336.

Table 2-2. *List of Permissible Nonbank Activities for Bank Holding Companies, 1971–86*

Year	By regulation	By specific order
1971	Making and servicing loans	Pooling loss reserves of banks with small business loans
	Industrial banking	
	Trust company functions	
	Investment or financial advice	
	Leasing personal or real property	
	Community development	
	Data processing (significantly expanded in 1982)	
	Insurance sales (limited)	
1972	Underwriting credit life, accident, and health insurance	Operating a thrift institution in Rhode Island
1973	Courier services	Buying and selling gold and silver bullion
1974	Management consulting to other depository institutions (expanded to nonbanks in 1982)	
1975	None	Operating a guaranty savings bank in New Hampshire
1977	None	Operating an investment company under New York law
1979	Issuing money orders, savings bonds, and travelers checks	Retail check authorization and check guaranty services
		Providing consumer-oriented financial management courses and materials
1980	Real estate appraising	None
1982	None	Engaging in commercial banking overseas through branches of a nonbank Delaware company
		Operating a distressed savings and loan
1983	None	Operating a limited-purpose bank that conducts credit card activities only

of 1986 when the Circuit Court of Appeals for the District of Columbia upheld a Federal Reserve ruling that banks were not prohibited under the act from privately placing commercial paper on behalf of corporate clients.[102] Technically, this decision did not permit banks to *underwrite* commercial paper, that is, to purchase the securities and then to resell them. Rather, the court approved the narrow activity of banks to place commercial paper with ultimate purchasers for a fee without actually

102. *Securities Industry Association* v. *The Board*, 807 F. 2d 1052 (D.C. Cir. 1986).

Table 2-2 *(continued)*

Year	By regulation	By specific order
1984	Arranging commercial real estate equity financing	Issuing consumer-type payment instruments having face value of not more than $10,000
	Discount securities brokerage	Operating a nonbank bank
	Underwriting and dealing in government obligations and money market instruments	FCM brokerage of futures contracts based on a municipal bond
	Foreign exchange advisory and transactional services	Providing financial studies and expert testimony for private corporations
	Acting as a futures commission merchant (FCM)	
1985	None	FCM brokerage of futures contracts based on stock indexes (and options on such contracts)
		Tax preparation services
		Credit card authorization services and lost or stolen credit card services
		Employee benefits consulting
		Expanded student loan servicing activities
		Insurance and sale of official checks
		Underwriting and reinsuring home mortgage redemption insurance
1986	Consumer financial counseling	None
	Tax planning and preparation	
	Futures and options advisory services	
	Operating a collection agency and credit bureau	
	Performing personal property appraisals	

Sources: *Appendices to the Statement by Paul A. Volcker, Chairman, Board of Governors of the Federal Reserve System,* before the House Subcommittee on Commerce, Consumer and Monetary Affairs of the Committee on Government Operations (Board of Governors of the Federal Reserve System, 1986), attachment I-D; Monica Langley, "Fed to Allow New Services by Bank Firms," *Wall Street Journal,* June 26, 1986.

taking title to the securities. Nevertheless, this aspect of the ruling adds yet another crack in the Glass-Steagall barriers designed to separate commercial and investment banking.[103]

In April 1987 the Federal Reserve Board issued a highly controversial ruling that could punch another gaping hole in the wall that Glass-Steagall

103. The Board's ruling, however, puts a significant constraint on bank placement of commercial paper, limiting it to no more than 5 percent of the gross revenues generated by the bank's underwriting affiliate.

was supposed to have erected between commercial and investment banking. This decision granted requests by Citicorp, J. P. Morgan, Bankers Trust, and other money center banking organizations to underwrite commercial paper, mortgage-backed securities, municipal revenue bonds, and securities backed by consumer installment debt (auto loans and credit card receivables) through separate securities subsidiaries "not principally engaged" in these underwriting activities. According to the Board, a securities subsidiary will meet the "not principally engaged" test as long as the gross revenues from the underwriting of the newly approved securities constitutes no more than 5 to 10 percent of the subsidiary's total gross revenues and if the subsidiary holds no more than a 5 percent market share in the underwriting of those securities.[104] The Board's ruling, however, was immediately challenged in federal court by the Securities Industry Association, and its effective date will be delayed until March 1988 if the Senate-passed moratorium on expanded BHC powers is enacted into law.

Perhaps even more significant, the Comptroller issued a ruling in June 1987 permitting national banks directly to underwrite securities backed by mortgages the banks originate, without the percentage limitations required by the Federal Reserve's ruling. If this opinion survives legal challenge by the securities industry (and any limited moratorium that may be imposed by Congress), it would pave the way for bank underwriting of a broad array of asset-backed instruments.

As significant as the recent federal regulatory approvals may be, American banking organizations still have less freedom in their domestic underwriting activities than they have in foreign markets, where the Federal Reserve has given broad permission to American BHCs to compete.[105] Although the Board limits American BHCs to $2 million in uncovered commitments of corporate equities in foreign securities markets, it does not restrict BHCs from participating in underwriting

104. The "not principally engaged" test has been interpreted more liberally by the Superintendent of Banking for the state of New York, who issued a ruling in December 1986 permitting banks chartered in that state to underwrite otherwise impermissible securities through separate bank subsidiaries, provided that the underwriting of those securities represented no more than 25 percent of the "activity" of the subsidiaries.

105. Under the Board's Regulation K, BHCs headquartered in the United States are permitted to engage in foreign nonbank activities as long as they are of a "financial nature." Under this standard, the Federal Reserve has authorized BHCs to engage in a number of permitted foreign businesses that are not on the approved domestic nonbank list, including general insurance agency and brokerage, managing a mutual fund (whose shares are not sold in the United States), travel agency, and corporate securities underwriting (subject to the limits noted in the text above).

debt securities abroad. As a result, subsidiaries of American BHCs are making inroads into foreign debt markets. In 1985 five American banking organizations ranked among the world's thirty largest underwriters of Eurobonds.[106]

Unless the Glass-Steagall Act is further liberalized soon, large American banking organizations are likely to concentrate increasing resources and effort in underwriting activities abroad where financial deregulation has been moving at a faster pace than in the United States. Canada has just dropped its long-standing financial product-line barriers by allowing common ownership of banks, trust companies, savings institutions, insurance companies, and securities firms. Of even greater significance are recent developments in the United Kingdom. In 1986 that country launched its "Little Bang," which opened London's securities markets to foreign firms, notably to leading U.S. banks. "Big Bang" followed later the same year, eliminating fixed brokerage commissions and the historic distinction in the United Kingdom between securities dealing and trading. Both liberalizations will accelerate the interest of American firms in financing their activities through underwritings in foreign markets where competition for their business is more intense than here.[107]

As American corporations turn more to the Euromarkets for new funds, pressures to repeal Glass-Steagall will mount in Congress. Although the foreign affiliates of American banks and securities houses will capture much of this foreign underwriting business, they will face stiff competition (discussed in the next chapter) from foreign-based institutions, particularly those headquartered in Japan.

The disparity between the strength of competition in the United States and in the European securities markets will only grow more difficult to defend. Indeed, at present, the United States and Japan are alone among the major industrialized countries in the world where commercial and investment banking are separated (table 2-3).[108] Moreover, dissatisfac-

106. M. S. Mendelsohn, "U.S. Banks Keep a Hand in International Bonds," *American Banker*, July 18, 1986. The Eurobond market has grown exponentially since the early 1970s, when $10 billion in new issues represented a good year. In 1986 new issues totaled $186 billion, and total trading in all Eurobond issues exceeded $3 trillion. See John J. Duffy, "The Eurobond Market Faces Regulation," *American Banker*, January 29, 1987.

107. Indeed, between 1981 and 1984, roughly one-third of all bond offerings by American corporations were sold in the Euromarkets. See *Restructuring Financial Markets*, p. 102.

108. However, the Japanese Finance Ministry reportedly is planning to allow foreign banks to engage in the Japanese securities business. Doug Tsuruoka, "Japan Planning Moves to Widen Finance Markets," *Wall Street Journal*, December 17, 1986.

Table 2-3. *Powers of Banks in Foreign Countries*

Country	Other significant bank powers
Bank underwriting of securities permitted	
Belgium	Banks may also hold equity shares of nonbank firms
Canada	Banks permitted to own securities firms as of July 1987
France	Banks may hold up to 20 percent of shares in a nonbank firm
Germany	Banks free to engage in any financial activity
Hong Kong	Banks may hold up to 25 percent of capital in nonbank company shares
Italy	Banks may hold up to 2 percent of capital in nonbank company shares
Netherlands	No restrictions on bank activities; equity participation above 5 percent in nonbank firms subject to approval
Singapore	Banks may hold up to 25 percent of capital in nonbank company shares
Switzerland	No activity restrictions
United Kingdom	No activity restrictions
Bank underwriting of securities prohibited or severely restricted	
Japan	Banks may underwrite public-sector securities and most securities abroad through subsidiaries; Japanese government may soon allow foreign banks to engage in the securities business
United States	Banks may underwrite general obligation municipals and arrange private placements; bank holding companies may engage in activities "closely related to the business of banking," and are generally free to underwrite all types of securities abroad through subsidiaries

Sources: Richard M. Levich, "A View from the International Capital Markets," in Ingo Walter, ed., *Deregulating Wall Street* (Wiley, 1985), p. 281; Doug Tsuruoka, "Japan Planning Moves to Widen Finance Markets," *Wall Street Journal,* December 17, 1986; and Michael Bobad, "Securities Deregulation Set to Get Under Way in Canada," *Washington Post,* June 30, 1987.

tion with Glass-Steagall will intensify as foreign banks, again especially those from Japan, acquire interests in American investment banks.[109] At

109. In 1986 Sumitomo Bank, the most profitable bank in Japan, acquired a limited partnership interest in Goldman Sachs, one of the strongest privately held investment banks in the United States. As a bank holding company, Sumitomo's purchase was governed by the Bank Holding Company Act, which permits BHCs to own only up to 5 percent of the voting securities of prohibited nonbanking activities. After a hearing on the issue, the Federal Reserve nevertheless held that Sumitomo's investment was exempt from these provisions because the Japanese banking organization had acquired only a passive ownership interest (as a limited partner) in Goldman Sachs.

Table 2-4. *Authorized Activities of State-Chartered Banks in Selected States*[a]

Item	Alabama	Alaska	California	Florida	Iowa	New York	North Carolina	Ohio	South Dakota
Insurance									
Underwriting	$	$					$		$
Brokerage	$	$			$		$		$
Securities									
Underwriting	$	$	$			$	$	$	
Brokerage	$	$	$				$		
Real estate									
Development	$	$	$	$		$	$	$	
Brokerage	$	$	$	$	$	$	$		$
Travel agency	$	$	$		$	$	$	$	$
Management consulting	$	$	$			$	$	$	

Source: Conference of State Bank Supervisors, as of August 1985.
a. This list is not exhaustive.

some point the Glass-Steagall Act may come to look so anachronistic that its repeal will become politically acceptable, if not inevitable.

Second, states are likely to provide broader authority for banking organizations by expanding the powers of their state-chartered banks. Indeed, as shown in table 2-4, many states already allow their banks to engage in a wide variety of nonbank businesses.[110] A recent survey conducted by the National Conference of State Legislatures indicates that thirteen states are likely to expand the powers of banks in their states in the 1987 legislative session.[111] Moreover, over one-third of the states—including Arizona, California, Florida, Ohio, and Texas—have allowed their thrift institutions to invest directly in real estate and other assets, permission not extended to federally chartered thrifts.[112]

Liberalization of state bank powers will be slowed by concerns about the health of the banking industry as a whole. And the expansion of interstate banking rights will almost certainly have to play itself out

110. A number of states permit their banks to participate in all or virtually all of the nonbank activities shown in the table. For a detailed enumeration of state bank powers in specific states, see Peter J. Wallison and Donald J. Toumey, "Continued Banking Deregulation Seems Inevitable," *Legal Times,* March 5, 1984; and Victor L. Saulsbury, "Bank Product Deregulation,"in Federal Deposit Insurance Corporation, Division of Research and Strategic Planning, *Regulatory Review,* May 1987, pp. 1–14.

111. Bureau of National Affairs, *Daily Report for Executives,* January 22, 1987.

112. James R. Barth, R. Dan Brumbaugh, Jr., and Daniel Sauerhaft, "Failure Costs of Government-Regulated Financial Firms: The Case of Thrift Institutions," Federal Home Loan Bank Board, June 1986. See also *Federal Regulation of Direct Instruments by Savings and Loan Associations,* H. Rept. 99-358, 99 Cong. 1 sess. (GPO, 1985).

before most states will turn with the same vigor to broadening the set of permissible bank activities. But if history is any guide, it is inevitable that an increasing number of states will liberalize bank authority as a way of attracting financial service firms and jobs to their locales. As they do, banks currently operating with a national charter will have increasing incentives to convert to state charters.[113] Such conversions will in turn place increasing pressure on Congress to liberalize activity authority for national banks or bank holding companies, or both, to level the federal-state playing field.[114]

Third, banking organizations may acquire broader activity authority by converting to unitary thrift holding companies (those that own a single thrift institution), which as previously noted, are not subject to the activity restrictions of the Savings and Loan Holding Company Act.[115] Recently, however, this option has become less attractive because the FHLBB, in an effort to supplement the dwindling reserves of the FSLIC, has added a special assessment to the deposit insurance premiums federally insured thrifts must pay.[116] Nevertheless, as nonbanking organizations continue to eat away at bank markets, the unitary THC device may prove to be more popular.

In sum, market forces, abetted by competition between federal and state regulatory authorities, will continue to erode the effectiveness

113. Significantly, in April 1987, shortly after New York liberalized the securities underwriting powers of its state-chartered banks, Citicorp converted its Rochester, New York, banking subsidiary from a national to a state charter. The Citicorp bank became the first subsidiary of a multinational holding company to leave the Comptroller's jurisdiction in more than a decade.

114. Significantly, the FDIC has anticipated the movement toward broader state banking powers. In 1984 the agency issued a rule requiring state-chartered banks not belonging to the Federal Reserve System—or those the FDIC directly supervises—to conduct any corporate securities underwriting that their states may allow solely through "bona fide" subsidiaries. According to the FDIC, a bona fide subsidiary is one that is capitalized at levels commensurate with the industry standard and that operates with employees, officers, and directors separate from those of the bank. In 1985 the FDIC proposed a similar rule that would require *all* insured banks to conduct any insurance underwriting or real estate development activities that their states may allow them through bona fide subsidiaries. The FDIC's actions are discussed in chapter 5.

115. See Victor L. Saulsbury, "Commercial Banks: An Endangered Species?" Federal Deposit Insurance Corporation, Division of Research and Strategic Planning, *Regulatory Review*, March 1986, pp. 1–9.

116. The FHLBB has also requested Congress for authority to impose a penalty on thrifts that withdraw from the FSLIC.

of the Depression-era financial product-line restrictions. The critical challenge facing policymakers, therefore, is not whether to halt this process, but whether to guide and manage it, and if so, in what manner. The subsequent chapters of the book help shed light on how this challenge can best be addressed.

CHAPTER THREE

Benefits from Financial Product Diversification

THE REMOVAL of barriers separating banks from other financial institutions can theoretically produce three types of social benefits. Relaxing product-line restrictions would permit new entrants to compete away excess profits that certain providers of financial services earn. Expanding activity freedom would permit financial "supermarkets" to deliver banking, securities, insurance, and real estate services together, yielding "economies of scope," cost savings from joint production and delivery of services or products. Allowing activity diversification would permit depository organizations in particular to smooth their earnings fluctuations, thereby reducing the risk that the federal deposit insurance agencies would need to rescue insured bank depositors.

This chapter assesses the potential benefits, while chapter 4 examines the potential risks, of allowing broader financial product freedom. These assessments relate only to the *social*, not the *private*, benefits and risks. The fact that private firms may choose to exercise wider activity powers does not prove that financial product diversification is socially beneficial. Managers of financial institutions, like those of nonfinancial enterprises, may seek to build financial conglomerates to enhance their personal prestige and compensation. When financial supermarkets are built to aggrandize an empire rather than to exploit market opportunities, society would be no better off and perhaps worse off if financial product-line restrictions were relaxed.

The evidence surveyed in this chapter, however, indicates that society would in fact benefit from financial product diversification. To be sure, most financial service markets are already highly competitive and thus unlikely to benefit from added entry by banking organizations. But competition in investment banking is imperfect enough that repealing the Glass-Steagall Act may lead to a modest reduction in fees charged for securities underwriting and other investment banking services.

Economies of scope from the joint provision of multiple financial services—that both producers and consumers would realize—are likely to be more significant. Finally, the typical depository organization should be able to reduce the variance of its earnings substantially without impairing its average profitability if banks or their holding companies were permitted to engage in a broader set of activities than allowed under current law.

The analysis in this chapter concentrates on potential bank entry only into "financial" nonbank activities, specifically the underwriting and brokerage of insurance, securities, and real estate. These activities are singled out because they are the most controversial and frequently mentioned targets of expansion by banks and thrifts.[1] The policy recommendations surveyed in chapter 5, however, address the possibility of bank entry into a broader array of nonbanking activities.

Benefits from Enhanced Competition

Financial product diversification will inevitably enhance the strength of competition in banking and nonbanking markets. The social benefits of new entry will be greatest in those financial service markets that are now imperfectly competitive, whether because of high natural barriers to entry or as a result of legal restrictions on financial product-line expansion. Where markets are already highly competitive, however, the social benefits of new entry are likely to be insignificant, although new competitors with different product and marketing strategies may prod existing suppliers to improve their own service offerings.

Theoretical Overview

Imperfect competition exists when suppliers in a market are able to exert some control over the prices they charge, specifically to set prices

---

1. See American Bankers Association, *Assessment of Business Expansion Opportunities for Banking* (Arthur Young and Company, 1983). The ABA study analyzed the potential opportunities for bank entry into thirteen service markets. The study was based on available financial data for each activity and on interviews with representatives of thirty-two banks of different sizes. The service markets found not to be moderately or highly attractive or suitable for bank entry included travel agency, nonfull payout leasing, telecommunications, and insurance underwriting. Of these less attractive activities, only insurance underwriting is examined separately in this chapter.

above marginal cost. When imperfect competition occurs, consumers pay higher prices and thus purchase a smaller volume of services than if the market were competitive. Costs are also likely to be inflated because firms do not face strong pressures to be efficient.[2] As shown in appendix A, these adverse effects of imperfect competition are to be distinguished from the economies of scope that diversified organizations may be able to realize by offering banking and nonbanking services jointly.

Unfortunately, marginal costs of firms are not readily observable, particularly for firms using common production, marketing, and distribution facilities to deliver multiple products or services. Accordingly, market power must be detected indirectly. A commonly used approach is to examine both the level of concentration in a market—the percentage of sales that the largest firms collectively capture—and the profitability of firms in that market. Industrial organization economists have traditionally maintained that in markets dominated by a few sellers, average profits are likely to be "supranormal"; that is, rates of return on equity or assets will exceed those required to compensate firms for the risks of competing in such markets.[3] Recent research suggests that the likelihood of imperfect competition significantly increases at four-firm concentration levels in the neighborhood of 50 percent and at eight-firm concentration levels in the 70 percent range.[4]

---

2. Harvey Leibenstein has labeled this behavior "x-inefficiency" in his seminal article "Allocative Efficiency vs. X-Efficiency," *American Economic Review*, vol. 56 (June 1966), pp. 392–415. See also William S. Comanor and Harvey Leibenstein, "Allocative Efficiency, X-Efficiency, and the Measurement of Welfare Losses," *Economica*, vol. 36 (August 1969), pp. 304–09.

3. Joe S. Bain was the first to find that profits and hence prices tended to be higher in concentrated industries, particularly where barriers to entry were also very high. See Bain, "Economies of Scale, Concentration and the Condition of Entry in Twenty Manufacturing Industries," *American Economic Review*, vol. 44 (March 1954), pp. 15–39; and Bain, *Barriers to New Competition: Their Character and Consequences in Manufacturing Industries* (Harvard University Press, 1956). Other studies have since supported the main thrust of Bain's early findings. See the summary discussion in Frederic M. Scherer, *Industrial Market Structure and Economic Performance* (Houghton Mifflin, 1980), pp. 276–95.

4. Ralph M. Bradburd and A. Mead Over, Jr., "Organizational Costs, 'Sticky Equilibria,' and Critical Levels of Concentration," *Review of Economics and Statistics*, vol. 64 (February 1982), pp. 50–58; and James W. Meehan and Thomas E. Duschenau, "The Critical Level of Concentration: An Empirical Analysis," *Journal of Industrial Economics*, vol. 22 (September 1973), pp. 21–35.

An alternative measure of concentration known as the Herfindahl-Herschman index (HHI) considers the market shares of all competitors in a market but assigns greater weight to the largest firms by summing the squares of the market shares (expressed in absolute numbers rather than in percentages) of all competitors. In 1982 the Department

A number of economists in recent years, however, have challenged the traditional view, arguing that observed linkages between market concentration and industry profitability reflect the superior efficiency of the leading firms rather than their market power.[5] Accordingly, a market that is highly concentrated may not indicate that it is imperfectly competitive. If this is the case, additional entry cannot automatically be expected to bring down prices.

In the financial services context, however, sound reasons are present for believing that a link exists between market concentration and imperfectly competitive behavior. As highlighted in chapter 2, the current legal framework severely restricts cross-industry entry by banking and nonbanking firms. Banking organizations, in particular, are generally precluded from offering many other financial services that for reasons discussed later in this chapter, are well suited to be delivered with banking services. One should not presume, therefore, that the existing market structure, at least in nonbanking financial industries, reflects the most efficient set of producers or suppliers. Accordingly, a high degree of concentration, together with a pattern of consistently high profitability in a nonbanking financial activity, is more likely to signal imperfectly competitive conditions in the financial services sector than in other sectors of the economy not burdened by legal barriers to entry.[6]

The Evidence

Table 3-1 summarizes recent profitability and concentration data for various financial service industries (excluding real estate, where com-

---

of Justice and the Federal Trade Commission replaced four- and eight-firm concentration ratios with the HHI in assessing the competitive effects of proposed mergers. Both agencies view HHI levels of 1,800 and above as indicating a highly concentrated market. For example, a market where four competitors have market shares of 40, 30, 20, and 10 percent, respectively, would have an HHI of 3,000 (1,600 + 900 + 400 + 100).

5. See, for example, Harold Demsetz, "Industry Structure, Market Rivalry, and Public Policy," *Journal of Law and Economics*, vol. 16 (April 1973), pp. 1–10; and Yale Brozen, "Concentration and Structural and Market Disequilbria," *Antitrust Bulletin*, vol. 16 (Summer 1971), pp. 241–48. For an excellent summary of the recent doctrinal debate between the traditionalists and their critics in the field of industrial organization economics, see Frederic M. Scherer, "On the Current State of Knowledge in Industrial Organization," in H. W. de Jong and William G. Shepherd, eds., *Mainstreams in Industrial Organization* (Dordrecht, The Netherlands: Martinus Nijhoff, 1986), pp. 5–22.

6. Because they are protected by legal barriers to entry, the various financial service markets are not perfectly "contestable," as that term recently has been used by some theorists. See William J. Baumol, John C. Panzar, and Robert D. Willig, *Contestable Markets and the Theory of Industry Structure* (Harcourt, Brace, Jovanovich, 1982).

Table 3-1. *Market Statistics for Financial Service Industries*

Industry	Number of firms	Concentration	Average after-tax return on equity (ROE) 1975–84 (percent)	Standard deviation of ROE (percent)
Commercial banks[a,b]	14,481 (1984)	Top twenty-five held 33 percent of assets in 1984	12.3	1.3
Thrift institutions[a,b]	3,393 (1984)	Top twenty-five held 25 percent of assets in 1984	3.4	10.7
Securities brokers[c,d]	4,885 (1983)	Top twenty-five accounted for approximately 75 percent of revenue and capital in 1984	13.0[e]	4.0
Securities underwriters[c]	n.a.	Moderately concentrated	16.4	5.7
Large investment banks only[d]	n.a.	See table 3-2	21.5	7.7
Life insurance underwriters[a,d]	2,193 (1985)	Top twenty-five held 53 percent of assets in 1983	13.7	2.3
Property-casualty insurance underwriters[a,d,e,f]	3,474 (1984)	Top twenty-five accounted for approximately 60 percent of all premiums in 1983	11.9	6.4
Insurance brokers and agents[g,h]	Approximately 70,000 (1981)	n.a.	12.2[i]	4.1
All manufacturing[j]	...	...	13.1	2.0

n.a. Not available.
a. U.S. Department of Commerce, Bureau of the Census, *Statistical Abstract of the United States, 1987* (Government Printing Office, 1986), pp. 482, 485, 499.
b. U.S. General Accounting Office, Staff Study, *Deposit Insurance: Analysis of Reform Proposals*, GAO/GGD-86-32A (Washington, D.C.: GAO, 1986), p. 24.
c. Securities Industry Association Yearbooks, 1983–84, for figures for 1976–83.
d. Richard H. Mead and Kathleen A. O'Neil, "The Performance of the Banks' Competitors," Federal Reserve Bank of New York, *Recent Trends in Commercial Bank Profitability* (The Bank, 1986), p. 364; underlying data supplied by staff at the Federal Reserve Bank of New York.
e. 1975–83.
f. Insurance Information Institute, *1984–85 Property/Casualty Fact Book* (New York: III, 1984), p. 11.
g. Mead and O'Neil, "Performance of the Banks' Competitors," p. 297.
h. Robert Morris and Associates, *Annual Statement Studies* (Philadelphia, Pa.: RMA, 1979, 1983, 1985). Since this source publishes profit data only on a pretax basis, after-tax returns on equity are calculated on the assumption that firms paid the maximum 48 percent corporate income tax rate.
i. 1976–85.
j. *Economic Report of the President, January 1987*, table 13-88.

prehensive data are not available). The profit data are shown as after-tax returns on equity. The concentration measures vary because the data come from diverse sources.

The information reported in table 3-1 indicates that of all the financial services industries, only investment banking shows evidence of significant imperfect competition. In all other lines of financial activity, thousands of firms compete, and markets are unconcentrated. Similarly, between 1975 and 1984, after-tax returns on equity for all financial services industries—except thrift institutions and securities underwriting—are in the 12 to 13 percent range. In the aggregate, therefore, the potential competitive benefits alone from further financial diversification appear to be limited. A more disaggregated look at the specific industries where some competitive improvement may be possible follows below.

Investment Banking. Because of its association with the Depression, broader bank participation in investment banking generally and in securities underwriting specifically is one of the more controversial aspects of the debate over financial product deregulation. However, of all financial service industries in the United States, investment banking also displays the strongest signs of imperfect competition: supranormal profitability and market concentration.

Table 3-1 indicates that between 1975 and 1984 securities underwriters as a group earned 16.2 percent on equity after taxes. This return on equity is the highest profit level recorded by any of the financial services listed. However, profits were even higher at the ten largest investment banks, which as discussed further below, dominate corporate securities underwriting in the United States (see table 3-2). These institutions earned an average of 21.5 percent on equity after taxes between 1975 and 1984, or more than nine percentage points more than commercial banks. Even if the variability (or riskiness) of profits that these institutions recorded is considered, their profits still outdistance those of other financial services. Thus, for example, the lower bound of after-tax returns on equity by the large investment banks at one standard deviation from the mean over the 1975–84 period, or 13.8 percent (21.5 percent minus 7.7 percent as shown in table 3-1), ranks above the mean profit level for every other financial service.[7]

7. Fisher and McGowan have persuasively argued that drawing inferences about the extent of monopoly power from accounting rates of return is difficult because accounting profits may not relate to the true economic rate of return on investment. Franklin M. Fisher and John J. McGowan, "On the Misuse of Accounting Rates of Return to Infer

Table 3-2. *Measures of Securities Underwriting Concentration in the U.S. and European Securities Markets, 1980–85*[a]

Percent

Market	1980	1981	1982	1983	1984	1985
Banks may not under-write securities						
U.S. corporate securities[b]						
Top five	59	64	54	56	71	70
Top ten	83	84	71	79	91	91
Municipal and state revenue bonds[c]						
Top four	23	27	27	27	n.a.	n.a.
Top ten	43	50	50	49	n.a.	n.a.
Dealer-placed commercial paper[e]						
Top five	n.a.	n.a.	99	99	98	96
Banks may underwrite securities						
Eurobonds[d]						
Top five	33	37	41	n.a.	n.a.	n.a.
Top ten	47	52	57	n.a.	n.a.	n.a.
Municipal and state general obligations[e]						
Top four	15	14	14	18	n.a.	n.a.
Top ten	31	29	29	32	n.a.	n.a.

n.a. Not available.

a. Concentration data based on dollar volume of lead managers for securities offerings.

b. Mead and O'Neil, "Performance of the Banks' Competitors," p. 364.

c. Public Securities Association, *Statistical Yearbook of Municipal Finance: The New Issue Market* (New York: PSA), 1980–83 editions.

d. Richard M. Levich, "A View from the International Capital Market," in Ingo Walter, ed., *Deregulating Wall Street* (Wiley, 1985), p. 273.

e. Data supplied by the Federal Reserve Board.

The high profits among securities underwriters conceal the high salaries and profit-sharing draws that investment banks pay their personnel, a fact consistent with the tendency of firms in imperfectly competitive markets to incur excessive costs. In 1985, for example, five of the top twenty-five highest paid executives in the United States at

Monopoly Profits," *American Economic Review*, vol. 73 (March 1983), pp. 82–97. However, because the Fisher-McGowan critique relies heavily on departures between accounting and economic rates of depreciation on capital investment, the critique is less relevant to firms in the financial services sector where the overwhelming proportion of assets are financial rather than physical.

publicly held corporations were officers of investment banks.[8] In the same year, personnel costs for the largest investment banks (which accounted for over 40 percent of the securities industry's profits in 1985) averaged over $100,000 per employee (including partners), compared with approximately $50,000 for the two leading wholesale commercial banks (Bankers Trust and Morgan Guaranty) and $33,800 for all twelve money center banks.[9] Bank entry into the full range of securities activities would compress these differentials in personnel costs since it would reduce profits that investment banks earn, as well as permit personnel that commercial banking organizations employ to be involved in a broader range of investment banking activities.[10]

Likewise, concentration among securities underwriters stands at levels at or near those traditionally associated with imperfectly competitive markets. As shown in table 3-2, in 1985 the top five investment banks were lead managers for 70 percent of U.S. corporate securities underwritten in that year—up from 54 percent as recently as 1982—and for 96 percent of all commercial paper placed through dealers. Significantly, Glass-Steagall bars banks from underwriting corporate debt and equity and severely restricts their underwriting of commercial paper.[11]

In short, the available profitability and concentration data indicate that the investment banking industry is imperfectly competitive. Repealing the prohibitions against commercial bank entry into securities underwriting would enhance competition. As shown in table 3-2, concentration in the Eurobond market, where banks are permitted to participate, has been substantially lower than in the American market

8. *Business Week,* May 5, 1986, p. 49. Four investment bankers made the "top 25" list in 1986. Ibid., May 4, 1987, p. 51.

9. Securities industry data are drawn from *Securities Industry Trends,* vol. 12 (May 30, 1986). Banking industry data are drawn from Thomas H. Hanley and others, *A Review of Bank Performance: 1986 Edition* (New York: Salomon Brothers, 1986), p. 74.

10. Commercial banks find it difficult to attract high-quality personnel from investment banks without paying the high six-figure (or even seven-figure) salaries these individuals now earn at investment banks. See Phillip Zweig, "Growing Pains," *Wall Street Journal,* August 13, 1986. However, commercial banks are competing for personnel in a market when the Glass-Steagall Act still protects investment banks from commercial bank competition. If that protection were removed, the added competition should reduce profits from investment banking activities. Such competition would, in turn, reduce the marginal revenue product that personnel employed by investment banks generate, causing salaries and profit shares to fall.

11. However, as discussed in chapter 2, a 1986 court decision has permitted banks to place commercial paper with purchasers without actually underwriting it.

for corporate securities offerings. Similarly, concentration levels have been far lower for underwritings of general obligation municipal bonds in the United States than for municipal revenue bonds that have been off limits to banking organizations.[12] Even if the Federal Reserve's recent ruling authorizing bank holding companies to underwrite commercial paper and revenue bonds through subsidiaries not "principally engaged" in such activities is upheld, banking organizations still would be restricted in the volumes of these securities they could underwrite and would therefore continue to operate at a competitive disadvantage, relative to their investment bank counterparts. In short, regulatory action by the Federal Reserve cannot provide the competitive benefits that could be supplied if the Glass-Steagall Act were simply repealed.

What benefits would added competition in investment banking bring? One clear advantage would be lower underwriting fees. Writing in 1979, William Silber reported that all twelve studies that had addressed the issue found that issuing costs and underwriting spreads (differences between prices that underwriters paid to issuers and those that underwriters charged to retail purchasers) were significantly lower for general obligation municipal and state bonds (which banks could underwrite) than for municipal and state revenue bonds (which banks could not underwrite). The differentials ranged between seven and thirteen basis points, equivalent to $150 million to $300 million per year in cost to issuers.[13] More recent studies making the same comparison give no reason to alter this estimate.[14]

It is unclear, however, whether the competitive benefits of permitting banking organizations to underwrite corporate securities would be as great as permitting them to underwrite revenue bonds. On the one hand,

12. The most recent data for the municipal revenue bond market suggest that that market has grown even more concentrated than the figures in table 3–2 indicate. In 1986 the top four underwriters of municipal revenue bonds (excluding state revenue bonds) held 35 percent of the market; the top ten garnered 62 percent. Concentration in the much larger market in underwritings of collateralized mortgage obligations was substantially greater: the top four underwriters held a 73 percent share; the top ten held a 96 percent share. See Phillip Zweig, "Fed Read to Hear Arguments for New Bank Powers," *Wall Street Journal*, February 2, 1987.

13. William L. Silber, *Municipal Revenue Bond Costs and Bank Underwriting: A Survey of the Evidence,* Monograph Series on Finance and Economics, 1979-3 (New York University Graduate School of Business Administration, 1979), p. 8.

14. For a listing of these studies, see Thomas A. Pugel and Lawrence J. White, "An Analysis of the Competitive Effects of Allowing Commercial Bank Affiliates to Underwrite Corporate Securities," in Ingo Walter, ed., *Deregulating Wall Street* (Wiley, 1985), pp. 128, 135.

since market concentration is higher for corporate securities issues than it is for municipal and state revenue bonds, the potential benefits of bank entry into the corporate securities market may be even greater than bank entry into municipal and state revenue bonds.

On the other hand, competition among corporate securities underwriters appears to have intensified in recent years, despite the increase in market concentration. This situation suggests that less room is available for improvement. The new factor is Rule 415, which the Securities and Exchange Commission (SEC) introduced in 1982. Rule 415 permits a company to register with the SEC all securities of a particular type that the company reasonably expects to issue over a two-year period.[15] By allowing issuers to pull securities "off the shelf," Rule 415 dramatically reduces the time required to complete an underwriting. While this provision has given larger investment bankers, with the capabilities to perform "due diligence" reviews and to purchase entire issues on short notice, an advantage over their smaller competitors, Rule 415 has also made each security more of a "commodity" and thus has intensified the vigor of competition among underwriters for business. Knowing the volume of securities "on the shelf," investment banks solicit issuers for business, while issuers themselves appear more willing to shop around, tendencies that lead to more competitive bidding.[16] Studies conducted by the SEC confirm that, on balance, Rule 415 has had a procompetitive effect, lowering spreads on equity issues by roughly 1 percent and spreads on bonds by approximately thirty to forty basis points.[17]

Moreover, continuing technological change in the securities markets should also dissipate the potential benefits of permitting banks to underwrite securities. Through their experience and established business relationships, investment banks have traditionally been able to locate potential purchasers of corporate securities more cheaply than the

15. By 1984 Rule 415 underwritings comprised 56 percent of all domestic underwritings. See Richard H. Mead and Kathleen A. O'Neil, "Performance of the Banks' Competitors," in Federal Reserve Bank of New York, *Recent Trends in Commercial Bank Profitability* (The Bank, 1986), p. 292.

16. See Pugel and White, "An Analysis of the Competitive Effects," pp. 114–16, 122–23.

17. See the following works by M. Wayne Marr and G. Rodney Thompson: "Shelf Registration and the Utility Industry," and "The Rule 415 Experiment: Equity Markets," Virginia Polytechnic Institute and State University, June 1983 and September 1983, respectively; and "Summary of 'Rule 415—The Ultimate Competitive Bid,'" Working Paper 171 (University of Tennessee, June 1983).

corporate issuers themselves. The diffusion of sophisticated computer-related telecommunications technology, however, threatens to reduce the underwriters' comparative advantage. Computer networks increasingly enable issuers and purchasers to be linked directly, without needing an intermediary. In time, underwriters may be left only with providing advice about securities offerings. Such a function will command a far lower price than the risk assumption activities underwriters currently perform.[18]

In contrast, corporate customers of advisory services offered by investment banks should benefit substantially from having the Glass-Steagall barriers removed. Securities underwriting now makes up only a small portion of total revenues that investment banks generate. A far more sizable proportion of investment bank earnings arises out of advisory fees, particularly those collected from mergers and acquisitions. For example, of the $10 billion in revenues earned by the ten largest investment banks in 1984, $6 billion originated from activities other than trading and underwriting; indeed, underwriting accounted for only $734 million, or little more than 7 percent of total revenues. This pattern holds true for the securities industry generally: in 1984 underwriting activities generated only $1.5 billion of $13.1 billion in revenue of all national full-line securities firms.[19]

To be sure, the Glass-Steagall Act does not bar banks from offering advisory services that compete with investment banks. However, by offering both underwriting and advisory services simultaneously, investment banks have a strong competitive advantage over commercial banks, since many mergers and acquisitions require financing through additional securities offerings to the public, whether through debt or equity. The rapid rise of Drexel Burnham Lambert to the upper echelons of the investment banking elite, for example, was made possible by the marriage of that firm's merger and acquisition (M&A) advisory talent to its extraordinary ability to place sub-investment grade securities ("junk bonds") with investors. Because of the Glass-Steagall Act, however, banks face a severe disadvantage in competing for M&A business since they cannot underwrite securities and may be unwilling

18. For an excellent discussion of the impact of technology on the securities markets and what it implies for securities regulation, see Donald C. Langevoort, "Information Technology and the Structure of Securities Regulation," *Harvard Law Review*, vol. 98 (February 1985), pp. 747–804.
19. Mead and O'Neil, "Performance of the Banks' Competitors," p. 354.

or unable to extend loans in the volumes required to complete the necessary financing.[20] Without this disadvantage, certain banks with extensive networks of customer relationships, which they could use to market or place securities, should be able to provide strong and effective competition with investment banks and thus bring down advisory fees.

Finally, relaxing the Glass-Steagall restrictions soon would have another, not widely recognized, benefit. As noted in chapter 2, recent liberalizations in the United Kingdom have enabled large foreign banks to affiliate with securities firms headquartered in London and thus to underwrite securities in the London market. As competition for under-writings in that market intensifies—particularly as it lowers underwriting spreads—American borrowers should increasingly turn to offering their securities through underwriters operating in the United Kingdom rather than in New York, accelerating a trend toward Euromarket financings by American corporations. Although some of this new business will be captured by London-based securities affiliates of American banking organizations, a large portion can be expected to flow to foreign financial organizations, particularly Japanese-owned banks and security houses, which has chapter 4 discusses, are now dominant in the world market and deeply involved in financial activities in London.

Securities business that is lost to foreign competitors reduces incomes of American banking and securities firms. Moreover, foreign-owned underwriters will inevitably want to lever their ability to market the securities of American corporate issuers into capturing other banking and financial business of these customers, posing the threat of greater losses in market share for American-based financial institutions. The sooner, therefore, that American banking organizations are allowed to compete without restriction in corporate securities underwriting activi-ties in the United States, the more quickly this expected loss of financial service jobs and income will be halted. Indeed, employment by foreign banks and securities houses operating in London jumped by over 11,000, or 26 percent, in 1986 alone, the largest single-year increase in the last two decades.[21] Citicorp already has 4,500 employees in the United Kingdom; Chase Manhattan more than 2,000; and Security Pacific more

---

20. It is not surprising, therefore, that between 1981 and 1984 banks participated as advisers in only five of the largest one hundred merger transactions during this period of intensive merger activity. See ibid., p. 321.

21. Michael Blanden, "Bigger Role for Foreign Banks in the City," *The Banker,* vol. 136 (November 1986), p. 69.

than 1,100.[22] Many of these employees would be working here rather than abroad if Glass-Steagall were repealed.

Insurance. Of all the financial service industries, only investment banking evidences strong signs of imperfect competition. Nevertheless, the profit levels in segments of at least two lines of financial activity—life insurance and insurance agency—appear high enough to attract entry by commercial banking organizations. Such additional entry could only have a procompetitive effect.

First, although the average profitability of life insurers appears similar to that of commercial banking (see table 3-1), the return on equity of stockholder-owned insurers has outpaced that of mutual insurers: 15.6 percent versus 10.6 percent over the 1975–84 period.[23] Moreover, while it is not heavily concentrated on a nationwide basis, the life insurance industry is still more concentrated than the commercial banking industry. As shown in table 3-1, the top twenty-five insurers control 53 percent of the assets among all life insurance companies.[24]

Larger banking organizations are natural entrants into life insurance underwriting, which tends to be less risky than property-casualty insurance underwriting.[25] And both traditional whole life insurance policies and the newer "single-premium" insurance policies are easily marketed as alternative savings vehicles to bank depositors.[26] Recent survey evidence suggests that banks might be more aggressive competitors in selling life insurance than existing insurers or their agents.[27]

22. "Yanks in Europe," *American Banker*, December 16, 1986.

23. Mead and O'Neil, "Performance of the Banks' Competitors," p. 270. The returns for mutual insurers are measured net of policyholders' dividends.

24. However, unlike large banking organizations, which are confined by law to just one or a few states, most large life insurers conduct business in all states. As a result, competition among banks in each state is generally less intense than the nationwide bank concentration statistics otherwise would indicate.

25. A recent survey of seventy-eight of the largest American banks found that twenty-three would be "very" or "somewhat" interested in underwriting life insurance; only thirteen expressed any interest in property-casualty insurance underwriting. See Lynn Brenner, "Insurance Underwriting Tempts Banks," *American Banker*, April 11, 1986.

26. Given the changes in the federal income tax law in 1986, single-premium life insurance policies are one of the few remaining attractive tax-deferred investment vehicles. Such policies require a purchaser to invest a lump sum, which not only covers all life insurance premiums for a given time period but also accumulates interest that is untaxed until the policy matures.

27. A recent survey conducted by the Consumer Federation of America found that bank-based life insurance agents were more willing to provide information—including

Second, insurance brokerage, too, is more profitable than it appears from the industrywide average return on equity figure shown in table 3-1. In particular, larger brokers have outperformed smaller insurance agencies by a wide margin: 22.5 percent versus 12.5 percent over the 1975–84 period.[28] This disparity in performance may indicate the presence of economies of scale in brokerage activities, a feature of the business that larger banking organizations would be well positioned to exploit.

Of all insurance activities, however, property-casualty insurance underwriting appears the least attractive for additional bank entry. Table 3-1 indicates that although the industry reported a return on equity (11.9 percent) that was close to that of commercial banking (12.3 percent) over the 1975–84 period, the earnings of property-casualty insurers were far more variable. Indeed, property-casualty insurers suffered through their worst years in the history of their industry in both 1984 and 1985. Underwriters have blamed much of their recent poor financial performance on expansive liability doctrines and have responded by significantly increasing premiums and withdrawing coverage.[29] Although certain representatives of the banking industry have cited this reaction as proof that the property-casualty industry could benefit from additional competition,[30] it is doubtful that many banking organizations would rush to fill the void if they were able. The strongest competition to property-casualty insurers has come from parties in perhaps the best position to assess and monitor the risks to which they are exposed—groups of (former) insureds themselves, or companies that have formed their own insurance syndicates. Given the highly volatile earnings pattern that property-casualty insurers have displayed in the past, it is unlikely that

---

premiums and premium cost comparisons—to customers over the telephone than were independent insurance agents. The study also estimated that, in the aggregate, American consumers could save between $5 billion and $7 billion per year in insurance premium payments by shopping more carefully. However, the study did not claim that those savings would necessarily be realized if banks were broadly permitted to sell life insurance. Consumer Federation of America, "The Potential Costs and Benefits of Allowing Banks to Sell Insurance," Washington, D.C., February 10, 1987.

28. Mead and O'Neil, "Performance of the Banks' Competitors," p. 270.

29. See Tort Policy Working Group, *Report of the Tort Policy Working Group on the Causes, Extent and Policy Implications of the Current Crisis in Insurance Availability and Affordability* (Washington, D.C.: Department of Justice, 1986).

30. Testimony of Edward Yingling, American Bankers Association, before the Subcommittee on Commerce, Transportation and Tourism of the House Energy Committee, April 22, 1986.

many banking organizations—with little or no experience in the field—would be eager entrants.[31]

Banking. Finally, opening up entry into banking by nonbanking organizations would only modestly enhance competition among depository institutions. Roughly 20,000 depositories—banks, thrifts, credit unions, and money market mutual funds—operate in the United States. This figure is widely believed to be higher than the number of firms required for effective competition. To be sure, competition in certain geographic markets, particularly in rural areas, is imperfect because of restrictions on intrastate branching and interstate expansion. However, available evidence suggests that concentration in local banking markets has been declining and that the efficiency costs of the current geographic barriers are small.[32] In any event, these costs are being reduced and should eventually be eliminated as interstate banking proceeds.[33] How much additional benefit would then be added by relaxing product-line restrictions is difficult to estimate, but it cannot be large.

Economies of Scope

A second way in which further financial product deregulation may yield social benefits is through economies of *scope,* cost savings from delivering multiple goods and services jointly through the same organi-

31. Indeed, for these reasons, the 1983 study on expanded bank powers commissioned by the American Bankers Association found that insurance underwriting was unattractive to banks.

32. Stephen A. Rhoades, "Interstate Banking and Product Line Deregulation: Implications from Available Evidence," *Loyola of Los Angeles Law Review,* vol. 18 (Fall 1985), pp. 1115–45. Using profit data over the ten-year period 1969–78 for 6,500 unit banks (those without branches) and thus avoiding any bias introduced by bank diversification, Rhoades estimated that the deadweight welfare loss of imperfect competition in the U.S. banking industry totaled only $11.9 million in 1978. Rhoades also found that where it existed, monopoly power in the banking industry had not led to increased costs. Nevertheless, Rhoades' study documented a sizable redistribution of income from consumers to banks in concentrated markets, totaling $1.3 billion in 1978. See Stephen A. Rhoades, "Welfare Loss, Redistribution Effect, and Restriction of Output Due to Monopoly in Banking," *Journal of Monetary Economics,* vol. 9 (May 1982), pp. 375–87.

33. One recent estimate suggests that aggregate banking costs would drop between $88 million and $600 million per year if interstate banking restrictions were lifted. Those figures exceed Rhoades' estimated welfare cost of the existing imperfect competition in the industry, but not his estimate of the redistribution of income from consumers to banks. See Mark J. Flannery, "The Social Cost of Unit Banking Restrictions," *Journal of Monetary Economics,* vol. 13 (March 1984), pp. 237–49.

zation rather than through specialized providers. These potential cost savings are to be distinguished from economies of *scale,* which represent lower costs per unit of a single good (or service) as total output of that good (or service) rises. As noted in chapter 2, a consensus of empirical studies has found that banking organizations do not display scale economies above $100 million in assets. Are there reasons for believing that greater opportunities exist for economies of scope as financial product diversification proceeds?

No clear answer emerges from studies that have examined the joint provision of services that banking organizations currently provide, although most investigators rely on a single data set, annual costs reported in the *Functional Cost Analysis* published by the Federal Reserve.[34] Much of the difference in results is due to variations in the number of bank "output" categories analyzed. Those studies that have measured cost savings across only two types of bank output—deposits and loans—have found significant scope economies, as large as 42 percent.[35] However, those researchers who have analyzed more than two bank output measures report conflicting results: one such study has found cost complementarities between most of the pair-wise output combinations among four bank outputs,[36] while another has found the opposite.[37] Most recently, in perhaps the most comprehensive empirical examination in this area thus far, Allen Berger, Gerald Hanweck, and David Humphrey explored five deposit and loan categories of bank output simultaneously and found evidence of only slight scope economies in commercial banking.[38]

The mixed evidence based on the costs of narrow deposit and loan

34. As observed in chapter 2, participating banks in the *Functional Cost Analysis* have deposit bases below $1 billion.

35. Thomas W. Gilligan and Michael L. Smirlock, "An Empirical Study of Joint Production and Scale Economies in Commercial Banking," *Journal of Banking and Finance,* vol. 8 (March 1984), pp. 66–67; and Thomas W. Gilligan, Michael L. Smirlock, and William Marshall, "Scale and Scope Economies in the Multi-Product Banking Firm," *Journal of Monetary Economics,* vol. 13 (May 1984), pp. 393–405.

36. Colin Lawrence and Robert P. Shay, "Technology and Financial Intermediation in Multiproduct Banking Firms: An Econometric Study of U.S. Banks 1979–1982," in Lawrence and Shay, eds., *Technological Innovation, Regulation, and the Monetary Economy* (Ballinger, 1986).

37. George J. Benston and others, "Economies of Scale and Scope in Banking," in *Proceedings of a Conference on Bank Structure and Competition* (Federal Reserve Bank of Chicago, May 1983). Interestingly, this study used essentially the same data that were analyzed in the Gilligan, Smirlock, and Marshall paper.

38. "Competitive Viability in Banking: Scale, Scope and Product Mix Economies," presented at the December 1985 meetings of the American Economic Association.

bank functions, however, should not be read to suggest that little potential exists for economies of scope as financial product diversification proceeds. Although cost data on the joint delivery of banking and nonbanking services are not available, strong conceptual grounds are present for believing that economies of scope among bank and nonbank activities would exist and could prove significant for those diversified firms willing to be patient for the economies to materialize.[39]

Two categories of potential scope economies must be distinguished. Firms may realize *internal* scope economies through joint *production and marketing,* whereas consumers may realize *external* scope economies through joint *consumption.* On the production side, economies of scope are likely to be available where facilities devoted to one objective or to serving a single market are not fully utilized and are capable of being deployed simultaneously to serve other objectives and other markets. On the consumption side, in contrast, economies of scope exist where providing multiple products or services at a single location or through a single firm saves consumers the time and expense of searching for and purchasing these items through specialized providers. Grocery stores, for example, realize economies of scope both from using their purchasing network to obtain many different food products and household supplies at the same time and from affording consumers the convenience to shop for all food and household supplies at a single time in a single location.

Financial supermarkets *that include banks* should be able to produce similar cost savings. Three production-related scope economies appear most likely.

First, diversified financial firms would be able to use the extensive network of customer relationships that their banking organizations have built up to lower the costs of the matching functions that both underwriters and brokers perform. For example, given their large customer base of corporate depositors and borrowers, many banks are likely to be able to match buyers and sellers of corporate assets (or of entire corporations) more efficiently and quickly than can many investment banks. Yet because the Glass-Steagall Act prohibits banks from underwriting the corporate securities that are often issued to finance these transactions, banks have only limited abilities to realize these savings.

---

39. For a similar view, see Edward J. Kane, "Technological and Regulatory Forces in the Developing Fusion of Financial-Services Competition," *Journal of Finance,* vol. 39 (July 1984), pp. 759–72.

Diversified financial organizations also may be able to use their banks to lower the costs of matching potential buyers and sellers of real estate.

Second, banking organizations can use the computer facilities that now store and process information required for delivering banking services to perform the same functions for providing other financial services.[40] Financial service firms have made significant investments in computer processing equipment in recent years. Although published data do not break out specific categories of investment, most of the plant and equipment spending by financial service firms—up 54 percent in real terms between 1983 and the second quarter of 1986, compared to just 22 percent for all industries—is likely to be devoted to computer- and communications-related facilities. These investment patterns reflect the fact that all financial service firms are essentially in the same business, providing and transferring information, which suggests the presence of scope economies across the broad range of financial services. A bank is primarily a computer data base that stores information about deposits and loans. An insurance company stores information about what to pay to whom if certain accidents or catastrophes occur. Securities and real estate brokers match buyers and sellers through computer-stored data bases. Any financial corporation doing business today should be capable of using the computer-stored data that lie at the core of one financial service to deliver other services and thus lower the costs of providing them all.

Third, diversified financial organizations should be able to realize economies in marketing and delivering multiple services jointly. Advertising and mailings that offer banking services can easily promote insurance, securities, and real estate services at the same time. Similarly, floor space in banks or in any other type of financial service firm can be used to deliver all financial services simultaneously more cheaply than they can be delivered by specialized providers of those services. For example, the current agency system for marketing, delivering, and servicing insurance is widely recognized as being inefficient, with many insurance brokers operating at less than optimal scale.[41] With their

40. One banker quoted in the recent staff study conducted by the Federal Reserve Bank of New York on the commercial banking industry has observed that "many operational service businesses conducted by banks have chronic excess capacity," and that once computer facilities are put in place, the marginal costs of adding an additional service drop "close to zero." See "Bankers and Bank Watchers on Bank Profitability," *Recent Trends in Commercial Bank Profitability*, p. 41.

41. Paul M. Horvitz, "Technological Innovation: Implications for Regulation of

branch networks and back-office capabilities, banking organizations should be able to realize scope economies in adding insurance to their service offerings. Indeed, premiums of life insurance provided by state-chartered savings banks in Massachusetts and New York are consistently among the lowest available throughout the nation.[42]

Of course, not all joint promotion and marketing of financial services need result in social benefit. To the extent financial product deregulation induces financial service firms to engage in trivial product differentiation and wasteful advertising services, all of which are conceivable, then no social economies from joint service marketing will be realized.

Finally, studies of economies of scope in the banking industry ignore the savings that joint consumption of financial services affords. As financial product diversification proceeds, such savings loom as perhaps the most important reason why many organizations are seeking to form financial supermarkets. For many consumers, particularly those in the rising number of two-earner households, the ability to obtain all financial services—banking, insurance, securities, and real estate—through the same organization would be an attractive convenience, yielding time savings that do not show up on firm balance sheets. A 1984 study published by the Federal Reserve Bank of Atlanta reported that 50 percent of the customers surveyed said that being able to obtain all their financial services through a single firm would be "somewhat" or "very" desirable. And of those favoring the single-firm approach, 93 percent said they would like that single firm to be a depository institution.[43] This finding is not surprising, since consumers contact their banks more consistently and frequently than they contact any other type of financial service firm. To be sure, there will always be customers who will want

Financial Institutions," in Lawrence and Shay, eds., *Technological Innovation, Regulation, and the Monetary Economy*, p. 117. Indeed, a recent study prepared for the American Insurance Association notes that the "distribution and service" sides of the insurance industry are the source of much of its current "expense problem" and that independent agents in particular duplicate functions that are performed at the underwriter level. American Insurance Association, *Expansion of Banks into Insurance* (New York, AIA, 1983), pp. 16–20.

42. "Life Insurance: Term Insurance," *Consumer Reports*, June 1986, pp. 383, 385; "Life Insurance: Whole-Life," *Consumer Reports*, July 1986, pp. 447–67. Savings banks in Massachusetts are not allowed to sell policies above $60,000 in face amount and are not permitted to sell insurance door to door or to pay salesmen on commission. New York restricts its mutual savings banks to selling life policies no larger than $30,000 in face amount. National banks have been permitted since 1916 to sell insurance only in towns with populations of 5,000 or less.

43. Veronica Bennett, "Consumer Demand for Product Deregulation," *Federal Reserve Bank of Atlanta Economic Review*, vol. 69 (May 1984), pp. 28–40.

Table 3-3. *Sample List of Major Diversified Financial Service Firms*

Company	Primary activity	Method through which engaged in banking	Other activities
Aetna Life and Casualty Company	Life and property-casualty insurance	Nonbank bank	Real estate development, financing
American Express	Travel services	Nonbank bank	Securities brokerage and underwriting, financing
Ford Motor Co.	Automobile manufacturing	Unitary thrift	Insurance underwriting, real estate development, consumer lending, financing
Gulf and Western	Diversified conglomerate	Nonbank bank	Insurance underwriting, motion picture production, real estate development, consumer lending, financing, leasing
Merrill Lynch and Co.	Securities brokerage	Nonbank bank	Insurance underwriting, real estate development, leasing
J. C. Penney Company	Retailing	Nonbank bank and unitary thrift	Insurance underwriting and brokerage, real estate development
Sears, Roebuck and Co.	Retailing	Nonbank bank and unitary thrift	Securities underwriting and brokerage, insurance underwriting and brokerage, real estate development and brokerage, mortgage banking

to deal with specialized providers, even if existing financial product-line restrictions were lifted. But the large potential market of consumers who apparently would prefer to patronize financial supermarkets provides powerful incentives for financial service firms to diversify their activities.

Perhaps the best evidence that scope economies are available through multiple financial services offerings is the movement that many organizations in recent years have made toward the financial supermarket model. Table 3-3 lists some of the more notable examples, identifying the range of services each provides. Significantly, although all of the companies listed in the table have traditionally been identified with nonbanking products and services, *each has entered banking,* either by opening a nonbank bank or a single thrift (thus escaping the activity restraints of the Savings and Loan Holding Company Act).

Of course, activity diversification need not prove rewarding for every firm that tries it. In 1986, for example, two financial supermarkets— American Express and Merrill Lynch—each repositioned its menu of service offerings.[44] Other diversified firms, such as Prudential-Bache,

44. American Express sold its property-casualty underwriter, Fireman's Fund;

have found that melding the sales, marketing, and personnel strategies of different financial service firms is more difficult than originally expected.[45] And the recent staff study published by the Federal Reserve Bank of New York found that profitability data for eight of the largest diversified financial conglomerates provided only inconclusive evidence of scope economies in financial services. While five of the eight finance companies owned by the diversified firms were more profitable than the typical large independent finance company, only four of the diversified giants reported earnings that were higher at the parent company level than the earnings for firms in the company's "primary" industry.[46]

However, it would be a mistake to conclude from the mixed experience of firms that have already diversified their service offerings that scope economies will not be available through the simultaneous delivery of banking and nonbanking activities. Although each of the diversified firms that the Federal Reserve staff study surveyed has entered banking by opening a nonbank bank, and significantly, has remained in banking, each of these banks is small compared with the rest of the firm with which it is affiliated. As a result, even with nonbanking organizations expanding modestly into banking, the marketplace has yet to witness what effects the joint delivery of banking and nonbanking services can offer.

To summarize, projecting the magnitude of future economies of scope from financial product diversification is difficult, if not impossible. Indeed, the notion that firms can realize synergies by forming multiproduct conglomerates has yet to be documented.[47] However, the changing nature of the financial services market suggests that different financial services are no longer (if they ever were) distantly related. Diversified financial service firms should come much closer to the grocery store model of enterprise than to the pure conglomerates that were the rage of the late 1960s. Economies of scope should be available in firms offering

Merrill Lynch withdrew from the real estate brokerage business in an apparent effort to devote greater resources to its worldwide securities business.

45. See Steve Swartz and Steve Weiner, "Stalled Synergy," *Wall Street Journal*, November 12, 1986.

46. Mead and O'Neil, "Performance of the Banks' Competitors," pp. 302–03. The diversified firms analyzed in the study included American Express, Beneficial Corporation, Household International, E. F. Hutton, Merrill Lynch, Aetna Life and Casualty Company, Transamerica Corp., and Sears, Roebuck and Co.

47. As noted in chapter 4, many mergers consummated in the 1970s have since become undone through sell-offs or spin-offs.

multiple financial services and products, even if these economies are currently difficult to quantify.

Activity Diversification

The final source of gains from further financial product deregulation lies in the benefits of activity diversification. As explained below, these benefits accrue to society if banking organizations can reduce the variability of their earnings at a given capital level and thus reduce their exposure to failure. Available data suggest that these benefits could be sizable.

The Importance of Diversification

As discussed in chapter 2, financial intermediaries are distinguished by their willingness to bear risks of several kinds: (1) *interest rate risks,* or the possibility that the cost of funds will rise above the return locked in on long-term assets; (2) *capital value risks,* which arise from the possibility that borrowers will default, leaving lenders with collateral whose value is often less than remaining loan balances; and (3) *liquidity risk,* or the sudden and unexpected redemption of an intermediary's liabilities—demand deposit withdrawals from banks or large unanticipated accident losses suffered by insurance companies—that can force emergency liquidations of relatively illiquid long-term investments at below market values.

Financial institutions endeavor to reduce the risks they face by shifting them to other parties and by diversifying their asset portfolios or activities. Risk shifting has increased in importance in recent years, particularly to thrift institutions, which once were locked in to long-term fixed-rate mortgages but now invest heavily in adjustable rate mortgages. Hedging interest rate risks through futures market transactions, for example, is also common.[48] And banks and thrifts have increasingly

48. A bank desiring to hedge against an increase in its cost of funds, for example, can sell a futures contract in Treasury bills, specifying a selling price on a certain future date. If interest rates rise before that date, the price of the Treasury bill will fall, enabling the bank to earn a profit on its futures contract. The profit on the futures transaction offsets the bank's higher cost of funds. For a guide to hedging transactions, see Michael T. Belongia and G. J. Santoni, "Hedging Interest Rate Risk with Financial Futures: Some Basic Principles," *Federal Reserve Bank of St. Louis Review,* vol. 66 (October 1984), pp. 15–25.

taken advantage of the exploding secondary market in mortgages and some consumer and commercial loans by selling those obligations to investment banks and other entities that package them and then sell securities backed by these packages.[49]

As long as they perform some intermediating function, however, financial institutions cannot shift all their risks to third parties. Indeed, the devices for shifting interest rate risk may enhance principal or default risks. For example, now that the interest rates on most commercial loans that banks extend float with market conditions, a prime objective of depository institutions is asset growth, since floating automatically builds in a positive interest rate margin on new loans. The drive toward maximizing assets may be pursued at the expense of credit quality, particularly if a bank's asset growth outstrips its ability to assess and monitor credit risks on new loans.[50]

These developments highlight the importance of *asset diversification* to all financial institutions, particularly to depository institutions. The advantage of diversification is that it allows institutions (as well as private investors) to combine in a single portfolio different assets with patterns of returns that over time are inversely related to some degree. This combination produces a smoothing effect, with the fluctuations in the earnings of some assets offsetting the fluctuations in the returns of other assets.[51]

In the nonbanking context, the private gains that firms may realize through diversification do not necessarily translate into *social* gains, because shareholders can offset any risk levels that individual firms assume by diversifying their own asset portfolios.[52] The federal insurance

---

49. For an excellent survey of the securitization movement, see Christine Pavel, "Securitization," *Federal Reserve Bank of Chicago Economic Perspectives,* vol. 10 (July–August 1986), pp. 16–31. Some observers have been concerned about the risks posed by securitization, particularly about the weakening of credit screening that the movement may entail. See Lowell L. Bryan, "The Credit Bomb in Our Financial System," *Harvard Business Review,* vol. 65 (January–February 1987), pp. 45–51.

50. Albert M. Wojnilower, "The Central Role of Credit Crunches in Recent Financial History," *Brookings Papers on Economic Activity, 2:1980,* pp. 277–326.

51. For expositions of the benefits of portfolio diversification, see Harry Markowitz, "Portfolio Selection," *Journal of Finance,* vol. 7 (March 1952), pp. 77–91; and *Portfolio Selection: Efficient Diversification of Investments* (Wiley, 1959). See also Eugene F. Fama, *Foundations of Finance: Portfolio Decisions and Securities Prices* (Basic Books, 1976).

52. Shareholders' abilities to diversify their own portfolios are nevertheless limited by the costs of assembling them. In addition, those shareholders who want to hold only

agencies, which bear the residual risk of bank failures, however, do not have such a luxury. Their "portfolios" are restricted by law to a single activity—banks for the Federal Deposit Insurance Corporation and thrift institutions for the Federal Savings and Loan Insurance Corporation.[53] Although the bank and thrift deposit insurance funds are designed to be self-financing through premium assessments on the insured institutions themselves, most depositors correctly believe that the United States Treasury or the Federal Reserve or both ultimately stand behind both funds.[54] Accordingly, risk-reducing activity (as well as geographic) diversification by bank or thrift organizations lowers the risk that taxpayers or the monetary authorities, or both, will be needed to rescue the insurance funds, either directly or indirectly, by propping up individual banks or thrifts threatened with failure.

Risk-reducing diversification by larger depository organizations in particular also can be important. In the past, the failure or near failure of larger banks has typically produced at least a short-term market perception that *all* large banks have become much riskier. This perception has raised the costs of funds for the banking system, increasing rates paid by borrowers and thus, at least temporarily, slowing investment growth during the perceived crisis. For example, the run on the Continental Illinois Bank in the spring of 1984 triggered an increase from 0.75 to 1.5 percentage points in the average spread that all large money center banks paid on three-month certificates of deposit relative to Treasury bills of the same maturity.[55] The CD-Treasury bill interest rate differential increased by an even larger three percentage points during 1974, when both the Franklin National Bank of New York and the Herstatt Bank in Germany went under.[56] Admittedly, these "spikes" in interest rate differentials disappeared shortly. But their occurrence suggests that diversification that has the effect of reducing the risk of large bank

---

a few stocks at a time gain from efficient diversification by the firms whose shares they hold.

53. The National Credit Union Association insures credit unions.

54. Both the FDIC and the FSLIC have only limited authority to borrow from the Treasury (up to $3 billion for the FDIC and only $750 million for the FSLIC). Nevertheless, it is widely believed that in an emergency either the Treasury or the Federal Reserve would provide far greater protection.

55. John J. Merrick, Jr., and Anthony Saunders, "Bank Regulation and Monetary Policy," *Journal of Money, Credit and Banking*, vol. 17 (November 1985), pt. 2, pp. 691–717.

56. Andrew S. Carron, "Financial Crises: Recent Experience in U.S. and International Markets," *Brookings Papers on Economic Activity, 2:1982*, pp. 395–418.

failures will lower the probability that society will be periodically subjected to the credit crunches associated with banking crises.

In theory, activity diversification can strengthen an insured bank and thus the federal insurance system, even if the nonbank activities are conducted outside the bank through the bank's holding company. This strengthening is possible because the earnings of the nonbanking affiliates may be flowed upstream (via dividends) to the parent holding company and from there back down to the bank in the form of capital infusions.[57]

At the same time, however, any opportunities open to depository institutions for reducing risks through diversification may not be realized, and indeed can be abused, because of the "moral hazard" that the present system of federal deposit insurance has created. As discussed more fully in the next chapter, this danger arises because deposit insurance premiums are not sensitive to the risks of bank or thrift failure and thus fail to deter depositories and arguably their holding companies from taking added risks. In the balance of this chapter, however, the assumption is made that banking organizations, considered collectively, would diversify in a risk-reducing way if given the opportunity to do so.

Pair-Wise Risk Comparisons to Estimate Benefits of Diversification

A critical issue for policymakers is to determine how significant the benefits of broader financial activity diversification would be. One way of analyzing this question is to compare the risks of commercial banking with those of a number of nonbanking activities for which comparable earnings information is available. Technically, this analysis can be accomplished by comparing the coefficient of variation of earnings, a standardized indicator of variability (computed as the standard deviation of earnings over a time period divided by the mean earnings level over the period) for banking and other activities. Banking organizations that enter nonbanking activities with lower coefficients of variation of earnings would experience a risk reduction. The same result could also be realized by combining banking with those nonbanking activities displaying offsetting earnings fluctuations. For example, a banking organization

---

57. Flows of funds in the other direction—from the bank to its holding company affiliates—are regulated by the Federal Reserve. Nevertheless, as discussed in chapters 4 and 5, bank holding companies may seek to circumvent these restrictions if the nonbank affiliates are threatened with failure.

could lower its risk exposure by entering insurance underwriting, even if considered in isolation the latter activity posed greater risk, if the earnings pattern of the bank were negatively correlated with that of insurance.

No set of data is ideal for estimating these relationships. The Department of Commerce collects and reports industry profitability data, but these data unfortunately are not disaggregated by the major types of financial product lines or activities. Other disaggregated data do exist, as discussed in the first part of this chapter, but they are generally unavailable before the mid-1970s. Finally, stock market prices, analyzed in certain studies,[58] are available only for banks (or their holding companies) whose stocks are publicly traded, or only a fraction of the nearly 15,000 commercial banks chartered in the United States.

None of these problems, however, appears in the income data that the Internal Revenue Service (IRS) collects and reports in its Source Book of Statistics of Income for Corporations. The IRS documents include profit information for all the major bank and nonbank financial activities, except for securities underwriting, which is not separately broken out from securities brokerage. Although banks in certain states and under certain limited conditions already engage in some nonbank activities covered in the IRS survey, the nonbank activities that are separately identified are generally off limits to banks or their holding companies. The profits reported to the IRS are based on tax accounting methods, which provide only imperfect approximations to income measured either by economic or financial accounting principles. The IRS data nevertheless represent the only source of comparable and consistent profit information for all major financial services industries.

Table 3-4 reports the results of the pair-wise risk comparisons based on IRS return on asset (ROA) data for different time periods analyzed by this author and in several prior studies.[59] The time periods shown in

58. See Peter C. Eisemann, "Diversification and the Congeneric Bank Holding Company," *Journal of Bank Research*, vol. 6 (Spring 1976), pp. 68–77; and Roger D. Stover, "A Reexamination of Bank Holding Company Acquisitions," *Journal of Bank Research*, vol. 12 (Summer 1982), pp. 101–08.

59. Because of changes in methods of reporting, however, estimates are not available for all of the activities listed in table 3-4. For earlier estimates calculated through 1981, see Robert E. Litan, "Evaluating and Controlling the Risks of Financial Product Deregulation," *Yale Journal on Regulation*, vol. 3 (Fall 1985), pp. 1–52.

The following prior studies are summarized in the table: Arnold Heggestad, "Riskiness of Investments in Nonbank Activities by Bank Holding Companies," *Journal of*

Table 3-4. *Coefficients of Variation (CV) and Correlation Coefficients (CR) for Banking of After-Tax Earnings for Selected Industries, Selected Years, 1953–82*

Percent of Assets

Activity	Heggestad (1953–67) CV	CR	Johnson and Meinster (1954–69) CV	CR	Wall and Eisenbeis (1970–80)[a] CV	CR	Litan (1962–72) CV	CR	Litan (1973–82) CV	CR	Litan (1962–82) CV	CR
Banks (except mutual savings and holding companies)	0.25	...	0.33	...	0.21	...	0.23	...	0.20	...	0.22	...[b]
Bank holding companies	...	...	...	...	0.20	0.79	...	...	0.20[b]	0.63[b]	0.20[b]	0.63[b]
Savings and loan associations	0.11	0.31	0.58	0.65	0.34	−0.46	0.33	−0.72*	0.72	−0.23	0.54	−0.37
Personal credit agencies	0.27	0.60	0.44	0.48	0.33	−0.70	0.13	0.65*	0.56	−0.45	0.40	0.01
Business credit agencies	...	...	...	...	0.25	0.77	0.10	0.50	0.51	0.35	0.34	0.31
Security agencies	...	...	...	...	0.35	−0.40	0.24	−0.37	0.26	0.10	0.37	−0.08
Security brokers, dealers, and flotation companies	...	...	...	...	0.41	−0.42	...	...	0.31	0.06	0.45	−0.11[c]
Commodities contracts, brokers, dealers, securities and commodities exchange	...	...	...	...	0.21	0.66	0.18	−0.79*	0.29	0.51	0.28	0.35[c]
Insurance underwriting	...	...	...	...	0.18	0.41	0.13	−0.87*	0.29	0.23	0.25	−0.19
Life insurance	...	...	...	...	0.10	−0.40	0.59	−0.55	0.32	−0.04	0.26	−0.27
Mutual insurance	...	...	...	...	0.49	0.31	0.18	−0.46	0.41	0.44	0.52	−0.21
Other insurance	...	...	...	...	0.43	0.45	0.18	−0.62*	0.49	0.36	0.35	0.08
Insurance agents	0.12	−0.38	0.15	−0.42	0.19	0.70	0.10	−0.62*	0.23	0.21	0.17	−0.06
Real estate	...	...	...	...	0.22	0.78	0.05	−0.69*	0.20	0.82*	0.21	0.24
Operators, lessors of buildings	0.03	−0.46	0.18	0.09	0.20	0.81	0.04	−0.53	0.21	0.80*	0.25	0.24
Lessors of railroad property and other	0.38	−0.56	1.02	0.09	0.12	−0.61	0.24	−0.55	0.15	−0.11	0.23	−0.37
Subdividers and developers	0.14	0.36	0.51	0.29	0.31	0.75	0.06	−0.01	0.31	0.60	0.24	0.33
Agents, brokers, and managers	0.17	−0.76	0.31	−0.63	...	...	...	...	...	...	...	...

Source: Articles cited in the text and author; all use data from U.S. Department of the Treasury, Internal Revenue Service, Statistics of Income Division, *Source Book, Statistics of Income: Active Corporation Income Tax Returns* (Washington, D.C.: IRS), various annual issues.

* Statistically significant at 95 percent confidence level.

a. Correlation coefficients computed from reported coefficients of determination.

b. Data available only for 1974–82.

c. Data available only for 1965–82.

the table extend through 1982, the latest year for which the IRS data were available. In theory, as shown in greater detail in appendix B, return on equity (ROE) data are preferred to ROA data because managers of firms typically pay primary attention to maximizing ROE. However, in this context, ROA data may be more useful to analyze because bank holding companies tend to capitalize their nonbank subsidiaries differently from independent firms in the same lines of business. In addition, holding companies tend to engage in "double leverage," issuing debt at the holding company level to purchase equity in their subsidiaries. As a result, one cannot determine what the effect on a holding company's ROE will be if it expands into nonbank activities, without making arbitrary assumptions as to how these activities will be capitalized. This problem is avoided by examining ROA data.[60]

Taken as a whole, the estimates in table 3-4 clearly illustrate that in each of the time periods examined, the earnings of the typical banking organization could have been made more stable if it had been permitted to engage in several of the nonbanking activities. The coefficients of variation for banking (and bank holding companies) are actually higher than those reported for certain activities listed in the table in certain time periods—including the leasing of railroad property and buildings, insurance agency, and real estate agency. In addition, commercial bank earnings were negatively correlated with several nonbanking activities in each period shown, although none of these correlations is statistically significant in the most recent periods.

Nevertheless, the opportunities for reducing risk through pair-wise combinations of bank and nonbank activities appear impressive. Table 3-5 presents the coefficients of variation of earnings of hypothetical combinations of banks with various nonbank activities. These statistics are based on data for the 1962–82 period. The calculations are based on the assumption that 75 percent of the assets of the diversified firm are devoted to banking and 25 percent to the single other nonbanking activity.

Economics and Business, vol. 27 (Spring 1975), pp. 219–23; Rodney D. Johnson and David R. Meinster, "Bank Holding Companies: Diversification Opportunities in Nonbank Activities," *Eastern Economic Journal*, vol. 1 (October 1974), pp. 316–23; and Larry D. Wall and Robert A. Eisenbeis, "Risk Considerations in Deregulating Bank Activities," *Federal Reserve Bank of Atlanta Economic Review*, vol. 69 (May 1984), pp. 6–20.

60. Wall and Eisenbeis, "Risk Considerations." In any event, results of both ROA and ROE data in two of the prior studies shown in table 3-4 did not differ materially. See Heggestad, "Riskiness of Investments in Nonbank Activities"; and Johnson and Meinster, "Bank Holding Companies."

Table 3-5. *Coefficients of Variation of Pair-Wise Combinations of Banks and Other Selected Financial Activities, 1962–82*[a]

Item	Coefficient of variation
Banks alone	0.22
Banks plus savings and loans	0.18
Banks plus personal credit agencies	0.24
Banks plus business credit agencies	0.22
Banks plus securities and commodities brokers	0.22
Banks plus life insurance	0.15
Banks plus mutual insurers	0.29
Banks plus insurance agents	0.15
Banks plus real estate operators and lessors	0.20
Banks plus subdividers and developers	0.20

Source: Computations based on data from IRS, *Source Book, Statistics of Income,* various issues.
a. Calculations assume that 75 percent of the assets of the combined firm are devoted to banking and 25 percent are devoted to the other nonbank activity.

Under this assumption, the coefficients of variation of the earnings patterns of the diversified firms are equal to or lower than that for the typical bank in isolation for all but two of the activities. This picture grows less sanguine—that is, the relative risks of the diversified firms grow—as the percentage of assets that are devoted to banking in the combined firm decreases. Nevertheless, the results in table 3-5 indicate impressively the opportunities that banks have for reducing risk by entering at least one other financial activity.

As already noted, one shortcoming of the IRS data on which the calculations in tables 3-4 and 3-5 are based, however, is that they are not as finely disaggregated by industry as is ideally desired. Perhaps most significant, the data for securities activities do not distinguish between brokerage and underwriting. Given the intensity of the current debate over the continued wisdom of restricting banks from participating in underwriting corporate and certain governmental securities, it is important to consider at least conceptually if not empirically what risks exist if banks are permitted to underwrite these securities freely.

Considered in isolation, underwriting securities involves *less* risk than extending and holding loans. In a typical securities offering, the underwriter bears the risk of loss for only a few days, whereas a commercial bank bears the risk of a loan default until the loan is due. In addition, by definition, the underwriter deals in assets that are liquid and readily traded; despite the progressive securitization of commercial bank balance sheets, most bank loans remain illiquid because they are specific to the borrower.

Other researchers have recently reported findings demonstrating that the risks of corporate securities underwriting are, if anything, lower than for other types of securities that banks are permitted to underwrite under exceptions to the Glass-Steagall Act. Anthony Saunders has demonstrated that fluctuations in yields of corporate bonds (currently off limits to banks under Glass-Steagall) were actually lower between January 1978 and March 1983 than the fluctuations in yields of general obligation municipal bonds (which banks are allowed to underwrite).[61] Similarly, Ian Giddy has shown that corporate underwriting of equity securities (also off limits to banks under Glass-Steagall) was less risky between 1976 and 1983 than the underwriting of corporate bonds, based on variations in the spreads between the issue price and secondary market transactions prices during the underwriting periods these securities were offered for sale.[62] The first result suggests there is no risk-related basis for precluding banks from underwriting municipal revenue bonds. The second result contradicts those who say that bonds are necessarily safer instruments to underwrite than corporate equities.

Efficient Portfolios of Financial Activities

At best, pair-wise risk comparisons can only suggest that banking organizations could reduce their risk exposure by entering certain individual nonbanking activities. Such comparisons, however, do not consider that combining banking with a *number* of different nonbanking activities *simultaneously* could also offer opportunities to reduce risk.

This shortcoming can be addressed by estimating an *efficient frontier* of diversified portfolios of financial activities. The frontier represents for different levels of risk (measured by variance of earnings patterns) the maximum returns that can be achieved by assembling different combinations of assets or activities in a single portfolio. Roughly speaking, the larger the distance between the estimated frontier of diversified financial activities and the risk-return combination of com-

61. Anthony Saunders, "Bank Safety and Soundness and the Risks of Corporate Securities Activities," in Walter, ed., *Deregulating Wall Street*, p. 174.

62. Ian H. Giddy, "Is Equity Underwriting Risky for Commercial Bank Affiliates?" in ibid., pp. 145–70.

Figure 3-1. *Risk and Returns of Selected Financial Activities, 1965–82*

Standard deviation (10^{-3})

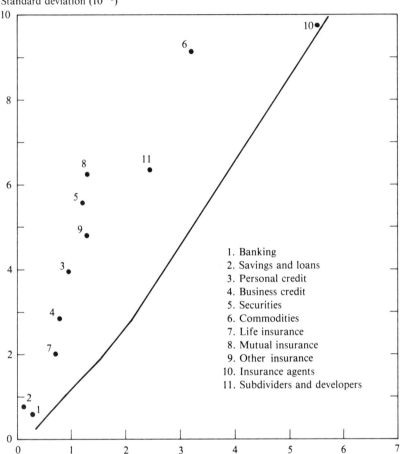

Mean after-tax return as a percent of assets (10^{-2})

1. Banking
2. Savings and loans
3. Personal credit
4. Business credit
5. Securities
6. Commodities
7. Life insurance
8. Mutual insurance
9. Other insurance
10. Insurance agents
11. Subdividers and developers

mercial banking, the greater the potential for reducing risk through financial product diversification.

Figure 3-1, which is based on the IRS data, shows the risk-return combinations of banking and various financial nonbank activities, as well as the estimated frontier of efficient diversified portfolios for 1965–82, respectively.[63] A similar picture appears when the risk-return com-

63. The 1965–82 period was chosen (rather than 1962–82) because the IRS did not report profit data for securities brokerage before 1965. In addition, because of computing limitations, efficient frontiers could be calculated for a maximum of eleven activities.

binations for the more recent 1973–82 period are plotted. The returns along the horizontal axis in figure 3-1 are measured in earnings as a percentage of assets. The vertical axis measures the standard deviation of earnings. The compositions of the efficient portfolios along the estimated frontiers illustrated for both time periods are shown in tables 3-6 and 3-7. The computational procedure for estimating the portfolios along the efficient frontier is described in the first section of appendix B.

Certain noteworthy conclusions can be drawn from the portfolio analysis. Significantly, the mean-standard deviation positions of commercial banking and the various activities are largely the same in both the shorter and longer time periods. Banking is the least risky and least rewarding activity; at the other extreme, insurance agency is the riskiest and highest earning activity.[64]

The most important result common to both time periods, however, is that the average banking organization could have significantly reduced risk if it had been able to diversify into other nonbank activities.[65] Table 3-6 shows, for example, that a diversified financial entity could have attained the same mean level of after-tax earnings as the nondiversified commercial bank, 0.285 percent of assets for 1965–82, with 27 percent less risk (because of a reduction in standard deviation in earnings from 0.00055 to 0.00040). Alternatively, the table demonstrates that at the same level of risk as commercial banking (0.00055), the diversified entity

---

Accordingly, several of the less important nonbank activities for which coefficients of variation and correlation coefficients are shown in table 3-4, and for which data for 1962–82 were available (operating and leasing of buildings, railroad leasing, and other insurance), were excluded from the efficient portfolio computations. These exclusions had little effect on the analysis, since as the results in tables 3-6 and 3-7 reflect, the estimated efficient frontiers generally contained no more than half of the eleven available activities.

64. The relatively low coefficient of variation of insurance agency across all time periods shown in table 3-4 conceals the fact that insurance agency appears to display considerable risk when measured by variance of earnings alone.

65. This result would not hold true in a deregulated climate if banks chose to maintain lower levels of capital, given their lower levels of earnings fluctuations. While this choice may be open to some banks, there is recent evidence that bank capital requirements are binding for most large bank organizations, or those most likely to broaden their services offerings if allowed to do so. That is, most banks have already been forced to raise their capital above levels they would choose in the absence of capital regulations. Accordingly, they would not be likely to offset reduced earnings variability with lower capital levels. See Larry D. Wall and David R. Peterson, "The Effect of Capital Adequacy Guidelines on Large Bank Holding Companies," Working Paper 85-3, (Federal Reserve Bank of Atlanta, December 1985).

Table 3-6. *Composition of Estimated Efficient Portfolios, 1965–82*
Percent

	Mean after-tax return target, percent of assets (top) and standard deviation (bottom)							
	0.25 *0.00037*	*0.285*[a] *0.00040*	*0.30* *0.00042*	*0.40* *0.00052*	*0.50* *0.0064*	*0.75* *0.00098*	*1.5* *0.0019*	*2.0* *0.0027*
Banking	0.636	0.667	0.670	0.743	0.743	0.552	0.318	0.145
Savings and loans	0.349	0.277	0.267	0.079	· · ·	· · ·	· · ·	· · ·
Personal credit	· · ·	· · ·	· · ·	· · ·	0.032	0.037	0.026	0.004
Business credit	· · ·	· · ·	· · ·	· · ·	· · ·	0.024	· · ·	· · ·
Securities	0.015	0.021	0.021	0.031	0.022	· · ·	· · ·	· · ·
Commodities	· · ·	0.004	0.004	0.007	0.015	0.048	0.111	0.149
Life insurance	· · ·	0.028	0.033	0.127	0.157	0.265	0.308	0.351
Mutual insurance	· · ·	0.003	0.004	0.014	0.013	0.009	· · ·	· · ·
Other insurance	· · ·	· · ·	· · ·	· · ·	· · ·	· · ·	· · ·	· · ·
Insurance agents	· · ·	· · ·	· · ·	· · ·	· · ·	· · ·	0.074	0.122
Subdividers and developers	· · ·	· · ·	· · ·	· · ·	0.018	0.065	0.163	0.228

Source: Underlying data from IRS, *Source Book, Statistics of Income,* various issues; computations by author.
a. Mean return for banking alone (standard deviation for banking alone is 0.00055).

Table 3-7. *Composition of Estimated Efficient Portfolios, 1973–82*

Percent

	Mean after-tax return target, percent of assets (top) and standard deviation (bottom)							
	0.25 ...	0.295[a] 0.00061	0.30 0.00058	0.40 0.00057	0.50 0.00070	0.75 0.00119	1.5 0.00261	2.0 0.00424
Banking	...	0.999	0.988	0.867	0.792	0.596	...	...
Savings and loans	...	...	...	...	...	...	...	...
Personal credit	...	0.0004	0.012	0.111	0.149	0.231	0.445	0.313
Business credit	...	...	...	...	...	...	...	...
Securities	...	...	...	...	...	...	...	...
Commodities	...	...	...	0.022	0.051	0.119	0.320	0.562
Life insurance	...	...	...	...	...	0.007	0.081	...
Mutual insurance	...	...	...	...	...	...	...	...
Other insurance	...	...	...	...	0.008	0.046	0.155	0.124
Insurance agents	...	...	...	...	...	...	...	...
Subdividers and developers	...	...	...	...	...	...	...	...

Source: Underlying data from IRS, *Source Book, Statistics of Income*, various issues; computations by author.

a. Mean return for banking alone (standard deviation for banking alone is 0.00061).

could have increased its earnings by approximately 47 percent (from 0.285 percent of assets for commercial banking to approximately 0.42 percent of assets at the frontier). Less significant but nevertheless noteworthy results are reported in table 3-7 for the more recent 1973–82 period: no reduction in risk for the diversified entity at the same earnings level as commercial banking (0.295 percent of assets), but a 45 percent earnings improvement (0.43 percent of assets versus 0.295 percent of assets) at the same level of risk as commercial banking. Similar results apply for bank holding companies, which for 1974–82 had the same mean-variance combination as banks alone.[66]

Nevertheless, other fundamental results from the efficient frontier analysis vary significantly across different time periods. Table 3-6 shows that over the longer period, 1965–82, the estimated portfolio contains significant proportions of nonbanking activities. For example, even at the same mean after-tax return that commercial banks earned alone (0.285 percent of assets), the efficiently diversified portfolio would have had 33 percent of total assets invested in nonbanking activities. In contrast, the corresponding proportions of nonbanking activities in efficient portfolios estimated for the 1973–82 period shown in table 3-7 would have been far lower—and virtually nonexistent at the mean level of after-tax earnings for commercial banks alone (0.295 percent of assets).

Similarly, the compositions of the efficient portfolios differ significantly across time periods. Between 1965 and 1982, for example, efficient portfolios contain at least six bank and nonbank activities at earnings levels equal to or higher than the average earnings of commercial banking alone. Significantly, at portfolio earnings levels of up to 0.30 percent of assets, savings and loan activities comprise a sizable proportion of the diversified portfolio (approximately 30 percent). At earnings above 0.50 percent of assets, the proportions of nonbank activities rise dramatically, with significant concentrations in life insurance underwriting and real estate development. During the more recent time period, however, relatively few nonbank activities enter the efficient portfolios and in less substantial proportions. Notably (and not surprisingly), savings and loan activities drop out of the efficient portfolios altogether. The only signif-

66. A banking organization may reduce its risk of failure even if in the process of diversifying its activities, it moves to a point on the efficient frontier with both higher earnings risk and return. The second section of appendix B discusses the conditions under which this situation can occur.

icant nonbank activities to enter the portfolios are personal credit (which banks can already engage in) and commodities brokerage.[67]

The foregoing results are broadly consistent with the findings of earlier studies of optimal portfolios of financial activities, based upon both accounting and market value data. Johnson and Meinster, the first to apply the portfolio theory framework to the risk implications of financial product diversification, found that on the basis of IRS profit data, portfolios constructed of commercial banking and twelve nonbanking activities either in equal weights or in weights proportionate to industry size showed lower risk over the 1954–69 period than those of commercial banking alone.[68] Using cash flows instead of profits, the same analysts later constructed an efficient frontier for two particular bank holding companies and obtained similar results.[69]

Two studies based on market valuations rather than on profit or cash flow data have reported even more substantial gains from financial product diversification. Using stock price data, Peter Eisemann has estimated that banking organizations could have more than doubled their expected returns at the same level of risk between 1961 and 1968 if they had entered a wide range of other financial activities.[70] But Eisemann also found that, as portfolio theory suggests, the benefits of diversification declined rapidly as the field of permissible nonbanking activities was expanded. For example, Eisemann's estimated efficient frontier was not materially different when the permissible range of nonbanking activities was broadened from a set including brokerage activities and savings and loans to a larger set also including insurance underwriting, real estate development, and investment banking.

Most recently, using a somewhat different technique based on both industry and firm data for 1959–68, Roger Stover determined that activity diversification would enhance the market value of the typical bank holding company (as measured by its debt capacity).[71] Stover's industry

---

67. This difference in results between the more recent and longer time periods is also reflected in efficient portfolios estimated through 1981 rather than through 1982. In particular, the percentages of nonbank activities in the efficient portfolios estimated for 1973–81 are substantially higher than those for 1973–82.

68. See Johnson and Meinster, "Bank Holding Companies," p. 319.

69. David R. Meinster and Rodney D. Johnson, "Bank Holding Company Diversification and the Risk of Capital Impairment," *Bell Journal of Economics,* vol. 10 (Autumn 1979), pp. 683–94.

70. Eisemann, "Diversification and the Congeneric Bank Holding Company."

71. Stover, "A Reexamination of Bank Holding Company Acquisitions."

and firm-specific results differed significantly, however. Based solely on industry data, only thrift, sales finance, and mutual fund activities, together with banking, entered the estimated efficient portfolio. However, when firm-specific data were examined, Stover found that the optimal portfolios of three randomly selected bank holding companies contained firms from almost every financial service industry.

The only exceptions to these findings are studies conducted by Boyd and his collaborators. These studies, which were based on Federal Reserve data on a sample of bank holding companies during the 1970s, show that only limited bank holding company diversification—no more than 2 percent of holding company assets—would minimize the risk of a worst case, or bankruptcy of the holding company.[72] Yet even these results suggest that holding company management slightly less risk averse—but still facing a risk of bankruptcy labeled "nil"—could have almost doubled their return on assets by investing just short of 10 percent of the typical firm's assets in nonbank activities.[73]

Qualifications and Conclusion

The results shown above and those reported in previous studies must be interpreted with several qualifications in mind.

First, the estimated gains from diversification presented here rest solely on historical data through 1982 and thus ignore the decline in earnings that banks and thrifts have suffered in recent years. Moreover, as already noted, the data used in this analysis are based on income

72. John H. Boyd, Gerald A. Hanweck, and Pipat Pithyachariyakul, "Bank Holding Company Diversification," *Proceedings of a Conference on Bank Structure and Competition* (Federal Reserve Bank of Chicago, 1980), pp. 105–21; and John Boyd and Pipat Pithyachariyakul, "Bank Holding Company Diversification into Nonbank Lines of Business" (Federal Reserve Bank of Chicago, 1984).

73. The results that Boyd and his collaborators reported in their studies merit several qualifications. First, the 1971–77 sample period analyzed in their work was one in which bank earnings were markedly more stable than they have been in recent years. An analysis that considers more recent Federal Reserve data could show greater potential benefits from diversification. Second, in contrast to the industry-wide IRS data, the Federal Reserve data examined in the Boyd studies do not cover the securities and real estate industries (underwriting, development, and brokerage) and contain information for only a limited number of insurance brokerage and underwriting firms—activities of central importance in the financial product deregulation debate. Moreover, the firm-specific data collected by the Federal Reserve reflect only the performances of subsidiaries of bank holding companies. This is an important limitation, since most nonbank enterprises operate independently of bank holding companies.

measured for tax purposes rather than on true economic income. This introduces some distortion because banks and insurance companies invest in tax-exempt securities, the income from which is not included in the income figures reported for tax purposes. As a result, the true economic earnings of banks and insurance companies are likely to be higher than shown in the tables and figures presented earlier.

This qualification notwithstanding, portfolio theory suggests that potential gains will always exist if investment choices are widened. Using more recent or different earnings data, therefore, should not disturb the *qualitative* conclusion that opportunities for reducing risk may be available if existing restrictions against financial product-line expansion were lifted. The IRS data are useful because they provide at least some indication of the *quantitative* significance of the risk reduction available.

Second, the foregoing results are based on industry-wide profit data, which necessarily conceals intra-industry variations among firms. As Boyd and his collaborators have noted, the use of industry-wide profit data is likely to bias downward the estimated risks of each individual activity. But using this data does not negate the likelihood that activity diversification may significantly reduce risk exposure. The results obtained by Roger Stover suggest that even *greater* gains from diversification are estimated when firm-specific rather than industry-wide data are used.

Finally, the portfolio theory framework treats the diversified financial organization as if it were a passively managed mutual fund containing the securities of each constituent activity. On the one hand, this treatment ignores the potential synergies or economies of scope that diversified entities may be able to achieve. On the other hand, the passive mutual fund assumption overstates the benefits of diversification where combining banking and nonbanking results in diseconomies, or where because of inexperience, diversified financial organizations find that their performance in new activities (measured by the mean and variance of earnings streams) is below average. This latter possibility is explored in greater detail in the next chapter.

In sum, the evidence suggests that financial product deregulation would offer potentially significant opportunities for reducing risk to the typical risk-averse bank or thrift organization. Nevertheless, the sensitivity of the estimated portfolio compositions to the time periods examined counsel strongly against relying on the IRS data to dismantle financial product-line restrictions *selectively*. Nonbank activities that may contribute to risk reduction in one period may subsequently increase the risk exposure of diversified banking organizations. Instead, the appropriate conclusion to draw is that given the freedom to participate in a wide range of financial activities, banking organizations at least would have the *opportunity* to reduce substantially the fluctuations in their earnings patterns and therefore their risk of failure.

CHAPTER FOUR

The Risks of Financial Product Deregulation

ACCELERATING the removal of financial product-line restrictions would be ill-advised if the risks outweighed the potential benefits identified in the last chapter. Opponents of expanding bank and thrift powers have raised three substantive objections. First, and most important, many fear that permitting depository institutions or their holding companies to engage in other lines of business could compromise the safety of a banking system already shaken by loan losses and bank failures. Second, they fear that certain large banking organizations and other financial conglomerates would accumulate too much economic and political power. Finally, some claim that banks would abuse greater product-line freedom by engaging in anticompetitive tying arrangements and exploiting conflicts of interest.

This chapter analyzes each of these objections. It concludes that although under certain circumstances these concerns could be justified, they are not so decisive that further product diversification by financial institutions should be prohibited. The preferable approach is to develop mechanisms for allowing banks and other financial institutions broader product-line freedom while minimizing the dangers. This challenge is taken up in chapter 5.

Financial System Risks

The continued good health of the American economy depends on a safe and sound banking system. At best, a shaky banking system weakens the confidence of investors—domestic and foreign—in making investments in this country; at worst, it can require massive federal expenditures or money creation by the Federal Reserve with undesirable inflationary consequences. Accordingly, legislative and executive policymakers can justifiably insist that proposals to accelerate the dismantling of financial product-line restrictions not be implemented without reasonable safeguards.

Reasons for Concern

It could be argued that society need not be concerned if further financial product diversification leads to increasing bank and thrift failures since policymakers can require the banking and thrift industries to bear any increased costs of failures by paying higher premiums for federal deposit insurance.[1] This view should be rejected. As a practical matter, a rising failure rate could easily enlarge the risks to the deposit insurance agencies, because Congress may be hesitant, even in the face of a significant increase in the bank failure rate, to authorize an increase in the deposit insurance premium. Recent experience reveals such hesitancy: despite a more than tenfold jump in the bank failure rate over the last six years, Congress has yet to allow either the Federal Deposit Insurance Corporation (FDIC) or the Federal Savings and Loan Insurance Corporation (FSLIC) to increase deposit insurance assessments or tie insurance premia to risk.[2]

To be sure, the insurance agencies or the Federal Reserve can always rescue a bank whose financial well-being is threatened by the impending failure of a nonbank affiliate. However, federal rescues have dangerous long-run effects because they undermine market discipline against excessive risk taking by banks and their affiliates.

In short, policymakers must consider whether financial product

---

1. To some extent, bank deposit insurance assessments are tied to the financial condition of the banking industry as a whole because, under current law, banks are entitled to a yearly rebate of a portion of the excess of the Federal Deposit Insurance Corporation's (FDIC) premium revenue over its losses and administrative expenses. Accordingly, if financial product deregulation caused the FDIC's losses to increase, the banking industry's effective premium assessment would rise (since rebates would fall). However, an increase in the bank failure rate that threatened to exhaust the resources of the FDIC would require an increase in the statutory premium assessment.

Although no rebate mechanism for federal thrift deposit insurance exists, in 1985 the Federal Home Loan Bank Board added a temporary "special assessment" of one-eighth of 1 percent of deposits to the regular insurance premium to supplement the dwindling reserves of the Federal Savings and Loan Insurance Corporation. This assessment could be made permanent or be increased, or both, if financial product deregulation led to an even higher thrift failure rate.

2. See the discussion of this issue in chapter 5.

Figure 4-1. *Performance Measures for the Banking Industry, 1972–85*

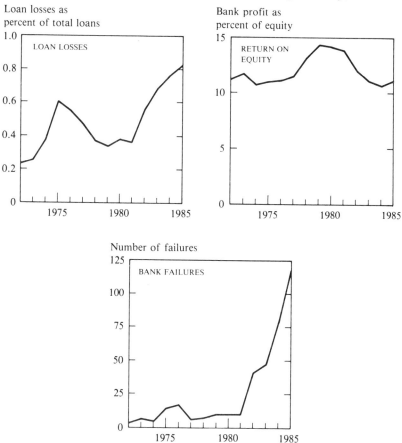

Sources: Federal Deposit Insurance Corporation, *Annual Reports*, 1972–85; and U.S. Bureau of the Census, *Statistical Abstract of the United States* (Government Printing Office, various issues).

deregulation would increase the risk of a major bank or thrift crisis that could not easily be contained with the limited resources of the FDIC and the FSLIC but instead would require direct Treasury assistance or a major lending effort by the Federal Reserve, or both.

The recent performance of the banking industry has underscored the potential fragility of the banking system. As shown in figure 4-1, both the number of bank failures and the aggregate volume of bank loan losses has soared since 1980. At the same time, bank profits have fallen dramatically, from over 14 percent of equity in the late 1970s to just 11.3 percent in 1985.

Severe problems have also plagued the thrift industry. Between 1980 and 1985, 581 thrift institutions, or 15 percent of all thrifts operating in 1980, failed.[3] Industry profits have been on a roller coaster: nearly $4 billion in 1985, but only $895 million in 1986. The decline of the thrifts in the poorest financial condition is especially worrisome. Unprofitable thrifts lost a total of $3.6 billion in 1985 and a staggering $8.3 billion in 1986. According to the General Accounting Office, as of September 1986, 445 thrifts had negative net worth measured by generally accepted accounting principles (GAAP) and would, if liquidated, cost the FSLIC more than the available reserves of the thrift insurance fund.[4]

The difficulties experienced by the banking and thrift industries have been cited by some observers as a reason for not relaxing financial product-line restrictions.[5] They argue that the performance of depositories demonstrates that many such institutions or their holding companies are ill-equipped to engage in other activities in which they have little or no experience. Referring to the portfolio analysis framework outlined in the last chapter, this argument suggests that many depository organizations that diversify into other activities may find that their inexperience would cause their earnings from these activities to be lower and more variable than the industry average. As a result, the diversified entities may not only fail to reach the efficient frontier, but may move to mean-variance positions that also imply a higher risk of failure than the earnings performance of banks or thrifts alone may indicate. The limited research

3. James R. Barth, Donald J. Bisenius, R. Dan Brumbaugh, Jr., and Daniel Sauerhaft, "The Thrift Industry's Rough Road Ahead," *Challenge*, vol. 29 (September–October 1986), p. 39.

4. U.S. General Accounting Office, "Thrift Industry: The Treasury/Federal Home Loan Bank Board Plan for FSLIC Recapitalization," GAO/GGD-87-46BR (Washington, D.C., 1987). Beginning in 1980, the Federal Home Loan Bank Board (FHLBB) allowed thrifts to use more liberal regulatory accounting principles (RAP) in order to give capital-short institutions breathing room to recover. Regulatory accounting principles permitted thrifts to amortize losses on sales of assets with below-market yields (GAAP does not allow such deferrals), recognize as income up to 250 basis points of up-front fees on loans (GAAP requires such fees to be booked as income over the life of loans), and include as capital for RAP purposes capital certificates that the FHLBB issues to troubled thrifts. As a result of these provisions, the number of RAP-insolvent thrifts has consistently run far below those insolvent as measured under GAAP. In May 1987, however, the FHLBB issued a rule requiring thrifts to move back toward GAAP accounting.

5. Congressman Fernand J. St Germain, chairman of the House Banking Committee, has opposed broader bank powers for this reason. See John M. Berry, "Banks in Turmoil: Can the System Sustain Shocks?" *Washington Post*, May 27, 1984.

that has examined the performance of bank holding company (BHC) activity diversification is not comforting: holding companies that have entered consumer finance, mortgage banking, and equipment leasing, at least in earlier periods, have failed to perform as well as independent enterprises engaged in these activities.[6] More recent evidence is mixed. Between 1980 and 1984, BHC-owned finance subsidiaries reported lower returns on equity than nonbank finance companies did; the reverse was true, however, for BHC-owned mortgage banking subsidiaries and their competitors.[7]

Depository organizations can also choose to expose themselves to greater risks through activity diversification. In the portfolio framework, such institutions would take advantage of product deregulation to move to mean-variance combinations on or off the efficient frontier. These combinations imply a higher risk of failure than that represented for banking or thrift activities alone.[8] To be sure, banks or thrifts do not need additional product-line authority to take added risks; to increase earnings each can extend higher yielding but riskier loans. Nevertheless, the activities that banks are allowed to pursue are subject to close (and increasingly intense) federal and state supervision and examination. Nonbank financial activities, in contrast, are generally not as intensely scrutinized and thus could serve as convenient outlets for risk-seeking depository organizations.

The likelihood that certain depository organizations would diversify in a risk-enhancing fashion is not easily dismissed because of the "moral hazard" effects created by the current system of federal deposit insurance. Since the insurance programs began, premiums have been assessed

---

6. Stephen A. Rhoades, "The Effect of Bank-Holding Company Acquisitions of Mortgage Bankers on Mortgage Lending Activity," *Journal of Business,* vol. 48 (July 1975), pp. 344–48, and "The Performance of Bank Holding Companies in Equipment Leasing," *Journal of Commercial Bank Lending,* October 1980, pp. 53–61; and Samuel H. Talley, "Bank Holding Company Performance in Consumer Finance and Mortgage Banking," *Magazine of Bank Administration,* July 1976, pp. 42–44.

7. Richard H. Mead and Kathleen A. O'Neil, "The Performance of the Banks' Competitors," in Federal Reserve Bank of New York, *Recent Trends in Commercial Bank Profitability* (The Bank, 1986), p. 274. This study suggests that the relatively poor performance of BHC finance companies may be due to BHC efforts to increase market share in anticipation of nationwide interstate banking. Meanwhile, the study speculates that the comparative superior performance of BHC mortgage banking subsidiaries may be due to their ability to rely more on earning a spread rather than on loan origination and servicing fees.

8. For a detailed discussion of how this outcome could arise, see appendix A.

as a constant percentage of (domestic) deposits.[9] As numerous commentators and the FDIC have observed, this feature of the insurance system encourages risk taking because it allows federally insured depository institutions to gather funds at costs that do not reflect the risks that their asset and liability structures may pose.[10] The banking system as a whole can suffer from such behavior. In attempting to attract necessary funds, risk-seeking banks and thrifts can drive up deposit interest rates that more conservatively managed institutions must also pay.[11] Since there is ample evidence that managers (as well as customers) of bank holding companies tend to view their organizations as integrated entities,[12] the incentives that depository institutions have to take risks as a result of flat-rate deposit insurance premiums can also induce their parent holding companies to assume risks in diversifying their activities.

The critical question policymakers must address, however, is not whether certain *individual* depository organizations or firms seeking to acquire them would take added risks in their activity diversification decisions, as some enterprises inevitably would. Instead, it is whether the *banking system as a whole* would be subjected to greater risks if financial product restrictions were relaxed or effectively circumvented. The two inquiries are not identical. As argued in the last chapter, activity deregulation would permit the typical banking or thrift organization to *reduce* significantly its risk of failure by diversifying into activities capable of smoothing the earnings fluctuations from deposit taking and

9. The statutory deposit insurance premium for both banks and thrifts is one-twelfth of 1 percent. As noted in note 1 in this chapter, the Federal Home Loan Bank Board imposed an additional assessment of one-eighth of 1 percent of thrift deposits in 1985.

10. George J. Benston, "Deposit Insurance and Bank Failures," *Federal Reserve Bank of Atlanta Economic Review,* vol. 68 (March 1983), pp. 4–17; Mark J. Flannery, "Deposit Insurance Creates a Need for Bank Regulation," *Federal Reserve Bank of Philadelphia Business Review,* January–February 1982, pp. 17–27; and Dean Cobos and others, "Market Discipline and the Federal Deposit Insurance Program," in *Deposit Insurance in a Changing Environment* (Washington, D.C.: FDIC, 1983), chap. 3, p. 1.

11. Herbert Baer, "Private Prices, Public Insurance: The Pricing of Federal Deposit Insurance," *Federal Reserve Bank of Chicago Economic Perspectives,* vol. 9 (September–October 1985), p. 46.

12. See Stephen Rhoades, "Interstate Banking and Product Line Expansion: Implications from Available Evidence," *Loyola of Los Angeles Law Review,* vol. 18 (Fall 1985), pp. 1140–45; Robert A. Eisenbeis, "How Should Bank Holding Companies Be Regulated?" *Federal Reserve Bank of Atlanta Economic Review,* vol. 68 (January 1983), pp. 42, 45; and Lucille S. Mayne, "Bank Holding Company Characteristics and the Upstreaming of Bank Funds, *Journal of Money, Credit and Banking,* vol. 12 (May 1980), p. 209.

lending. If the depository institutions currently most susceptible to failure took advantage of more liberal activity authority to diversify in a risk-reducing fashion, other institutions could take greater risks when expanding into other activities without increasing the dangers to the banking system. Conversely, if additional risk seeking were concentrated among banks and thrifts already taking the greatest risks, then financial product deregulation could adversely affect the safety and soundness of the banking system, even if other banks and thrifts were able to reduce their risks of failure. The banking system could also be weakened if through relaxing current law, banks or thrifts were acquired or established by firms that are not engaged in depository activities and that have higher failure probabilities than the depositories.

Of course, the net effect that financial product deregulation would have on the safety and soundness of the banking system cannot be determined in advance. As argued in the next chapter, much would depend not only on the reactions of affected institutions themselves but on any conditions that are placed on organizations that do choose to diversify. Nevertheless, some insight into this important issue may be gained by examining the past behavior of the relevant actors. Have banking and thrift organizations expanded their activities within the constraints imposed by current law in a risk-reducing or risk-enhancing fashion? What do the earnings patterns of the diversified financial conglomerates most likely to engage in banking in a more fully deregulated environment suggest about the effect their further diversification would have on the banks they acquire or open? The answers below indicate that the greater risks to the soundness of the banking system are likely to arise from nonbanking organizations' efforts to diversify into banking rather than from bank and thrift organizations' efforts to branch into nonbanking activities.

Prior Bank Holding Company Diversification

Because activity diversification by BHCs has not been extensive,[13] the performances of diversified BHCs cannot indicate how BHCs would

13. In a sample of 267 diversified bank holding companies examined by Wall in a study discussed in the text below, nonbank activities accounted for an average of only 7 percent of the holding companies' investments between 1976 and 1984. Larry D. Wall, "Has Bank Holding Companies' Diversification Affected Their Risk of Failure?" *Journal of Economics and Business* (forthcoming).

Table 4-1. *Means and Coefficients of Variation of After-Tax Earnings for Bank Holding Companies and Their Subsidiary Banks, 1978–84*

Percent of assets

Banking organization	Bank holding companies		Subsidary banks	
	Mean	Coefficient of variation	Mean	Coefficient of variation
AmeriTrust Corp.*	1.087	0.088	1.049	0.099
Bank of Boston Corp.*	0.697	0.098	0.581	0.099
BankAmerica Corp.	0.457	0.336	0.434	0.284
Bankers Trust New York Corp.	0.577	0.242	0.516	0.190
Barnett Banks of Florida*	0.957	0.062	0.841	0.265
Chase Manhattan Corporation	0.490	0.144	0.490	0.137
Chemical New York Corp.	0.511	0.172	0.464	0.132
Citicorp	0.577	0.120	0.677	0.088
Continental Illinois Corporation*	−0.107	−13.282	−0.007	−157.821
Corestates Financial Corp.*	0.861	0.230	0.800	0.256
First Atlanta Corp.*	0.903	0.236	0.993	0.264
First Bank System	0.814	0.139	0.797	0.068
First Chicago Corp.*	0.403	0.316	0.337	0.405
First Interstate*	0.691	0.107	0.580	0.176
InterFirst Corp.*	0.726	0.909	0.306	3.341
Irving Bank Corp.*	0.476	0.077	0.456	0.091
J. P. Morgan and Co.*	0.779	0.060	0.709	0.092
Manufacturers Hanover Corp.*	0.490	0.059	0.483	0.059
Marine Midland Banks	0.369	0.256	0.343	0.184
Mellon Bank Corporation*	0.743	0.106	0.696	0.227
NBD Bancorp	0.759	0.135	0.744	0.129
NCNB Corp.*	0.807	0.065	0.817	0.090
National City Corporation, Cleveland*	1.026	0.196	0.947	0.196
Northern Trust Corp.	0.506	0.273	0.494	0.245
Norwest Corporation*	0.774	0.260	0.599	0.299
PNC Financial Corp.*	1.049	0.026	0.900	0.086
Republic New York Corp.*	0.824	0.122	0.741	0.179
Security Pacific Corp.*	0.689	0.026	0.714	0.033
Texas Commerce Bancshares	1.063	0.083	0.801	0.051
U.S. Bancorp	1.110	0.167	1.061	0.067
Wells Fargo and Co.*	0.607	0.101	0.587	0.137
Simple average[a]	0.727	0.174	0.665	0.266
Weighted[a,b]	0.617	0.172	0.584	0.220

Sources: Thomas H. Hanley and others, *A Review of Bank Performance: 1984 Edition* (New York: Salomon Brothers, 1984), and *1985 Edition;* and *1000 Largest U.S. Banks,* 1982–85 editions (Austin, Texas: Sheshunoff and Co.).

* Coefficient of variation for the holding company is less than that for the bank.

a. Weights are 1984 bank holding company assets.

b. Computed excluding Continental Illinois Corporation.

behave with more liberal opportunities. Nevertheless, prior diversification by BHCs thus far has not been a cause for alarm; if anything, it mildly suggests that broader product-line freedom would enhance the safety of the banking system.

Consider first the aggregate evidence. According to the IRS data reviewed in the last chapter, BHCs as a group had not diversified in a risk-enhancing manner at least through 1982. As shown in table 3-4, between 1974 and 1982 the coefficient of variation of earnings for bank holding companies was equal to that for commercial banking alone (0.20).

Table 4-1 reports similar information for the thirty-one largest bank holding companies in the United States, or the banking organizations most likely to use expanded product powers. The table demonstrates that at least between 1978 and 1984, a period of considerable volatility in the banking industry, the large BHCs as a group experienced greater stability in their after-tax earnings (before securities transactions) than did their lead subsidiary bank. The average of the coefficients of variation for the earnings-asset ratios of the BHCs (excluding Continental Illinois, which had negative earnings over the period) was nearly 36 percent lower than that for the earnings-asset ratios for the lead subsidiary banks (0.174 versus 0.266); the corresponding average, weighted by 1984 bank assets, was 22 percent lower for the holding companies than for the banks (0.172 versus 0.220). Interestingly, these levels of risk reduction are roughly equal to the theoretical gains from portfolio diversification presented in chapter 3.

The performances of the individual BHCs reveals a somewhat different but nevertheless sanguine picture. Of the thirty holding companies (other than Continental Illinois) listed in table 4-1, nineteen reported more stable earnings patterns (as measured by the coefficient of variation of earnings) than their subsidiary banks. More significant, table 4-2 shows that eight of the ten riskiest banks listed in table 4-1 (excluding Continental Illinois) had parent holding companies that displayed equal or less risk than their subsidiary banks, suggesting that activity diversification thus far has had a risk-moderating effect for the largest banking organizations.[14] These results are consistent with a broader analysis of the 1976–84 earnings performance of 267 diversified bank holding com-

14. The earnings for the parent holding company for Continental Bank, too, had a lower coefficient of variation than those for the bank itself.

Table 4-2. *Coefficients of Variation of the Ten Riskiest Banks and Their Holding Companies from Table 4-1 (Excluding Continental Illinois Corporation), 1978–84*

Banking organization	Bank holding company	Bank
1. InterFirst Corp.	0.909	3.341
2. First Chicago Corp.	0.316	0.405
3. Norwest Corporation	0.260	0.299
4. BankAmerica Corp.*	0.336	0.284
5. Barnett Banks of Florida	0.062	0.265
6. First Atlanta Corp.	0.236	0.264
7. Corestates Financial Corp.	0.230	0.256
8. Northern Trust Corp.	0.273	0.245
9. Mellon Bank Corporation	0.106	0.227
10. National City Corporation, Cleveland	0.196	0.196

Source: Table 4-1.
* Holding company has higher coefficient of variation than the subsidiary bank.

panies recently completed by Larry Wall.[15] In his study, Wall found that nonbank subsidiaries reduced the risk of failure for 176 of the 267 bank holding companies in his sample.[16] As in the above analysis, the risk-moderating influence of activity diversification was concentrated among the riskier banking organizations; indeed, the five riskiest BHCs had become less susceptible to failure because of their nonbanking activities (although the risk-reducing effect in each case was small).

These results must be qualified, however, by several factors. First, because many of the largest bank holding companies own more than one bank, the relative stability or instability of earnings at the holding company level may be due as much to the earnings performance of their smaller (nonlead) banks than to diversification by the holding companies into nonbank activities. In addition, BHC activity diversification to date has been quite limited and precisely because of legal restrictions has not covered the nonbanking businesses that banking organizations are most eager to enter. The effects of diversification also can be quite sensitive to the time period examined. For example, Peter Eisemann found that BHCs had entered certain nonbank activities in the 1960s—including data processing, mortgage banking, and factoring—that were not in-

15. Wall, "Has Bank Holding Companies' Diversification Affected Their Risk of Failure?" This study was based on earnings data reported to the Federal Reserve.
16. Wall defined the risk of failure as the probability that losses in a single year would exhaust stockholders' equity.

cluded in his estimated risk-minimizing efficient frontiers,[17] a result suggesting that BHCs had diversified in a risk-enhancing fashion. Similarly, using Federal Reserve and other published data, Boyd and Graham found that a sample of sixty-four of the largest BHCs as a group had diversified in a risk-enhancing fashion between 1971 and 1977 but between 1978 and 1983 had broadened their activities in a way that did not systematically increase or decrease the risk of failure.[18] Finally, the results listed in table 4-1 are also sensitive to time period: by adding only one year of data (1984 profits), the number of parent holding companies that had less volatile earnings than their subsidiary banks increased from sixteen to nineteen.

In sum, prior activity diversification by BHCs can provide only limited comfort that relaxing financial product-line restrictions would not increase banking system risks.

Thrifts and Thrift Holding Companies

Recent thrift institution behavior provides another source of evidence for determining whether and to what extent depository institutions would diversify their activities in a risk-enhancing manner if financial product-line restrictions were relaxed. Since the financial difficulties experienced by the thrift industry have been substantially worse than those encountered by commercial banks, the potential for risk taking by thrifts takes on special significance. With so many insured thrifts having nothing to lose, the danger exists that many will endeavor to climb back to financial health by assuming greater risks if broader diversification is permitted.

This danger is precisely the issue that the Federal Home Loan Bank Board (FHLBB) attempted to address in 1985 when it promulgated its controversial rule requiring state-chartered thrifts to obtain supervisory approval for direct investments exceeding the larger of either 10 percent of assets or twice the level of net worth measured by federal regulators.

17. Peter C. Eisemann, "Diversification and the Congeneric Bank Holding Company," *Journal of Bank Research,* vol. 6 (Spring 1976), pp. 68–77.

18. John H. Boyd and Stanley L. Graham, "Risk, Regulation and Bank Holding Company Expansion into Nonbanking," *Federal Reserve Bank of Minneapolis Quarterly Review,* vol. 10 (Spring 1986), pp. 2–17. The authors attribute the different results in the two time periods to the Federal Reserve's tightening its regulatory supervision over BHC activity expansion during the second period, thus preventing BHCs as a group from diversifying in a risk-enhancing fashion. However, an alternative interpretation is that BHCs have acquired greater experience in nonbank activities over time.

The Bank Board issued its rule to curtail thrifts' investing in stocks, real estate, and commercial ventures in states such as California and Texas that have liberalized the authorized powers of their state-chartered savings and loans.

The evidence that the FHLBB cited in adopting its direct investment rule helps to shed light on how activity diversification by thrift organizations would affect their exposure to risk. The FHLBB reported that at least as of 1985, thrift institutions with significant direct investments in service corporations or real estate had grown more rapidly, had asset portfolios with significantly more credit risk, and had less stable liability structures than the average savings institution. In two cases, the Board noted, "loans" that amounted to direct investments were major contributing factors to the failure of a thrift.[19]

The FHLBB's findings were strongly criticized by George Benston, who in an industry-sponsored study examined the effects of thrifts that had engaged in direct investment activity. In the most recently updated version of this work, Benston found that between 1981 and 1984 the average annual returns on direct investments by these institutions (3.75 percent) far outperformed those on other assets (-0.16 percent).[20] More significant, he found that the standard deviation of returns on assets was lower with direct investments included than with those assets excluded, indicating that, on average, asset diversification by thrifts has thus far been risk moderating. Finally, in a multivariate analysis, Benston found no significant relationship between savings and loans that had failed during 1981–85 and the extent of direct investments that those institutions made.[21]

Resolving the controversial and visible debate between Professor Benston and the Bank Board is not necessary to draw some inferences from the thrift industry's direct investment experience. There appears

19. 50 Fed. Reg. 6900 (February 19, 1985).

20. Professor Benston submitted comments to the FHLBB on its direct investment proposal as well as on other regulatory changes recommended to the bank board. A lengthened version of these comments was later published. See George J. Benston, *An Analysis of the Causes of Savings and Loan Association Failures,* Monograph Series in Finance and Economics, 1985-4/5 (New York University Graduate School of Business Administration, 1985).

21. In his univariate analysis, however, Benston found that failed savings and loans in 1984 and 1985 had statistically significant higher fractions of their assets invested in direct investments than other thrift institutions had. Ibid., p. 36.

to be no dispute that for many thrifts, making direct investments—that is, diversifying activities and investments—would enhance earnings and reduce risk. The problem that the Bank Board has identified, however, is that those institutions that have failed have suffered unusually large losses on their direct investments. In a study of 324 thrifts that failed between December 1981 and October 1985, FHLBB investigators determined that direct investments were positively related to a statistically significant degree to the costs that the FSLIC incurred in closing failed thrifts or in assisting their merger with healthier institutions.[22] This level of loss is far greater than the average loss of 15 to 20 cents on the dollar that the FSLIC experiences on failed thrifts generally.[23] Moreover, according to Bank Board staff, of the thirty-seven thrifts that had made direct investments exceeding 10 percent of assets in December 1983, twenty-one had either failed or were near failure by October 1986.

These findings confirm that the moral hazard features of deposit insurance act most perversely for institutions that are near failure. Indeed, in apparent recognition of this fact, the Bank Board amended its direct investment rule in April 1987, by tying the level of permissible direct investment by thrifts to their capital position.

Nevertheless, until the many insolvent thrifts are closed or merged with healthier partners, the incentives for risk taking created by deposit insurance will continue to pose serious risks to the federal deposit insurance system, if not ultimately to taxpayers generally, regardless of whether thrifts are permitted to diversify their activities.[24] Accordingly, policymakers must remain concerned that as long as a significant number of depository institutions are financially unsound, a substantial number would take advantage of enhanced activity authority to expose themselves and the FSLIC to even greater risks.

---

22. James R. Barth, R. Dan Brumbaugh, Jr., and Daniel Sauerhaft, "Failure Costs of Government-Regulated Financial Firms: The Case of Thrift Institutions," Research Working Paper 123 (Federal Home Loan Bank Board, October 1986).

23. Testimony of Edwin J. Gray before the Senate Banking Committee, March 13, 1986, reprinted in the *American Banker*, March 28, 1986.

24. At this writing, Congress was considering legislation to supplement the FSLIC insurance fund with a capital infusion ranging between $5.0 billion and $10.0 billion. The Bank Board, however, has been able to take at least some direct action to strengthen the financial position of the industry. In September 1986 the Board issued new requirements for raising the net worth at all thrifts ultimately to a minimum of 6 percent of assets.

Potential Diversification into Banking by Nonbank Financial Conglomerates

Depository organizations would not be the only entities allowed to expand their product-line offerings in a fully deregulated environment. A level playing field would also permit entry into banking or thrift activities by financial organizations currently barred from such lines of business.

The recency of the financial conglomerate movement, however, causes some difficulty in assessing how additional entry by nonbanks into banking would affect the risks borne by the federal insurance agencies. In one of the only studies relevant to this question, Wall and Eisenbeis suggested that these risks might be insignificant, based on a finding that mergers between financial and nonfinancial firms were not associated with a statistically significant effect on bond prices of the surviving corporation.[25] Nevertheless, given the existing financial product-line restrictions, the Wall-Eisenbeis study was unable to isolate specifically the risk implications of entry by nondepository firms into banking.

This limitation can be overcome by using prior earnings patterns of financial conglomerates likely to enter banking in a fully deregulated environment to determine whether acquisitions of banks by such organizations would increase the susceptibility of those banks to failure. For this purpose, it is assumed that the likelihood of failure decreases as the coefficient of variation of an institution's return on equity grows smaller.[26] For illustrative purposes only, a second assumption is that each nonbanking firm in the sample analyzed acquires a bank with an earnings pattern identical to the industry average and that the equity of the acquired bank constitutes 50 percent of the resulting firm's net worth.[27]

25. Larry D. Wall and Robert A. Eisenbeis, "Risk Considerations in Deregulating Bank Activities," *Federal Reserve Bank of Atlanta Economic Review,* vol. 69 (May 1984), pp. 6–20.

26. For a justification of this assumption, see appendix A. In this case, returns on equity rather than returns on assets are used because the question analyzed focuses not on expansion by banking organizations into other activities (which can be capitalized very differently depending on whether they are bank owned) but instead on acquisitions by nonbanking firms of a single additional banking firm, which in the exercise is assumed to be capitalized at the industry average. Moreover, assets of financial and nonfinancial firms are not comparable. Returns on equity therefore provide a better common barometer of bank and nonbank earnings performance.

27. Allocating different proportions of the resulting firm's net worth to the banking subsidiary does not change the qualitative results of this exercise.

Table 4-3 reports the results of this exercise, using earnings data for 1977–85. For fifteen of the eighteen firms listed in the table, the coefficient of variation of earnings for the firm decreased when the typical bank was added to the enterprise. While this result would have lowered the risk for the conglomerate as a whole, in most cases it would have exposed the *bank* to larger risk. Specifically, for all but five of the eighteen firms already active in a number of financial service activities (and thus likely entrants into banking), the acquisition of the typical bank would have left the coefficient of variation of returns on equity for the resulting firm higher than that for the average bank. These results are the direct outgrowth of the fact that only seven of the eighteen firms had earnings patterns that were negatively correlated with the earnings pattern of the commercial banking industry; and more significant, the fact that the earnings of *all but one* of the nonbanking firms listed in the table were more variable than those of the average commercial bank. In short, the results shown here suggest that nonbank entry into banking would increase risks to the banking system because it would embed banks in organizations with more variable earnings profiles.

The foregoing exercise, of course, has its limitations. Financial conglomerates can always acquire or open banks with atypical earnings patterns such that risks facing the bank diminish when it is embedded in a diversified organization. More generally, prior patterns of earnings variations can provide only a limited glimpse of what future earnings may look like. Nevertheless, the results of the exercise are disquieting for what they show about the consequences of passive acquisitions of banks by nonbanking organizations. The risks may even be greater when the passive acquisition assumption is relaxed, since many nonbanking firms would bring a more aggressive, risk-taking attitude to the operation of the banks they purchase or open than is now found in the banking industry.

Risks to the Payments System

Finally, even if financial product diversification were to strengthen the financial health of banking organizations generally, the risk always exists that in isolated instances threatened failures of nonbanking affiliates may tempt banks (or their parent companies) to engineer a rescue that threatens the integrity of the payments system. Although, as discussed below, section 23A of the Federal Reserve Act constrains

Table 4-3. *Entry by Nonbanking Firms into Banking, 1977–85*[a]

Firm	Financial activities[b]	Mean return on equity (percent)	Standard deviation of returns	Coefficient of variation	Correlation of return on equity with average return on equity for banking industry
Aetna Life and Casualty Company	Banking	0.129	0.067	0.516	0.654
	Insurance underwriting	(0.127)	(0.039)	(0.307)	
	Real estate investment-development				
	Financing				
	Other				
American Can Company	Banking	0.077	0.088	1.132	−0.041
	Securities brokerage	(0.101)	(0.043)	(0.425)	
	Mortgage banking				
	Other				
American Express Company	Banking	0.175	0.027	0.157	0.775
	Securities underwriting and brokerage	(0.150)	(0.019)	(0.127)	
	Insurance underwriting and brokerage				
	Credit cards				
	Financing				
	Others				
American General Corporation	Securities brokerage	0.145	0.015	0.102	0.743
	Insurance underwriting	(0.135)	(0.014)	(0.104)	
	Real estate investment-development				
	Consumer lending				
	Mortgage banking				
	Other				

Company	Segments				
Avco Financial Services	Banking Insurance underwriting and brokerage Consumer lending Other	0.116 (0.120)	0.039 (0.022)	0.333 (0.188)	0.104
Beneficial Corporation	Banking Insurance underwriting and brokerage Consumer lending Financing Leasing Other	0.151 (0.138)	0.035 (0.179)	0.235 (1.333)	0.415
Control Data Corp.	Banking Insurance underwriting Consumer lending Financing Leasing	0.020 (0.072)	0.176 (0.092)	9.012 (1.282)	0.447
Ford Motor Co.	Insurance underwriting Real estate investment-development Consumer lending Financing Thrift	0.088 (0.106)	0.172 (0.083)	1.955 (0.782)	−0.694
General Electric Co.	Securities underwriting Insurance underwriting Mortgage banking Financing Leasing Other	0.182 (0.153)	0.006 (0.009)	0.034 (0.059)	0.626
General Motors Corp.	Insurance underwriting Mortgage banking Financing Leasing	0.131 (0.128)	0.070 (0.033)	0.532 (0.259)	−0.521

Table 4-3 (continued)

Firm	Financial activities[b]	Mean return on equity (percent)	Standard deviation of returns	Coefficient of variation	Correlation of return on equity with average return on equity for banking industry
The Greyhound Corporation	Insurance underwriting	0.118 (0.121)	0.023 (0.017)	0.197 (0.142)	0.682
	Financing				
	Leasing				
	Other				
Gulf and Western	Banking	0.101 (0.113)	0.078 (0.044)	0.774 (0.386)	0.460
	Insurance underwriting				
	Real estate investment-development				
	Consumer lending				
	Financing				
	Leasing				
	Other				
Household International	Banking	0.123 (0.124)	0.024 (0.013)	0.198 (0.105)	−0.013
	Insurance underwriting				
	Financing				
	Leasing				
	Other				
IBM Credit Corp.	Financing	0.226 (0.175)	0.021 (0.011)	0.094 (0.061)	−0.080
ITT Consumer Services Corp.	Securities underwriting and brokerage	0.095 (0.110)	0.025 (0.017)	0.261 (0.155)	0.329
	Insurance underwriting				
	Consumer lending				
	Financing				

Merrill Lynch and Co.	Thrift	0.137	0.062	0.449	0.548
	Securities underwriting and brokerage	(0.131)	(0.036)	(0.275)	
	Insurance underwriting				
	Real estate investment-development				
	Real estate brokerage				
	Leasing				
	Other				
J. C. Penney Financial Corp.	Banking	0.131	0.019	0.148	−0.229
	Thrift	(0.128)	(0.009)	(0.066)	
	Insurance underwriting and brokerage				
	Real estate investment-development				
	Credit cards				
Sears, Roebuck and Co.	Thrift	0.116	0.018	0.156	−0.352
	Securities underwriting and brokerage	(0.120)	(0.007)	(0.060)	
	Insurance underwriting and brokerage				
	Real estate investment-development				
	Real estate brokerage				
	Mortgage banking				
	Credit cards				
	Other				
Banking industry as a whole	. . .	0.124	0.013	0.105	. . .

Sources: *Moody's Industrial Manual*, 1974–85, annual editions (New York: Moody's Investors Service); *Moody's Bank and Finance Manual*, 1975–85, annual editions; *Moody's Transportation Manual*, 1977 and 1985, annual editions; *Standard & Poor's Corporation Records*, 1984–85 (New York: Standard and Poor's Corporation); Deborah J. Danker and Mary M. McLaughlin, "Profitability of Insured Commercial Banks in 1984," *Federal Reserve Bulletin*, vol. 71 (November 1985), p. 842; Danker and McLaughlin, "Profitability of Insured Commercial Banks in 1983," *Federal Reserve Bulletin*, vol. 70 (November 1984), p. 809; Barbara Negri Opper, "Profitability of Insured Commercial Banks," *Federal Reserve Bulletin*, vol. 68 (August 1982), p. 460; and "Insured Commercial Bank Income in 1977," *Federal Reserve Bulletin*, vol. 64 (June 1978), p. 441.

a. The first set of numbers refers to current nonbanking firms. The second set (in parentheses) refers to these firms after merger with a bank with an industry average earnings profile (shown in the last line of the table) that comprises 50 percent of the combined firm's equity. All calculations use annual data for 1977–85.

b. Other activities include factoring, investment advisory services, mutual fund management, data processing services, purchasing of installment contracts, trust services, venture capital services, merchant banking, pension fund management, travelers' checks, and money orders.

banks in the total amounts they can lend to any of their affiliates, that section does not cover intraday extensions of credit to affiliates. Since the Federal Reserve ultimately guarantees the integrity of the payments system by standing ready to step in to cover transfers due banks at the end of each business day, the monetary authority itself is at risk if banks were to cause a payment shortfall through their attempts to rescue ailing affiliates.[28] To be sure, this risk exists now with the restricted set of nonbanking activities in which bank holding companies have been permitted to engage. However, it could be magnified in a deregulated environment, particularly as the largest banking organizations diversify into a range of other activities.

Summary

In sum, what limited evidence is available suggests that the potential risks to the banking system from relaxing financial product-line restrictions are more likely to arise from entry by nonbanking firms into banking than from expansion by banks and thrifts into other activities. However, quantifying the precise magnitude of these risks is impossible because predicting which organizations would take advantage of looser activity restrictions and in what manner is infeasible. Moreover, the nature and magnitude of the risks depend primarily on the conditions under which organizations are permitted to diversify their activities and product offerings. This important subject is explored in detail in chapter 5.

Aggregate Concentration

Americans have long been suspicious of large concentrations of power, both political and economic. Federalism—the separation of political power at the federal and state levels—has survived and been strengthened because of suspicions of centralized political authority. Federalist tendencies have been especially evident in governmental supervision of the financial sector of the economy. Since the founding of the republic, banks have been chartered, regulated, and supervised at both the state and federal levels. In contrast, the insurance industry

---

28. For a description of the Federal Reserve's role in protecting the integrity of the payments system, see Martin Mayer, *The Money Bazaars* (Dutton, 1984).

has only been systematically regulated by the states, but never by the federal government.

In the economic arena, objections to concentration date from the early fight between Hamiltonian and Jeffersonian forces over the establishment of the First and Second Banks of the United States. Later in the nineteenth century, Congress reacted to the formation of large trusts and holding companies by enacting the Sherman Antitrust Act of 1890 to prohibit monopolization. In 1914 Congress strengthened the antitrust laws by passing the Clayton Act, which prohibits mergers that could be anticompetitive. Although the antitrust statutes were aimed at eliminating and preventing the classic evils of monopoly power in individual markets, they also reflected a widespread fear of the social and political dangers of undue concentration of economic resources. As Judge Learned Hand observed in his noted opinion requiring the breakup of the Aluminum Corporation of America: "Throughout the history of these [antitrust] statutes it has been constantly assumed that one of their purposes was to perpetuate and preserve, *for its own sake and in spite of possible cost,* an organization of industry in small units which can effectively compete with each other [emphasis added]."[29]

This same attitude was reflected one decade later in the congressional decision to enact the Bank Holding Company Act of 1956 and thereafter the amendments to that act adopted in 1970, which together have restricted banking organizations from both interstate and product-line expansion. As a representative of the Nixon administration explained to the Senate Banking Committee in 1970, the bank holding company restrictions were necessary to prevent the United States from copying the "zaibatsu" arrangements between banks and industrial enterprises for which the Japanese were (and still are) well known.[30] Moreover,

---

29. *United States* v. *Aluminum Co. of America,* 148 F. 2d 416, 429 (2d Cir. 1946). Recent antitrust policy, especially that pursued during the Reagan administration, has rejected the "bigness is bad" view in favor of a narrower focus on competitive characteristics of individual markets. This new approach was highlighted by the Justice Department's decision in 1981 to abandon its antitrust suit against IBM and to settle its antitrust challenge against AT&T.

30. Testimony of Charls E. Walker, Undersecretary of the Treasury, *Hearing on One-Bank Holding Company Legislation,* Hearing before the Senate Committee on Banking and Currency, 91 Cong. 2 sess. (Government Printing Office, 1970), p. 13. The Federal Reserve Board has also expressed concern about the threat of "undue concentration of economic resources" in deciding a number of BHC applications to engage in activities "closely related to the business of banking." Stephen Halpert, "The

within the banking industry, state and federal law has traditionally favored "widely dispersed control," a concept recently reaffirmed by the Supreme Court's decision upholding the constitutionality of regional banking compacts.[31]

Given this long history of opposition to concentration of economic power, particularly in the financial sector, the appropriate question to ask is whether the trend toward financial product diversification by banks and other financial institutions may produce an unwanted increase in the concentration of ownership of assets. This inquiry involves two issues. Will financial product diversification in fact lead to greater aggregate concentration of economic power? And if it does, how much concentration would be socially undesirable?

Impact of Financial Product Diversification
on Aggregate Concentration

Allowing banks and other financial institutions broader product-line freedom is often assumed to lead inevitably to greater aggregate concentration. If product diversification would enable banks and other financial institutions to realize economies of scope and to reduce risk, then it must also promote the growth of larger financial institutions at the expense of their smaller competitors. Bank holding companies, it is often argued, would be in the best position to reach outward. As one recent congressional report has noted, the top ten BHCs alone control over $700 billion in assets, an amount equal to the total assets of all life insurers and nearly three times the assets of the property-casualty insurance industry; just the top three BHCs have capital roughly equal to that held by the entire securities industry.[32]

This line of analysis, however, overstates the capability of large banking organizations to acquire other nonbank entities, at least in the next few years. Although they have caught up significantly in recent

---

Separation of Banking and Commerce Reconsidered" (University of Miami, August 1986).

31. *Northeast Bancorp, Inc.* v. *Board of Governors of the Federal Reserve System.* Significantly, the Court's majority opinion in this case was authored by Justice Rehnquist, now chief justice.

32. *Restructuring Financial Markets: The Major Policy Issues,* Committee Print, Report from the Chairman of the Subcommittee on Telecommunications, Consumer Protection, and Finance of the House Committee on Energy and Commerce, 99 Cong. 2 sess. (GPO, 1986), pp. 227, 233.

Figure 4-2. *Price-Earnings Multiples, 1979–85*

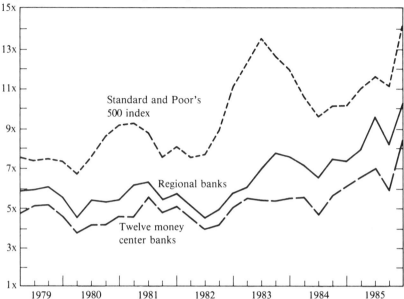

Source: Thomas H. Hanley and others, *A Review of Bank Performance: 1986 Edition* (New York: Salomon Brothers, 1986).

years, the twelve leading money center banks continue to have weaker capital positions than their large regional counterparts.[33] With the recent increases in capital requirements mandated by the federal regulatory agencies now in effect, the largest banking organizations are not likely to expand vigorously by acquisition until they have built up some margin of safety over the required capital minimum of 6 percent. Equally significant, the larger banking organizations are constrained, at least relative to their large regional counterparts, in their abilities to use their common stock to acquire other firms by the historically low price-earnings multiples that investors have assigned to their shares, as shown in figure 4-2.

Indeed, the largest banking organizations have been disadvantaged

33. In 1981 a group of twenty-three of the largest regional banking organizations followed by Salomon Brothers had an average capital-to-asset ratio of 5.5 percent, as compared with a 4.1 percent average for the twelve money center banks. By the end of 1985, the gap between the two groups of banks narrowed substantially, 6.2 percent for the regionals versus 5.9 percent for the money center institutions. Thomas H. Hanley and others, *A Review of Bank Performance: 1986 Edition* (New York: Salomon Brothers, 1986), p. 59.

Figure 4-3. *Percentage of Total Bank Deposits Held by the Ten Largest U.S. Banks, 1940–85*

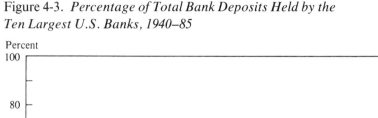

Sources: L. Michael Cacace, "Special Purpose Banks Post Top Deposit Gains," *American Banker*, March 18, 1986; Conference of State Bank Supervisors, "The Dynamic American Banking System—An Analysis of Geographic Structural Constraints," Policy Study, April 1983, p. 17.

in recent years by the discrimination against New York and California banks in most regional or reciprocal interstate statutes. Figure 4-3 shows that between 1950 and 1980 the ten largest banks acquired a steadily rising share of all bank deposits in the nation; since 1980, however, the share held by the top ten has leveled off at a plateau no higher than it was in 1940. Much more significant, however, is that since 1980 the ten leading banks have suffered a significant loss in deposit share among the fifty largest banks, as shown in figure 4-4. Banks in the bottom tiers of the top fifty have taken up the slack, reflecting the emergence of super-regional banking organizations, particularly in areas of the country such as the southeast, where state legislatures have promoted regional inter-state banking.

The gaining strength of regional banks is reflected in their recent profit performance relative to their larger money center competitors. The average 14.5 percent return on equity (ROE) of regional bank holding companies in 1985 was almost identical to the 14.6 percent ROE recorded in 1979–81, a period of peak profitability. In contrast, the ROE of large

Figure 4-4. *Concentration of Domestic Deposits among the Fifty Largest U.S. Banks, 1980, 1985*

Percentage of domestic deposits

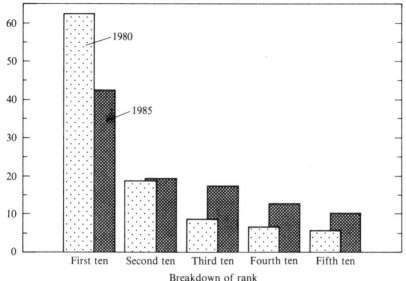

Breakdown of rank

Source: See figure 4-3.

multinational bank holding companies in 1985 stood at just above 11 percent, over three percentage points lower than its level in 1979.[34]

In short, by the time nationwide interstate banking arrives, the nation's banking system should be considerably less concentrated at the top than it was a few years ago. This greater equality among the nation's largest banks, in turn, significantly reduces the likelihood that a few major banking organizations will dominate the ownership of financial assets as financial product-line barriers are eased or circumvented.

Of course, financial product deregulation may allow the largest banking organizations as a group—including the money center and "super-regional" institutions—to grow faster than smaller banks. But writing off the ability of smaller banks to compete in a fully deregulated environment would be a mistake. Many customers in many markets will continue to want the personalized attention they receive from smaller institutions. And states such as California and New York that have

34. Federal Reserve Bank of New York, *Recent Trends in Commercial Bank Profitability*, pp. 9, 12, 13.

liberal intrastate branching provisions provide ample evidence that small independent banks can survive the competition of larger banking organizations.[35]

Finally, one of the important lessons learned from the conglomerate merger movement elsewhere in the economy is that many of the alliances that may be formed between banks and other financial or nonfinancial firms as financial product deregulation proceeds will not last. A recent study by McKinsey and Company found that in twenty-eight of fifty-eight major acquisitions completed between 1972 and 1983, the acquired firm failed to earn a return sufficient to cover the parent firm's cost of capital.[36] The poor postmerger performance of many acquired firms helps explain why in recent years divestiture transactions account for about one-third of both the number and value of all merger and acquisition transactions.[37]

This analysis does not dismiss the possibility that as firms succeed in diversifying the range of financial services they offer over time, aggregate concentration of the ownership of resources will increase, perhaps significantly. But this result cannot be assured.

How Much Aggregate Concentration Is Undesirable?

It is not clear that any trend toward further concentration of financial assets would be undesirable. In a world of growing interdependence between nations, policy cannot reliably be based only on projections of domestic economic effects. American financial institutions, like American manufacturers, are competing in a world market. Financial institu-

35. Testimony of Paul A. Volcker, Chairman of the Federal Reserve Board, in *Interstate Banking,* Hearings before the Subcommittee on Financial Institutions Supervision, Regulation, and Insurance of the House Committee on Banking, Finance, and Urban Affairs, 99 Cong. 1 sess. (GPO, 1985), p. 9; Stephen A. Rhoades and Donald T. Savage, "Can Small Banks Compete?" *Bankers Magazine,* vol. 164 (January–February 1981), pp. 59–65; and B. Frank King, "Upstate New York: Tough Markets for City Banks," *Federal Reserve Bank of Atlanta Economic Review,* vol. 70 (June–July 1985), pp. 30–34.

36. Joan M. O'Connell, "Do Mergers Really Work?" *Business Week,* June 3, 1985, p. 89.

37. *Economic Report of the President, February 1985,* p. 195. See also F. M. Scherer and David J. Ravenscraft, *Mergers, Sell-Offs, and Economic Efficiency* (Brookings, forthcoming). A recent study by Michael Porter found that of 1,601 acquisitions made by thirty-three major corporations between 1950 and 1980, 53 percent had been undone by 1987. Michael E. Porter, "From Competitive Advantage to Corporate Strategy," *Harvard Business Review,* vol. 65 (May–June 1987), pp. 43–57.

Figure 4-5. *Shares of Total Deposits of the World's 500 Largest Banks Held by the U.S. and Foreign Banks, Selected Years, 1970–85*

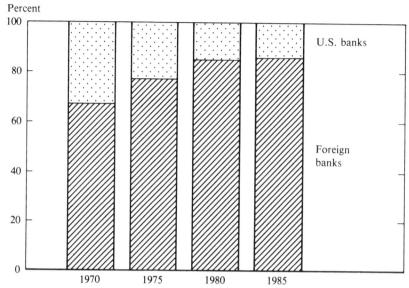

Source: Bureau of the Census, *Statistical Abstract of the United States, 1986* (GPO, 1986), p. 497.

tions from other countries compete not only with American financial intermediaries through their branches or subsidiaries in the United States but also with each other for deposit-taking, lending, and investment business in worldwide markets. If the trend toward financial product diversification by American financial intermediaries produces larger financial firms in our market, this trend may enhance the competitive positions of these firms on the world stage.

In fact, American banks have slipped badly in recent years relative to their foreign competitors. Figure 4-5 shows that the share of total deposits of the world's 500 largest banks held by American institutions has fallen substantially in just the last fifteen years, from 32 percent in 1970 to just 14 percent in 1985. The declining position of American institutions is especially noticeable among the world's twenty largest banking organizations. As shown in table 4-4, American banks occupied the first three positions in this elite group in 1970; indeed, eight of the eleven largest banks in the world were based in the United States. By 1986 the rankings had changed dramatically. Only three American banks were ranked in the world's top twenty. The largest bank in the world in 1970—Bank of

Table 4-4. *Ranking of the World's Twenty Largest Banking Organizations, 1970, 1986*

Banking organization

Rank	1970	1986
1	BankAmerica Corp. (U.S.)	Dai-Ichi Kangyo Bank, LTD. (Japan)
2	Citicorp (U.S.)	Citicorp (U.S.)
3	Chase Manhattan Corporation (U.S.)	Fuji Bank, LTD. (Japan)
4	Barclays PLC (U.K.)	Sumitomo Bank, LTD. (Japan)
5	Manufacturers Hanover Corp. (U.S.)	Mitsubishi Trust and Banking Corp. (Japan)
6	J. P. Morgan and Co. (U.S.)	Banque Nationale de Paris (France)
7	National Westminster Bank PLC (U.K.)	Sanwa Bank, LTD. (Japan)
8	First Interstate Bancorp (U.S.)	Credit Agricole (France)
9	Banco Nazionale del Lavoro (Italy)	BankAmerica Corp. (U.S.)
10	Chemical New York Corp. (U.S.)	Credit Lyonnais (France)
11	Bankers Trust New York Corp. (U.S.)	Norinchukin Bank, LTD. (Japan)
12	Royal Bank of Canada (Canada)	National Westminster Bank PLC (U.K.)
13	Fuji Bank, LTD. (Japan)	Industrial Bank of Japan, LTD. (Japan)
14	Westdeutsche Landesbank Girozentrale (Germany)	Société Generale (France)
15	Banque Nationale de Paris (France)	Deutsche Bank AG (Germany)
16	Mitsubishi Trust and Banking Corp. (Japan)	Barclays PLC (U.K.)
17	Sumitomo Bank, LTD. (Japan)	Tokai Bank, LTD. (Japan)
18	Sanwa Bank, LTD. (Japan)	Mitsui Trust and Banking Corp., LTD. (Japan)
19	Canadian Imperial Bank of Commerce (Canada)	Chase Manhattan Corporation (U.S.)
20	Midland Bank PLC (U.K.)	Midland Bank PLC (U.K.)

Sources: *The Banker*, vol. 136 (August 1986), pp. 79–171; and Susan Chira, "The Japanese Bank That Is Now No. 1," *New York Times*, September 8, 1986.

America—was ninth in 1986; Citicorp, its replacement beginning in 1981, gave way to Dai-Ichi Kangyo Bank of Japan.

Perhaps more significant, American banks have slipped relative to foreign financial institutions in market value capitalization, which measures the ability of an organization to purchase other assets and companies. By the end of 1976, the largest two financial institutions in the world, measured by market value capitalization, were American: Bank of America and Citicorp. By the end of 1986, Bank of America had fallen off the top fifty list, Citicorp was down to twenty-ninth, and the highest ranking American financial firm—American Express—was not even primarily a bank and was no higher than seventeenth. Significantly, the nine top ranking institutions were all Japanese.[38]

38. Rosamund Jones and Neil Osborn, "The Power League," *Euromoney*, February 1987, pp. 83–95.

These international trends notwithstanding, those who fear that financial product diversification by financial institutions will lead to a greater concentration of assets held by American financial firms advance three arguments why such a trend would be undesirable. Of course, each of these arguments is valid in the extreme. Few would defend the desirability of having the ownership or control of all financial assets concentrated in a handful of corporations. The relevant question, however, is whether the detrimental effects of extreme concentration would also surface at the concentration levels that financial product diversification could reasonably be expected to produce.

One concern, for example, is that increasing the concentration of financial assets would reduce the diversity and multiplicity in decision-making units that arguably facilitate innovation and economic expansion.[39] Under this line of argument, a lending market that may be unconcentrated enough to ensure that it is competitive—that no individual lender has the power to set credit terms—does not guarantee that scarce loanable funds will be allocated toward the most attractive investment opportunities. In making lending decisions, large financial institutions tend to use formal and technical criteria, which can have the effect of discriminating against smaller and newer business borrowers. Since much of the American economy's dynamism lies in its newer businesses,[40] economic growth could be dampened if further financial product deregulation allowed larger financial institutions to expand at the expense of their smaller competitors.

The lending behavior of larger banks, however, generally does not bear out this concern. There is little evidence, for example, that larger banks consistently discriminate against small business borrowers. Indeed, at least one survey has found that larger banks are *more* willing than their smaller counterparts to make loans to new, small businesses, reflecting greater abilities to diversify their risks and to accumulate experience by extending credit in a broader range of activities.[41] Another

39. *Restructuring Financial Markets*, pp. 197–98.
40. Between 1980 and 1983 businesses less than ten years old added a total of 750,000 employees to their payroll, whereas the companies listed in the Fortune 500 lost 3 million jobs. Peter F. Drucker, "Our Entrepreneurial Economy," *Harvard Business Review*, vol. 62 (January–February 1984), pp. 58–64. More recently, the Small Business Administration has reported that employment in industries that small businesses dominate (notably construction, finance, real estate, insurance, and other services) expanded at more than twice the rate over the 1982–84 period than employment in industries characterized by larger firms. See U.S. Small Business Association, *The State of Small Business: A Report to the President* (GPO, 1985), pp. 17–19.
41. Bernard Shull, "Changes in Commercial Banking Structure and Small Business

more recent study has found that the credit needs of smaller businesses tend to be denied more in liberal branching states, but when credit needs are met in such states, the terms are generally considered satisfactory.[42] In any event, it is well established that larger banks in the United States are more willing lenders—reflected in higher loan-to-asset ratios—than smaller banks.[43] As a result, even if larger banks tended, on balance, to be less favorable toward small business borrowers than smaller banks, the higher loan-to-asset ratios at larger banks could produce a greater volume of loans to small business as average bank size in the United States increases.[44]

Evidence from other countries, meanwhile, fails to substantiate any clear linkage between bank concentration and economic growth. Table 4-5 shows estimates of the five-firm concentration ratios among banks and related lending institutions for the United States and for five other leading industrialized countries, coupled with real GNP growth recorded in these countries between 1950 and 1985. The concentration estimates are presented as ranges, with the upper bounds generally representing concentration only among banks and the lower bounds including related depository institutions (such as savings and loans or credit unions). Significantly, although the United States has the lowest five-firm con-

Lending," in Interagency Task Force on Small Business Finance, *Studies in Small Business Finance* (December 1981).

42. Peter L. Struck and Lewis Mandell, "The Effect of Bank Deregulation on Small Business: A Note," *Journal of Finance*, vol. 38 (June 1983), pp. 1025–31.

43. In 1984 banks with assets below $100 million had approximately 52 percent of their assets invested in loans; for banks with assets over $1 billion, the loan-to-asset ratio was 62 percent. Karl A. Scheld and Herbert Baer, "Interstate Banking and Intrastate Branching: Summing Up," in Herbert Baer and Sue F. Gregorash, eds., *Toward Nationwide Banking: A Guide to the Issues* (Federal Reserve Bank of Chicago, 1986).

44. A related fear often expressed by opponents of interstate banking is that larger banks tend to channel funds collected in smaller, rural areas to urban borrowers. This concern was examined by a Carter administration task force, which found no evidence to support the claim that banks use outlying branches to transfer funds to head offices in urban areas; rather banks transfer funds among rural offices as dictated by needs. Department of the Treasury, *Geographic Restrictions on Commercial Banking in the United States: The Report of the President* (Department of the Treasury, 1981), p. 15. See also Robert A. Eisenbeis, "Regional Forces for Interstate Banking," *Federal Reserve Bank of Atlanta Economic Review*, vol. 68 (May 1983), p. 30. The concern about the lending attitudes of large banks toward local communities also ignores the fact that banks in rural or less populated areas already are a major source of federal funds for money center banks in New York. See Scheld and Baer, "Interstate Banking and Intrastate Branching: Summing Up," pp. 75–83.

Table 4-5. *Five-Firm Bank Concentration Ratio and GNP Growth for Six Major Industrialized Countries, 1950–85*

Country	Concentration ratio	Real GNP growth (percent)	
		1950–85	*1973–85*
United States (commercial lending)	14.9–19.0	197	30
Japan	22.0–32.0	768	57
Germany	26.0–56.8	403	24
United Kingdom	50.0–73.0	125	15
Canada (commercial lending)	70.7–85.0	341	37
France	73.0–87.0	327	29

Sources: Herbert Baer and Sue F. Gregorash, eds., *Toward Nationwide Banking: A Guide to the Issues* (Federal Reserve Bank of Chicago, 1986); and International Monetary Fund, *International Financial Statistics: Yearbook 1986* (Washington, D.C.: IMF, 1986).

centration ratio of all the countries listed, its economic growth has fallen short in both 1950–85 and 1973–85 of all those countries, except the United Kingdom. However, the table also indicates that of the countries outside the United States, those with the lowest financial concentration ratios—Japan and Germany—have grown considerably faster than those where only five banks clearly dominate the banking system.

A second concern of those who fear that further financial product diversification would increase concentration in the financial sector centers on the destabilizing effect an increase in concentration could have on the financial system as a whole. These critics argue that a larger number of independent decisionmakers minimize the chance that speculative activities will cause destabilizing "bandwagon effects" that lead to panics. Similarly, they contend that diversity in decisionmaking units helps reduce the chance that problems among a few financial firms will affect the health of others.[45]

However, no reliable evidence that fewer decisionmakers would increase the likelihood of bandwagon effects is available. The speculative fever that culminated in the stock market crash of 1929 occurred at a time when the market was much less dominated than it is today by large institutional investors. Indeed, provided they are well diversified, a fewer number of financial institutions can actually strengthen an economy's stability. During the Depression, for example, not one of Canada's banks failed, a result consistent with that country's long-standing refusal to limit the geographic range of its banks. In contrast, the United States lost roughly one-third of its banks between 1930 and 1933.

45. *Restructuring Financial Markets*, pp. 197–98.

Finally, and perhaps most significant, many in this country have long been concerned that excessive concentration of economic resources would adversely affect the stability of our political system. A healthy democracy requires an effective balance of competing interests or factions.[46] Achieving this balance may become more difficult as the number of independent decisionmaking units in an economy declines. The greatest threat may indeed arise from concentration among financial institutions, given their essential role in channeling society's savings toward investment projects. Again, if financial product diversification were to aid the concentration of assets in the financial sector, under this view, it would have undesirable implications for the functioning of our political system.

This line of argument, however, ignores the powerful role of countervailing nonbusiness interest groups in our society. Sweeping environmental and safety regulation was established in the 1960s and 1970s despite strong opposition from the business community.[47] Similarly, Congress enacted comprehensive tax reform legislation in 1986 despite intense lobbying from powerful business interests. These events are consistent with a recent empirical analysis that found that neither firm size nor industry size significantly influenced federal legislation enacted during the 1976–80 period,[48] and with several studies that have failed to find a statistically significant relationship between aggregate *bank* concentration and political power.[49]

In sum, most would concede that extreme concentration in the ownership of financial assets would be undesirable, both economically and politically. However, the same cannot be said of trends toward mildly increasing levels of aggregate concentration. In particular, modest increases in aggregate concentration would not be likely to reduce

46. Alexander Hamilton, James Madison, and John Jay, *The Federalist, or The New Constitution* (Oxford: Basil Blackwell, 1948).

47. Robert E. Litan and William D. Nordhaus, *Reforming Federal Regulation* (Yale University Press, 1983).

48. Daniel C. Estey and Richard E. Caves, "Market Structure and Political Influence: New Data on Political Expenditures, Activity, and Success," *Economic Inquiry*, vol. 21 (January 1983), pp. 24–38.

49. Cynthia A. Glassman, "The Impact of Banks' Statewide Economic Power on Their Political Power: An Empirical Analysis," *Atlantic Economic Journal*, vol. 9 (July 1981), pp. 53–56; Stephen A. Rhoades and Roger D. Rutz, "Economic Power and Political Influence: An Empirical Analysis of Bank Regulatory Decisions," *Atlantic Economic Journal*, vol. 11 (July 1983), pp. 79–86; and John T. Rose, "Aggregate Concentration in Banking and Political Leverage: A Note," *Industrial Organization Review*, vol. 6 (1978), pp. 193–97.

economic growth, destabilize the financial system, or produce unwelcome political effects. Nevertheless, for those who still remain concerned, measures may be taken to minimize the concentrating effect of financial product diversification without detracting from the economic benefits diversification may produce. This subject is explored in chapter 5.

Specific Abuses

The final set of concerns about further financial product diversification centers on two specific potential dangers that stem from the ability of diversified financial institutions to offer multiple financial services. One commonly voiced fear is that diversified financial firms would tie the sales of their various services together. Some in the insurance industry, for example, have feared that if banking organizations were permitted to sell or underwrite insurance, they could directly or indirectly force borrowers to purchase insurance from their nonbanking affiliates as a condition for receiving credit and other banking services. Independent providers of other nonbanking services have expressed similar fears. They argue that such tying arrangements deprive consumers of choice and foreclose market opportunities of other providers of the competing services.

A second concern is that diversified financial organizations may be able to exploit conflicts of interest and thus to distort the allocation of credit, as well as to compromise the safety of the banking system. Some argue that banks in diversified financial organizations would find ways—explicit or implicit—to channel funds to their nonbanking affiliates on conditions and terms that are not arm's length. Others assert that in their eagerness to generate up-front fees, banks will tend to favor customers of their nonbank affiliates in making credit decisions.

As developed further below, existing statutes are designed to address most of these concerns. However, even if current laws should be deemed to provide insufficient protection, less drastic remedies than activity separation are available.

Tying

The fear that financial product diversification will lead to unwanted tie-ins must be assessed in a broader context. From both an economic and a legal perspective, the act of tying *by itself* is not objectionable. To the contrary, consumers prefer to purchase numerous products and services on a tied basis—such as automobiles with stereo tape decks and air conditioners, or household appliances with service contracts. The practice warrants concern only when tying effectively denies consumers who want the choice the ability to purchase products or services separately.

The antitrust laws reflect this principle. Section 3 of the Clayton Act, as interpreted in numerous judicial decisions, bars tying arrangements involving *goods* where the producer establishing the tie-in has substantial market power in the tying goods market *or* where the tie-in will foreclose a "not insubstantial" volume of sales in the tied goods market.[50] For example, consider an arrangement under which an oil company ties the sale of its gasoline to the purchase of its engine oil. In applying section 3 of the Clayton Act to this practice, courts will ask whether the oil company has significant market power in the sale of gasoline or the tie-in arrangement involves more than a *de minimis* volume of goods. As a practical matter, either of these tests will generally be satisfied if the tying arrangement can be established, and no justifiable business purpose for the tie-in is present.[51]

Tying arrangements involving *services* rather than goods are judged under the somewhat more rigorous standards of section 1 of the Sherman Act (which prohibits agreements or conspiracies in restraint of trade) and section 5 of the Federal Trade Commission Act (which prohibits unfair trade practices). The Sherman Act standards have been construed to require the proof of *both* market power in the tying product *and* the foreclosure of a not insubstantial volume of commerce.[52]

---

50. *Times-Picayune Publishing Co.* v. *United States,* 345 U.S. 594 (1953).

51. Whether a justifiable business purpose will be found depends on industry practice, that is, whether the two products are generally sold together (such as a right glove and a left glove).

52. In *U.S. Steel Corp.* v. *Fortner Enterprises, Inc.,* 429 U.S. 610 (1977), a 1977 case relevant to the debate over financial product deregulation, the Supreme Court demonstrated the significance of this dual requirement. At issue was an arrangement in which the purchase of low-cost prefabricated houses (the tied product) was tied to granting loans to acquire and develop land (the tying product). Although the Court found that the $200,000 in sales of prefabricated housing was not an insubstantial amount of commerce, it did conclude that on the evidence before it, no showing had been made that U.S. Steel had market power in providing credit. The fact that Fortner may have felt compelled to agree to the tie-in did not prove that U.S. Steel had the requisite market power in the credit market to establish an antitrust violation.

Until 1970, banking services were treated the same as other types of services under the antitying provisions of the antitrust laws. However, in 1970 Congress recognized the unique importance of credit in the economy by amending the Bank Holding Company Act to prohibit *any* tying of bank credit to any other service offered by a bank or its holding company. The prohibition was meant to apply regardless of the bank's size or its market power. A similar prohibition was extended to tying by federally chartered thrift institutions in 1982. Accordingly, if financial product-line restrictions were suddenly dropped, current antitying restrictions more stringent than those of the Clayton or Sherman acts would flatly *prohibit* tied offerings of bank credit and nonbank services.

Critics of financial product deregulation recognize that these legal restrictions exist, but fear that such restrictions would be ineffective in a deregulated environment. They argue that many victims of tie-ins may not be aware that the arrangements are unlawful, and even if they were aware, would lack the resources to challenge large banking organizations in court. In addition, some claim that because of pressure applied by a loan officer, consumers may erroneously believe that they are required to purchase another nonbanking service as a condition for obtaining a bank loan.[53]

If consumers accept tie-ins out of ignorance, the problems with the arrangements are easily rectified without imposing the far more drastic measure of completely separating banking from other activities. All financial institutions can be required to advise their customers—in advertisements, in person, and in contract language—that they need not purchase any service offered by any arm of the organization as a condition for obtaining credit or any service in which the customers are primarily interested.[54] If consumers are forced to accept unlawful tie-ins because

---

53. The American Council of Life Insurance (ACLI), for example, has pointed to a 1979 Federal Reserve staff study that found that nearly two-thirds of bank borrowers also purchase credit life or health insurance from the bank, and over 40 percent of such borrowers purchased the insurance because they believed it was "required" or "strongly recommended." Testimony of Richard S. Schweiker, President of the ACLI, in *Competition in Financial Service,* Hearings before the Subcommittee on Commerce, Transportation, and Tourism of the House Energy and Commerce Committee, 98 Cong. 1 sess. (GPO, 1983), pp. 104–17. See also Robert A. Eisenbeis and Paul R. Schweitzer, "Tie-ins Between the Granting of Credit and Sale of Insurance by Bank Holding Companies and Other Lenders," Federal Reserve Board Staff Study, February 1979.

54. In fact, the Federal Reserve has previously imposed this condition in connection

they lack incentives to challenge them, the standing requirements in the antitying provisions of the antitrust and banking statutes can be liberalized to give other parties the right to sue. The Reagan administration's financial product deregulation bill proposed in 1983, for example, would have allowed trade associations as well as private individuals and corporations to challenge tying arrangements that bank holding companies and thrift institutions imposed.[55]

Ultimately, however, the practical ability of diversified financial organizations to engage in anticompetitive tying arrangements, implicitly and explicitly, will depend on the market power held by these organizations. In competitive markets, banks and other financial institutions that also try to enforce tying arrangements that consumers do not wish to take part in will inevitably lose business to other firms. In fact, as discussed in chapter 3, the markets for the various nonbanking services that banks seek to provide are generally highly competitive.[56] Equally significant, competition among depository institutions is generally intense, particularly with the growing competition in both depository and lending services between commercial banks and thrifts.[57] Where depository markets are concentrated, the exceptions are largely in rural areas or smaller communities, certain of which could benefit from additional entry into banking in a more fully deregulated environment from such financial institutions as insurance companies or securities brokers. But even if competition should remain imperfect in certain of

with its approval of specific nonbank activities that are deemed to be "closely related to the business of banking."

55. The bill also would have required banks to inform potential borrowing customers in writing that they would not be required to purchase insurance from holding company affiliates as a condition for obtaining a loan.

56. The only exception—securities underwriting—would probably become much more competitive if banks were permitted entry.

57. The Antitrust Division of the Justice Department, for example, recently cited the highly competitive nature of the banking industry in concluding that the fears about the dangers of tying credit to other nonbanking services were unfounded. The Division stated its views in response to an advance notice of proposed rulemaking by the FDIC in 1983 seeking comments on the need for rulemaking to govern involvement by insured banks in a variety of nonbanking activities. 49 Fed. Reg. 48552, 48553 (December 13, 1984).

It is noteworthy that even a recent study commissioned by an insurance trade association concludes that "deposit-taking institutions generally do not dominate their markets to such an extent that substantial market power could be used to force their way into the markets by compelling the purchase of an insurance product by their depositors." American Insurance Association, *Expansion of Banks into Insurance* (New York: AIA, 1983), p. vii.

these markets, the most efficient way to deter anticompetitive tie-ins is to attack that problem directly by using broader disclosure requirements and liberalized standing provisions, rather than by prohibiting depository and nondepository financial institutions from engaging in each other's business.

Conflicts of Interest

Conflicts of interest involving the banking industry have long attracted the special attention of policymakers. Because of their role in accepting deposits, banks are viewed as owing a duty to deposit holders as well as to the federal deposit insurance agencies to operate in a safe and sound manner. Because of their role in supplying credit, banks are viewed as owing a duty to the entire public to make impartial lending decisions and not to favor any particular class of potential borrowers.

As banking organizations move into other businesses, however, there is some fear that they will have increasing incentives to pursue objectives that are inconsistent with each of these duties. Some argue, for example, that managers of diversified financial organizations may be tempted, particularly at times when the nonbanking subsidiaries or divisions may be subject to financial distress, to pressure their wholly owned bank to channel funds to its nonbanking affiliates. A related concern is that banks belonging to diversified financial conglomerates will be reluctant to lend to competitors of the conglomerates' nonbanking subsidiaries. Finally, some fear that lending officers may be pressured or have incentives to favor customers of the nonbank affiliates. In short, the concern is that lending officials in diversified financial organizations may face incentives to produce results that may be in the organization's short-run interest, but which could nevertheless expose the organization—and society as a whole—to the risk of larger losses over the long term.

Bank Favoritism toward Nonbank Affiliates. The first fear—that banks in diversified financial organizations would be tempted to favor nonbanking affiliates—can be largely addressed under existing law. The Federal Reserve Board monitors interaffiliate transactions to ensure that bank subsidiaries of holding companies do not divert income to their nonbank affiliates by overpaying for assets and services they buy from those firms.[58] In addition, banks are subject to restrictions on payments

58. The Board has the power to take formal action—obtaining written agreements

of dividends and capital reductions, while savings and loan subsidiaries of multithrift holding companies must give advance notice to the FSLIC of proposed dividends.[59]

Perhaps most important, however, is that transactions between banks and their nonbank affiliates are tightly controlled by section 23A of the Federal Reserve Act, which limits "covered transactions" between a bank and any one nonbank affiliate to 10 percent of bank capital and surplus, and the sum of all covered transactions to all affiliates to no more than 20 percent of bank capital and surplus. "Covered transactions" include loans, purchases of securities or assets, the acceptance of securities as collateral, and the issuance of guarantees, acceptances, or letters of credit. In fact, banking organizations have kept their bank-to-affiliate transactions far below the permissible limits. In their study of 224 bank holding companies for 1975–80, Rose and Talley found that downstream transfers of funds from nonbank subsidiaries to their affiliated banks dominated extensions of bank credit to the nonbank affiliates.[60] Savings and loans belonging to multithrift holding companies are even more tightly controlled: the Savings and Loan Holding Company Act Amendments *prohibit* savings and loan subsidiaries of multithrift holding companies from investing in or making loans and guarantees to holding company affiliates.

As controlled as interaffiliate transactions may be, however, insured depositories belonging to diversified financial organizations can still exploit conflicts of interest by favoring nonbank affiliates. At a minimum, bank holding companies may use various *sub rosa* mechanisms to channel resources from their banks to their nonbank corporations: by imposing higher services or management fees on their banks, by increasing their depositories' tax reimbursements to parent companies, or by making subtle adjustments in interaffiliate pricing.[61] Each of these

---

or issuing cease-and-desist orders—where interaffiliate pricing distortions have a material and adverse effect on the bank. Larry D. Wall, "Insulating Banks from Nonbank Affiliates," *Federal Reserve Bank of Atlanta Economic Review,* vol. 69 (September 1984), pp.18–29.

59. In the absence of prior regulatory approval, all national and member bank dividends are limited to the sum of the current year's earnings and the prior two years' retained earnings. Insured state nonmember bank dividends generally are limited by similar state restrictions. Ibid., p. 24.

60. John T. Rose and Samuel H. Talley, "Financial Transactions Within Bank Holding Companies," *Journal of Financial Research,* vol. 7 (Fall 1984), pp. 209–17.

61. Anthony G. Cornyn and Samuel H. Talley, "Activity Deregulation and Bank

techniques may be difficult to detect and can be used as a device for systematically bolstering the nonbank activities at the expense of bank loan customers.

Why would a profit-maximizing banking organization use its bank subsidiary to support nonbanking operations that may offer lower returns on invested capital at the margin than banking activities? The answer lies in the interest of any financial organization in preserving its reputation for soundness in *all* activities, specifically in preventing a run on the bank by depositors who may erroneously believe their funds would be threatened if nonbank affiliates were to become insolvent. As former Citicorp Chairman Walter Wriston has observed: "It is inconceivable that any major bank would walk away from any subsidiary of its holding company. If your name is on the door, all of your capital funds are going to be behind it in the real world. Lawyers can say you have separation, but the marketplace is persuasive, and it would not see it that way."[62] In fact, many banks during the 1970s rescued real estate investment trusts (REITs) that they had sponsored and advised even though the REITs were not technically part of their organizations. Perhaps more significant, several bank failures in the 1970s were attributable to problems with nonbank affiliates.[63] Most recently, federal regulatory authorities felt compelled to save the Continental Illinois holding company as well as its subsidiary bank. Among other things, the regulators feared that the demise of Continental's holding company or its nonbank subsidiaries could trigger still additional runs on the beleaguered bank.

In short, despite all the restrictions on transactions between banks and their affiliates, banks are likely to be sorely tempted or forced by their holding companies to assist troubled affiliates.[64] Such action poses

Soundness," in *Proceedings of a Conference on Bank Structure and Competition* (Federal Reserve Bank of Chicago, 1983), pp. 34–35.

62. *Financial Institutions Restructuring and Services Act of 1981,* Hearings before the Senate Committee on Banking, Housing, and Urban Affairs, 97 Cong. 1 sess. (GPO, 1981), 589–90.

63. See Cornyn and Talley, "Activity Deregulation and Bank Soundness," pp. 33–34, discussing the failures of the Hamilton National Bank of Chattanooga and Beverly Hills Bancorp; and Lucille S. Mayne, "New Directions in Bank Holding Company Supervision," *Banking Law Journal,* vol. 95 (January 1978), pp. 729, 731, discussing the failures of American City Bank Trust Co. of Milwaukee, Wisconsin, and Palmer First National Bank Trust Co. of Sarasota, Florida.

64. A recent report on financial product diversification by the U.S. General Accounting Office comes to the same conclusion. See GAO, *Bank Powers: Insulating Banks from the Potential Risks of Expanded Activities,* GAO/GGD-87-35 (Washington, D.C.: GAO, 1987).

a potential conflict of interest because the rescues divert resources that could otherwise be loaned to bank customers; in the extreme case, the drain on the bank could pose serious risks to the continued soundness of the bank itself. As already discussed, financial product diversification should strengthen most banking organizations, reducing the risks that banks would be confronted with opportunities to exploit potential conflicts of interest arising from supporting their nonbank affiliates. However, some banking organizations may use widened activity authority to take greater risks; furthermore, the entry of nonbanking corporations into banking could expose certain banks to greater risks than those experienced by the industry now. If these patterns emerge, the risks of bank favoritism toward affiliates would be greater than they are now.

Bank Discrimination against Competitors of Nonbank Affiliates. Further financial product diversification may create a second potential conflict of interest by providing disincentives for banks in diversified conglomerates to lend to competitors of their nonbank affiliates. Thus, for example, a bank affiliated with an insurance agency might not be as willing to lend to other insurance agencies as banks not affiliated with such enterprises.

From a purely economic perspective, discrimination of this sort would only be rational if the opportunity cost from refusing loans to qualified borrowers outweighed the indirect advantages such behavior might provide to the bank affiliates that compete against those potential borrowers. Where loan markets are competitive, however, this condition would never be met because the borrowers who may be denied credit by a conglomerate's bank subsidiary would be able to obtain funding on the same (if not better) terms from other institutions. The same would be true if the relevant product or service markets were competitive, for then the nonbanking enterprises within financial conglomerates would gain nothing from the loan discrimination practiced by their bank affiliates.

Not all markets, however, are perfectly competitive. As discussed in chapter 3, although the lending markets in most geographic regions throughout the country are highly competitive, banking markets in less populated areas tend to be concentrated. Perhaps more important, in a world of complete financial product-line freedom, it is conceivable that as the number of conglomerates engaged in both banking and nonbanking activities increases, the lending markets confronting competitors in those nonbanking lines of business not large enough to have access to the public securities markets or to lenders in other geographic areas could radically change. The independent insurance agency or real estate brokerage office in a small- to medium-sized town, for example, could have difficulty in obtaining bank financing if all or most of the insured lending institutions (or their holding companies) in the area were also engaged in selling insurance and real estate. In the limit, independent agents or brokers could be totally replaced in such regions by bank-affiliated enterprises.

Clearly, where such transitions occur, individual businesses and their owners would be harmed. This concern is why smaller businesses offering financial services have so strongly opposed the expansion of banks into nonbanking activities. But just as the antitrust laws are concerned with injury to *competition* and not to *competitors*, the relevant question for the nation as a whole is whether loan discrimination by diversified banking organizations would produce an anticompetitive result. If such discrimination merely caused bank-affiliated suppliers to substitute for independent suppliers, the strength of competition in the relevant product or service market would remain unchanged. Indeed, if financial product expansion enabled banking organizations to realize economies of scope and gains from portfolio diversification, the non-banking affiliates would be able to offer products and services at lower prices than consumers are being charged. However, in certain instances, financial product diversification could be associated with a decrease in the number of suppliers providing specific services. Such a decrease in less populated regions would reduce competition. Consumers would be worse off if the adverse effects of the decline in competition outweighed the efficiency gains from financial product consolidation.

Yet even in lesser populated regions of the country where borrowers and consumers already may face limited choices, continuing advances in the delivery of financial services should constrain the ability of diversified banking organizations to profit from attempts to discriminate against competitors of their nonbank affiliates. The marketing of insurance, in particular, is likely to be revolutionized as financial product diversification proceeds. Customers in rural areas can be identified by mail and served out of regional locations, opening up local markets to competition from national financial conglomerates. The greater the competition in such service markets as insurance, the less incentive a local diversified banking organization has to refuse to lend to borrowers with whom nonbank affiliates may be competing.

In short, adverse effects to competition in product and service markets from potential loan discrimination are most likely to be felt only in geographic regions where lending and product markets may already be less than perfectly competitive. The magnitude of these effects is highly uncertain and depends on a combination of market-related factors: the extent to which banking organizations in such regions would diversify their service offerings; the extent of lending discrimination that those diversified banking organizations would practice; and the present and future strength of competition in local lending and product markets, which depend heavily on continuing advances in the nationwide delivery of financial services. Finally, and perhaps most important, the dangers from lending discrimination would depend on the conditions under which banking organizations will be permitted to diversify their service offerings, particularly whether highly diversified financial institutions will be permitted to fund their lending operations with federally insured deposits. This important issue is addressed in the next chapter.

Bank Favoritism toward Customers of Nonbank Affiliates. A third source of potential conflicts to which critics of financial product deregulation have pointed stems from the incentives that diversified banking organizations could have to steer loans toward customers of their nonbank affiliates. For example, banks (or thrifts) belonging to financial conglomerates could make special efforts to extend mortgage loans to customers of their real estate brokerage affiliates or to their co-venturers in their holding company's real estate development activities. Indeed, similar arrangements between banks and customers of their securities underwriting affiliates motivated Congress to enact the Glass-Steagall provisions. Banking organizations that practiced such favoritism would not explicitly tie banking and nonbanking services together—an act barred by existing bank holding company law—but rather would subtly channel loans to customers of affiliates in a fashion that bolstered the business of those affiliates.[65]

Why would a diversified financial organization permit or direct its bank to favor borrowers who may also be customers of nonbanking affiliates? Such favoritism implies that the bank would lend to otherwise

65. One of the abuses uncovered during the Pecora hearings was that certain banks had loaned more freely to actual or potential corporate customers of their securities affiliates to help the distribution of securities by those customers than to people or firms that were not customers of the security affiliates. Edward J. Kelly, III, "Conflicts of Interest: A Legal View," in Ingo Walter, ed., *Deregulating Wall Street* (Wiley, 1985), pp. 231–54.

unqualified borrowers or to qualified borrowers on terms that do not adequately reflect the risks of default simply to secure business for a nonbank affiliate. What incentives would a bank have to cross-subsidize its affiliate in this manner?

One incentive, paradoxically, arises primarily from the strict restrictions on direct interaffiliate transactions under current law or under any supplemental provisions that may be added as financial product deregulation progresses. Any new venture requires a certain amount of capital investment. Often the venture may also require continuing operating assistance, at least until it is firmly established. For a new nonbanking affiliate, a parent holding company may rationally decide that this ongoing assistance is more productively provided as favorable credit extension to customers of the affiliated new ventures rather than as direct cash transfers, either from the holding company or from the bank subsidiary. As just noted, current law limits the amount of funds a bank subsidiary may channel to an affiliate. More important, by using their bank lending as a marketing tool to enhance sales by their nonbank affiliates, diversified financial organizations may be able to build a customer base for those affiliates more rapidly than would otherwise be possible. Thus even subtle bank favoritism toward customers of nonbank affiliates would be a more cost-effective form of investment than direct cash infusions.

A second reason why a diversified financial organization might have its bank favor customers of nonbank subsidiaries is to take advantage of the convenience this practice may provide those customers. Some home purchasers, for example, may find that it is not worth looking around for a cheaper mortgage if the bank or thrift affiliated with their real estate broker stands ready to approve and extend a mortgage quickly. In certain cases, the added customer convenience may strengthen the marketing position of both the bank and its nonbanking affiliates. Like the grocery stores that periodically advertise "loss-leader" food items as a way of attracting customers to their stores, diversified financial organizations can implicitly offer access to credit as a way of attracting consumers to purchase a wide range of financial services from the same firm. Indeed, given the inertial nature of many consumers' relationships with financial institutions, the carrot of offering bank credit (on terms that do not fully reflect the risks of default) can be useful in building a base of long-term customers for all of the services diversified financial firms are capable of delivering.

If favoritism in bank lending is motivated by each of the foregoing factors, more damage would be inflicted on competitors of the nonbanking affiliates than on the banks themselves. To be sure, a biased lending policy of the sort just discussed can weaken a bank. However, imprudent lending is already encouraged by the moral hazard features of the flat-rate system of deposit insurance, which makes the cost of bank funds largely insensitive to the credit risks of bank investments. Accordingly, as a general rule, the likelihood that bank affiliations with nonbank activities can increase the *overall* risks of bank loan portfolios is small. Rather, any bias in lending decisions would show up in the kinds of risky loans banks choose to make. When those loans have the effect of drawing customers toward nonbanking affiliates, they will inevitably cause competitors of those affiliates not themselves related to a bank to lose business. In some areas, this activity could reduce the strength of competition in those nonbanking markets by in effect raising entry barriers to the markets for nonbanking services and products.

Under certain circumstances, however, bank favoritism toward customers of affiliates could raise risks to the bank itself. Organizations with very short time horizons can find profit in generating fee-based income for their affiliates by bending their lending policies to favor their customers. The temptation to assist customers of nonbank affiliates through liberal bank lending can be especially great if the affiliates are in financial difficulties, for then the reputation of the bank is at risk. The added risk to the bank in either event—which the federal deposit insurance system fails to deter—may never materialize, or if it does, may happen many years later when the relevant bank loan officers or even upper level bank management have probably moved on to other jobs.

Predicting or forecasting how significant any lending bias toward customers of nonbank affiliates would prove to be in a more fully deregulated environment is difficult. Some comfort can be drawn from the absence of abuses in those securities underwriting activities in which American commercial banks have been allowed to engage.[66] In addition,

---

66. A 1975 study by the Department of the Treasury, for example, found no evidence of actual conflicts arising from commercial bank underwriting of general obligation municipal bonds. U.S. Department of the Treasury, Office of Capital Markets Policy, *Public Policy Aspects of Bank Securities Activities* (Treasury Department, 1975). More recently, a comprehensive study of the Eurobond market, where U.S. banks can and do underwrite securities, found no evidence of imprudence. Richard M. Levich, "A

the strong disclosure regulations under the securities acts could easily be amended to require banks to disclose any loans they may have made to customers of their underwriting affiliate.[67]

Nevertheless, prudent public policy must consider potential biases in bank lending in other contexts. Although banks are limited in how much they can lend to a single customer, they are not constrained in lending to customers of affiliates.[68] Several possible supplemental remedies for preventing potential conflicts arising from bank favoritism toward customers of their affiliates are reviewed in the next chapter.

View from the International Capital Markets,'' in Walter, ed., *Deregulating Wall Street*, pp. 255–86.

67. Under current regulations issued pursuant to the 1933 Securities Act, issuers of securities must file registration statements with the Securities and Exchange Commission. These statements must contain information about the nature of the underwriter's interest in the issuer as well as the term of the underwriting arrangement itself. 17 C.F.R. 229.508 (1986). These regulations could easily be clarified or amended to require disclosure of the nature of any relationship the issuer may have with any affiliate of the underwriter, including its affiliated bank.

68. National and state banks are generally limited to lending no more than 15 percent of capital to any single customer.

CHAPTER FIVE

Policy Alternatives

A CENTRAL thesis of this study is that unless Congress affirmatively prohibits them, banks and other financial institutions will inevitably find ways of offering a full range of financial services. Some organizations will exploit loopholes in the complicated maze of statutes and regulations that govern financial institutions. Others will eventually be able to take advantage of the liberalizations that will ultimately come from the states, perhaps from federal regulators as well. But in the absence of federal legislation, transforming the financial marketplace will probably be inefficient and beset by legal uncertainties that impede an orderly transition to a more competitive financial system.

The critical challenge for policymakers, therefore, is to establish the legal conditions under which financial product diversification can best proceed. Specifically, what steps should be taken to ensure that the social benefits of diversification identified in chapter 3 are realized without running the risks examined in chapter 4?

This chapter outlines two broad but not necessarily exclusive approaches for meeting this challenge. They share a fundamental feature that virtually all experts in this area agree will be necessary as financial product diversification proceeds: banking and nonbanking activities should be conducted in separate corporate entities. Beyond this minimum requirement, the two approaches significantly diverge.

The first approach would address piecemeal the risks that financial product diversification poses, each handled by a specific remedy. The specific policy measures identified could be implemented individually or in a package. Risks to the safety and soundness of the banking system could be reduced by increasing capital requirements or deposit insurance premiums. Risks of excessive concentration could be minimized by placing ceilings on the ownership of financial assets by diversified organizations. Risks of potential conflicts of interest that financial conglomerates could exploit could be prevented by using disclosure requirements or by prohibiting bank transactions with nonbank affiliates and their customers.

144

The second approach is more comprehensive than the piecemeal approach. It would require any highly diversified firm—financial or nonfinancial—choosing to offer insured depository services to isolate the depository in a separate corporate subsidiary and to restrict the depository's investments to highly liquid "safe" securities. Lending activities would have to be conducted through another subsidiary or affiliate and funded by noninsured liabilities and equity. In short, such an approach would break the Gordian knot between deposit taking and commercial lending. That link has long defined commercial banking and has long made banks the object of special government regulation. The analysis presented here suggests that the benefits of adopting a "narrow" or "safe" banking structure for firms seeking to engage in a wide range of banking and nonbanking activities would outweigh its costs, would be preferable to the piecemeal approach to minimizing risks, and would help speed the delivery of the social benefits of financial product diversification.

The Case for Structural Separation

It is conventional wisdom that financial product diversification will not be allowed to proceed—by state or federal regulators or by lawmakers—unless banking and nonbanking activities are carried out in separate, albeit related, corporations. The Reagan administration's financial institutions deregulation proposal (S. 1609 and H.R. 3537) of 1983, for example, would have permitted banking and thrift organizations to engage in a virtually unlimited range of financial activities (except corporate securities underwriting) but only through separate nonbank subsidiaries of a parent holding company. The narrower product deregulation bills that the Senate passed in 1984 (S. 2851) and the Senate Banking Committee considered in 1986 (S. 2592), as well as the deregulation initiative (H.R. 50) that Representative Doug Barnard (D-Georgia) proposed in 1987, are premised on the same model. The deregulation proposal that E. Gerald Corrigan, president of the Federal Reserve Bank of New York, advanced in early 1987 is also based on the administration's model.[1]

One motivation for requiring the separation of banking and nonbank-

1. See E. Gerald Corrigan, "Financial Market Structure: A Longer View," *Federal Reserve Bank of New York Annual Report, 1986* (The Bank, 1987), pp. 3–6. The Corrigan proposal is discussed further below.

ing corporations is to minimize the likelihood that bank deposits would be used or called upon to rescue ailing nonbanking operations, thus exposing banks in diversified organizations to greater risks of failure. How effective separation would be in achieving this objective, however, is disputable. On the one hand, some commentators maintain that separation would be highly effective; courts would be unlikely to "pierce the corporate veil" of the banking subsidiary to hold it liable for the debts of its affiliates.[2] On the other hand, despite the separate legal status of related banking and nonbanking corporations, there is evidence that banks will find ways of assisting their nonbanking affiliates if these affiliates encounter financial trouble.[3]

A second related motivation for requiring separate corporations is to prevent banks belonging to diversified financial conglomerates from using federally insured deposits—purchased at interest rates below those required to attract uninsured funds—to fund nonbanking activities, to the competitive detriment of independent competitors providing nonbanking services. Indeed, this concern was one of the arguments that the Reagan administration pressed in advocating its 1983 financial product deregulation proposal.[4]

2. Sam Chase and Donn Waage, "Corporate Separateness as a Tool of Bank Regulation," reprinted in *Competitive Equity in the Financial Services Industry, Part II*, Hearings on S. 2181 and S. 2134 before the Senate Committee on Banking, Housing and Urban Affairs, 98 Cong. 2 sess. (Government Printing Office, 1984), p. 249. For a legal analysis of the potential liability of a bank for actions taken by nonbank affiliates, see Robert Charles Clark, "The Regulation of Financial Holding Companies," *Harvard Law Review*, vol. 92 (February 1979), pp. 789–863.

3. This point was discussed in chapter 4. See also Fischer Black, Merton H. Miller, and Richard A. Posner, "An Approach to the Regulation of Bank Holding Companies," *Journal of Business*, vol. 51 (July 1978), pp. 379–412.

4. See Testimony of Peter J. Wallison, General Counsel, Department of the Treasury, in *Competition in Financial Services*, Hearings on H.R. 3397 and H.R. 3537 before the Subcommittee on Commerce, Transportation and Tourism of the House Committee on Energy and Commerce, 98 Cong. 1 sess. (GPO, 1983).

A variation of this second motivation for corporate separateness was behind the decision by the Federal Communications Commission (FCC) to require AT&T and, after the AT&T breakup, the Bell operating companies (BOCs) to offer unregulated products and services in subsidiaries separate from the entities offering regulated telephone service. The FCC reasoned that without the separate subsidiary requirement the combined entity could use accounting techniques to generate higher costs and therefore higher regulated prices for the regulated telecommunications services and thereby apply the added revenue to subsidize the offerings of the unregulated products and services at predatory prices. Critics of the separate subsidiary requirement currently applicable to AT&T and the BOCs, however, argue that it has led to costly duplication

A third motivation for requiring separate corporations is to help regulate and supervise the different activities. Each of the major financial services industries—banking, securities, and insurance—is subject to its own regulations that different federal and state agencies administer. If banks were directly permitted to offer these other financial services, the overlap in regulatory jurisdictions would lead to wasteful duplication and confusion. At worst, the effectiveness of each regulatory body would be impaired until it acquired sufficient expertise to supervise activities in which it currently has no experience.

The corporate separateness requirement may be implemented in either of two ways. Subsidiaries of depository institutions can perform non-banking functions, as now occurs with certain state-chartered banks or service corporation subsidiaries of thrift institutions. Alternatively, banking and nonbanking affiliates may coexist as subsidiaries of a common holding company, as now occurs through existing bank and thrift holding companies.[5] Which organizational form should be preferred?

Allowing nonbank activities to be conducted directly through subsidiaries of insured institutions would have several benefits. It would ensure that any benefits of activity diversification and economies of scope that could be realized through multiproduct offerings would directly flow to those institutions. Whether the benefits would be as great if nonbank activities were placed in a parallel subsidiary of a holding company is uncertain: it would depend on the amount of freedom that federal regulators permit the holding companies and their bank and nonbank subsidiaries to operate as integrated entities.[6] The direct subsidiary approach could also be less costly because it would eliminate the need for creating new holding companies. This consideration is particularly important for smaller banks and thrifts.[7]

---

of efforts, distorted investment decisions, discouraged research and development, and resulted in needless and expensive litigation. See William J. Baumol and Robert D. Willig, "Telephones and Computers: The Costs of Artificial Separation," *Regulation*, March–April 1985, pp. 23–32.

5. Special corporate forms must be provided for mutual insurance companies that are allowed to diversify into other activities. Because they are owned by their policyholders, mutual insurers cannot be subsidiaries of a holding company. This point is discussed further below.

6. As discussed in chapter 4, there already is ample evidence that bank holding companies operate on an integrated basis.

7. To minimize this cost, the financial institutions deregulation bill that the Reagan

In this author's view, these benefits are outweighed by factors favoring
the holding company mechanism. Requiring all nonbank activities to be
operated within a holding company structure would end the growing
disparity between the range of nonbank activities open to bank holding
companies, which the Federal Reserve (Fed) regulate, and those open
to state-chartered banks in certain states where banks may directly
engage in nonbank activities not approved for bank holding companies.
More important, the holding company approach, however imperfect, is
more likely to prevent deposit insurance from subsidizing nonbanking
activities, as would occur if banks were allowed to invest directly in
nonbank enterprises. In the holding company mechanism, the nonbank
activities do not appear on the asset side of the bank's balance sheet;
under the alternative structure, they clearly would. Finally, requiring
that financial activity diversification proceed only through the holding
company mechanism would vest agencies at the federal level with all
responsibility for supervising the transactions and affiliations between
the nonbank and bank activities. This requirement would minimize
jurisdictional overlaps between state and federal agencies, as well as
unnecessary duplication in overseeing nonbank activities in which
depository organizations may be engaged.[8]

Reducing the Risks of Financial Product Diversification Piecemeal

Corporate separateness alone does not adequately address all the
risks of further financial product diversification identified in chapter 4.
As already noted, legal separation may not remove the safety-related
risks of banks' attempts to rescue nonbanking affiliates. Nor does it

administration proposed in 1983 would have exempted simple conversions of banks and
thrifts to holding company structures from the registration requirements of the securities
laws and from the regulatory approvals required under the Bank Holding Company Act
and the Savings and Loan Holding Company Act Amendments.

8. For a summary of arguments favoring the holding company approach to financial
product deregulation, see Wallison Testimony, *Competition in Financial Services*, pp.
64–65. A significant drawback to federal-state uniformity, however, is that it would eliminate the competition between legislators and regulators at the two levels of government,
which as chapter 2 demonstrated has been an important source of regulatory innovation
in the banking arena. See Kenneth E. Scott, "The Dual Banking System: A Model of
Competition in Regulation," *Stanford Law Review*, vol. 30 (November 1977), pp. 1–50.

answer the concerns about aggregate concentration and conflicts of interest.

The piecemeal approach could satisfactorily contain most, perhaps all, of the risks of further financial product diversification. However, as demonstrated below, none of its components is free from practical or theoretical drawbacks.

Minimizing Safety-Related Risks

Earlier chapters suggested that although further financial product deregulation would enhance the stability of many banking organizations, certain firms, particularly those not engaged in banking activities, could use the opportunities that product deregulation creates to increase the risks of the banks they charter, acquire, or currently operate. Five commonly discussed mechanisms or techniques, individually or in combination, could reduce this danger.

Strengthened Separation Requirements. The first approach is to strengthen the corporate separateness provisions themselves by requiring banks and their related nonbank corporations to be operated as distinct entities. Requiring banks and their affiliates to be operated in different locations and under different names, for example, could reduce the likelihood that depositors would withdraw funds from their bank upon hearing news that nonbank affiliates are in financial trouble.[9] Prohibiting bank and nonbank corporations from sharing common officers and directors would limit the danger that any moral hazard effects from flat-rate deposit insurance would affect the conduct of the nonbank subsidiary or affiliate. Such a requirement would also help ensure that nonbank operations are staffed by individuals knowledgeable in the relevant fields rather than by bankers or thrift managers who are likely to have little or no experience in nonbank activities. Separate managements can especially be helpful in preventing interaffiliate transactions that could potentially weaken a depository institution, while favoring its nonbank affiliates or subsidiaries.[10] In late 1984 the Federal Deposit

---

9. The financial product deregulation bill that the Senate passed in 1984 (S. 2851) would have precluded the securities affiliates of bank holding companies from having a name similar to the bank's or from advertising in any way that the bank subsidiary was responsible for the obligations of the affiliate. The administration proposal contained the second restriction but not the first.

10. Clark, "Regulation of Financial Holding Companies," p. 803.

Insurance Corporation (FDIC) imposed all these separate operating requirements on state nonmember banks that may be authorized to underwrite corporate securities and proposed in 1985 that the requirements also apply to all insured banks permitted to underwrite insurance and invest in real estate.[11]

Detailed separateness provisions, however, could be costly. Prohibiting the use of common employees, officers, directors, and locations would detract from the potential economies that could be realized from activity diversification. Similarly, banning the use of common trade names could reduce some of the marketing advantages of diversification.[12]

Unfortunately, there exist no reliable empirical data to assess the costs and benefits of various separate operating requirements. Whether any are advisable, therefore, should depend on what other mechanisms, if any, are implemented to contain the potentially adverse effects financial product deregulation might have on the safety and soundness of the banking system. The more effective these other steps are, the less likely the added benefits of the FDIC approach would be to outweigh the costs.

Enhancing Disclosure. A second method for minimizing adverse safety-related impacts of product-line diversification by depository organizations is to strengthen existing disclosure requirements.

Bank regulatory agencies require all banks to file regular reports disclosing their current financial condition. For national banks, the Comptroller of the Currency recently revised these "call reports" to require quarterly disclosure of past-due loans, a detailed list of the remaining maturity of loans and other interest bearing assets (to reflect interest rate risk), and information on off-balance sheet transactions.[13] The 3,300 banks that are publicly held (directly or through holding

11. The Glass-Steagall Act's restrictions against bank underwriting of corporate securities do not extend to state-chartered banks that are not members of the Federal Reserve System. The FDIC's 1985 proposal would not, however, impose detailed separate operating requirements on banks engaged in *selling* insurance or real estate. In March 1987 the FDIC proposed abandoning its requirement that securities underwriting subsidiaries of state-chartered banks carry different names and be accessed through a different entrance from their parent banks.

12. The FDIC's requirements attempt to minimize this disadvantage by permitting diversified organizations either to market separate bank and nonbank services jointly or to advertise that a nonbank entity is affiliated with a bank or its holding company.

13. Gary G. Gilbert, "Disclosure and Market Discipline: Issues and Evidence," *Federal Reserve Bank of Atlanta Economic Review*, vol. 68 (November 1983), pp. 70–76.

companies), representing 23 percent of all banks, are also subject to the additional disclosure rules of the Securities and Exchange Commission (SEC), which requires these institutions to report the past-due status and concentration of loans as well as dealings involving insiders.[14]

Critics of existing bank disclosure requirements, however, argue that they fail to provide the public with up-to-date information about the true financial health of banks. Without such information, it is alleged, bank depositors, creditors, and shareholders cannot discipline banking organizations that take imprudent risks.

One frequently cited flaw of bank call reports, for example, is that they do not reflect the examination results of regulatory supervisors, who may have less sanguine assessments of the quality of a bank's loan portfolio than the banks themselves or their certified auditors have. Similarly, bank regulators do not publish enforcement actions taken against banks.[15] Finally, and perhaps most important, banks are not required to "mark their assets to market"—that is, to report their assets at market value rather than at historical cost. As a result, banks with loans of questionable quality continue to show higher levels of capital under current accounting conventions than if these loans were written down to reflect their worth on the open market.[16]

Strengthening bank disclosure rules to address each of these defects, however, has its complications. A policy of disclosing the results of examination data could reduce the quality of information that the examinations themselves produce. The current system of secrecy enhances the examiners' ability to draw out information from bank officers and employees, who would probably be less cooperative if examination reports were routinely made public.

Other difficulties attach to market value accounting, a favored approach among some commentators for enhancing market discipline

14. See Edmund Coulson, "Full Disclosure: The SEC's Requirements Relating to Bank Holding Companies," *Federal Reserve Bank of Atlanta Economic Review,* vol. 68 (November 1983), pp. 62–69; and Gilbert, "Disclosure and Market Discipline."

15. The federal bank regulatory agencies have the authority to issue "cease-and-desist" orders to compel banks to refrain from engaging in practices that the agencies believe unduly threaten bank solvency. The agencies can also order the removal of bank employees, officers, or directors.

16. Under current regulations, banks can be required to set aside reserves against loans on which borrowers are not making timely payments of principal and interest. However, secondary market prices of bank loans to a number of developing countries are currently well below the book values of these loans net of reserves, confirming that the current loan loss reserve policy is not equivalent to market value accounting.

against excessive risk taking by banks.[17] Clearly, loans cannot be "marked to market" if there are no secondary transactions that permit market values to be assessed. The market for private bank loans to foreign countries, for which a secondary market has been developing, is still immature.[18] More important, any requirement that banks list their loans at market value could have the counterproductive effect of deterring banks from selling their poor quality loans and thus from taking steps to enhance their liquidity and minimize their exposure to still further deteriorations in loan quality.[19]

Finally, increasing disclosure to enhance market discipline may also increase the risk of deposit runs, thus inviting the instability that policymakers aim at preventing. Indeed, fearing this risk, in 1986 the FDIC withdrew its proposal announced in May 1985 to publish in press release form all final enforcement orders issued against insured banks.[20]

Stronger Supervision. Historically, regulatory supervision has been the principal means through which the federal government has attempted to mitigate the incentives for bank risk taking that deposit insurance creates. In general, national banks are examined on-site by examiners from the Office of the Comptroller on the average of once a year. State-chartered banks are generally examined less frequently by their state bank regulators and by the Federal Reserve (if they belong to the Federal Reserve System) or by the FDIC (if they are not Federal Reserve members). Thrift institutions are examined by the Federal Home Loan Bank Board (FHLBB) (if they are federally chartered) or by their state regulators.[21]

17. See Edward J. Kane, *The Gathering Crisis in Federal Deposit Insurance* (MIT Press, 1985).

18. The total volume of foreign country debt exchanged in 1986 was an estimated $5 billion, as compared to the more than $240 billion in foreign debt held by American banks. S. Karene Witcher and Richard B. Schmitt, "Growing Market in Third World Debt Raises Questions on the Loans' Value," *Wall Street Journal,* October 7, 1986.

19. Indeed, this negative effect was the major reason that in 1985 a panel of the American Institute of Certified Public Accountants issued guidelines allowing banks taking a loss on the sale or swap of a foreign country loan not to reduce the book value of other loans to that country.

20. Significantly, however, publicly owned banking organizations are already required by the SEC to disclose enforcement actions.

21. The frequency of examinations, however, depends on an institution's financial condition. For banks, all federal regulators use some variant of the "CAMEL" rating system. The acronym stands for capital adequacy, asset quality, management and administration, earnings and liquidity. Each factor is rated on a scale from one (the best) to five (the worst); a composite rating on the same scale is based on a simple

Many knowledgeable observers agree that bank and thrift supervision is inadequate. The number of examiners at the three federal bank regulatory agencies was down to 4,400 in July 1985, as compared to approximately 5,000 in 1980.[22] In addition, there is concern about the high turnover and limited competence of examiners, particularly considering the increasing sophistication of the transactions they are required to review.[23]

Nevertheless, there are encouraging signs that federal regulators are attempting to upgrade their enforcement efforts. In 1985 the Federal Home Loan Bank Board moved its examiners off budget to the regional Federal Home Loan banks to increase the number of examiners and their pay. In 1986 federal bank regulators agreed to share confidential supervisory information with their counterparts at the state level.[24]

Still, there are limits to how effective any supervisory and enforcement program can be. Current systems for predicting bank failures well in advance are imperfect.[25] Prediction accuracy is unlikely to improve as financial product diversification proceeds. It may even worsen because of the additional uncertainties introduced as banking organizations try

---

average of the individual ratings. Banks receiving a composite CAMEL rating of two or less receive more than normal supervisory attention. Banks with a composite rating of three are closely supervised by the Comptroller and the Federal Reserve. Banks with ratings of four or five are placed on the FDIC's "problem list" and intensely supervised.

22. Monica Langley, "Federal Bank Examiners Are Drawing Fire," *Wall Street Journal*, July 16, 1985.

23. These problems are aggravated by the limited salaries of supervisory jobs relative to private-sector opportunities and by the frequent travel that diminishes the morale and quality of life for examiners over time. See Comptroller General of the United States, *The Federal Structure for Examining Financial Institutions Can be Improved*, Report to the Congress, GAO/GGD-81-21 (Washington, D.C.: GAO, 1981).

24. Edward J. Kane, "No Room For Weak Links in the Chain of Deposit Insurance Reform," Working Paper 1 (University of California, National Center of Financial Services, 1987).

25. See George J. Benston, "Financial Disclosure and Bank Failure," *Federal Reserve Bank of Atlanta Economic Review*, vol. 63 (March 1984), pp. 5–12. One recent study correctly predicted 64 percent of seventy-three bank failures between July 1, 1980, and July 1, 1983, using publicly available financial data compiled one year in advance. Prediction accuracy increased to only 67 percent, however, when examination data were added to the prediction model. See John F. Bovenzi, James A. Marino, and Frank E. McFadden, "Commercial Bank Failure Prediction Models," *Federal Reserve Bank of Atlanta Economic Review*, vol. 69 (November 1983), pp. 14–26. Recent models developed at the Federal Home Loan Bank Board may be more accurate in predicting failures of thrift institutions. See James R. Barth and others, "Thrift Institution Failures: Causes and Policy Issues," paper presented to the Conference on Bank Structure and Competition, Federal Reserve Bank of Chicago, May 1985.

new activities. In short, therefore, regulators would probably not be able through enhanced supervision alone to significantly reduce the safety-related risks from financial product deregulation.

Risk-Based Deposit Insurance Premiums. Inherent limits to the effectiveness of direct regulatory supervision of banks have prompted significant interest in risk-based deposit insurance premiums as an alternative or supplement to other techniques for disciplining depository institutions. Notably, the Garn–St Germain Act of 1982 directed each of the federal deposit insurance agencies to evaluate their programs and to consider whether insurance premiums could be adjusted to reflect the degree of risk that insured institutions assume. Following the publication of the required reports in 1983, both the FDIC and the FHLBB submitted legislative proposals to Congress in 1985.[26]

Specifically, the FDIC proposed to vary the amount of the rebate on premiums that insured banks pay—currently, up to 40 percent of the agency's net assessment income—with an institution's risk.[27] In addition, the agency proposed to charge banks for additional examinations and to use the proceeds to increase the rebate given to "normal risk" banks. The Bank Board's risk-based pricing proposal took a different tack. It suggested that an additional assessment be imposed on thrifts with asset investments exceeding the investment limitations applicable to federally chartered thrift institutions.

Although attractive in principle, establishing a risk-based deposit insurance system is not easy, as even proponents of the concept admit. The risks the failure of a particular bank may pose to the safety of the financial system as a whole, for example, are virtually impossible to assess. A crude compromise, however, would justify charging banks that are "too large to fail" higher premiums than all other banks. But even this apparently sensible idea would be difficult, perhaps unwise, to

26. The reports to Congress included the following publications: Federal Deposit Insurance Corporation, *Deposit Insurance in a Changing Environment* (FDIC, 1983); *Agenda for Reform: A Report on Deposit Insurance to the Congress from the Federal Home Loan Bank Board* (FHLBB, 1983); and National Credit Union Administration, *Credit Union Share Insurance: A Report to the Congress* (NCUA, 1983).

27. Although the FDIC's proposal did not spell out how the rebates would be related to risk, it requested comment on a plan announced in 1985 to rate bank risk on the basis of two independent criteria. The first test would be an objective evaluation of a bank's primary capital, net charge-offs, and net income. The second test would be based on existing examination criteria. The two tests would be used to determine if a bank is a "normal" risk and thus eligible for a full rebate or a "higher than normal" risk (in which case it would forfeit its rebate).

implement, since it would require regulators to tip their hand in advance as to what size threshold makes a bank too large to fail. Maintaining uncertainty about the location of that threshold is better so that at least some market discipline against risk taking may remain.[28]

A more severe problem preventing effective implementation of a risk-based deposit insurance system is the difficulty of objectively quantifying the credit risks of an institution's loan portfolio, especially on a timely basis. In the past, on-site bank examinations have been as long as three years apart.[29]

Tying a bank's deposit insurance premium to the risks of its loans *after the risks have become evident* could be counterproductive. The central objective of risk-based pricing of any type of insurance is to calibrate the premium to risk *ex ante,* that is, at the time the activity is insured and before the event to be insured against has occurred. Yet it would be almost impossible for any insurer to assess a bank's credit risk in advance. Instead, risk-based pricing proposals tie current premiums to an institution's performance *ex post,* which may or may not be correlated to any *ex ante* measure of risk.[30] As a result, a bank in trouble for reasons not predictable *ex ante* could be required to pay a higher

28. A number of commentators have suggested that, at a minimum, all banks be assessed deposit insurance premiums against their foreign deposits. Since the largest banks rely most heavily on foreign sources of funds, this proposal would increase the premiums paid by banks that are most likely "too large to fail." See Irvine H. Sprague, *Bailout: An Insider's Account of Bank Failures and Rescues* (Basic Books, 1986).

Sprague also explains in his book that the perceived need to rescue large failing banks is a reason that the FDIC had to abandon its "modified payout" plan. Under this procedure used by the FDIC in several situations in 1983 and 1984, uninsured depositors (those with accounts above $100,000) at failed banks were paid a percentage of their deposits, based on the FDIC's assessment of the ultimate value of their claims. The FDIC adopted this policy with the hope of instilling greater depository discipline against risk-seeking banks since the policy does not provide uninsured depositors with the *de facto* deposit insurance that comes through a federally arranged rescue or merger of the failing bank with a healthy institution. The FDIC did not apply the modified payout scheme, however, during the crisis surrounding the Continental Illinois Bank, fearing the wider deposit run on other institutions if Continental were closed.

29. FDIC, *Deposit Insurance in a Changing Environment,* pp. II-7, II-8.

30. Indeed, the recent study of bank profitability by the New Federal Reserve Bank of New York discussed in chapter 2 suggests that much of the increase in bank loan losses since 1980 has not been the result of greater risk taking *ex ante,* but instead the result of a combination of forces—including recession and commodity price deflation—over which banks have had no control. See Paul Bennett, "The Effects of Changes in the Interest Rate Environment on Large Bank Earnings," in Federal Reserve Bank of New York, *Recent Trends in Commercial Bank Profitability* (The Bank, 1986), pp. 73–87.

premium—at a time when it can least afford to—because of bad luck. It would be preferable but still very rough to relate risk to classes of asset investments or to measures of the industrial or geographic diversification of the entire loan portfolio.[31]

Similar problems would plague any attempt to tie a bank's deposit insurance premium to the extent of activity diversification by its parent holding company. The empirical analysis in chapter 3 suggests that banks in highly diversified organizations should pay *lower* deposit insurance premiums because diversification generally lowers risk exposure. Nevertheless, activity diversification may increase risk exposure when carried out by individual firms. That any system of risk-based deposit insurance pricing could identify *ex ante* which diversified organizations would deserve higher (or lower) premiums is doubtful.

Finally, even if the relevant risks could be quantified, risk-based insurance pricing would only be effective if it produced differentials in premiums that were large enough to affect behavior. The FDIC's premium rebate proposal of 1985, however, fails this test. Based upon historical levels of the rebate, the proposal would introduce a maximum risk penalty of about four to five basis points. Given typical spreads between marginal lending and borrowing rates of interest of one hundred or more basis points, a maximum penalty of five basis points would hardly deter the risk-seeking bank.[32] In recognition of this problem, FDIC Chairman William Seidman proposed in 1986 that the risk penalty be as high as the current deposit insurance premium itself, one-twelfth of 1 percent, or roughly eight basis points. But even a risk penalty of this size would fall far short of the levels required to deter excessive risk taking.[33]

Strengthened or Modified Capital Standards. Another technique for preventing or minimizing the adverse effects of enhanced risk taking under deregulation is to strengthen or modify existing bank capital

31. The risk-based capital requirements discussed below are tied to broad asset classes rather than to assessments of the quality of the assets within each class.

32. Laurie S. Goodman and Sherrill Shaffer, "The Economics of Deposit Insurance: A Critical Evaluation of Proposed Reforms," *Yale Journal on Regulation,* vol. 2, no. 1 (1984), p. 154.

33. A recent study made by staff members at the Federal Reserve Board intimated that for a small number of banks the insurance premium that fully compensated the FDIC for expected losses would exceed one hundred basis points. Robert B. Avery, Gerald A. Hanweck, and Myron Kwast, "An Analysis of Risk-Based Deposit Insurance for Commercial Banks," in *Proceedings of a Conference on Bank Structure and Competition* (Federal Reserve Bank of Chicago, 1985), pp. 227, 233–35.

requirements. If government-imposed standards cause banks to maintain greater equity than they otherwise would—behavior that has empirically been demonstrated—they can constrain bank risk taking and at the same time enlarge the cushion against losses to which the deposit insurance agencies are exposed.[34] For these reasons, larger capital requirements also reduce the need for intensive regulatory supervision and examination of banks.[35]

In December 1981, the three major federal bank regulatory agencies— the FDIC, the Comptroller, and the Federal Reserve—agreed for the first time on a common bank capital standard. After amendment in 1984, this policy required banks and bank holding companies of all sizes to maintain "primary" capital of at least 5.5 percent of assets.[36] Nevertheless, the continuing problems in the banking and thrift industries have spurred interest in even stronger capital standards, which could enable depositories to absorb risks that new activities may create.

One approach is to require higher standards specifically for diversified banking organizations. The FDIC's 1985 capital standards proposal could be used as a model. Under the FDIC's proposal, all insured banks would gradually raise their primary capital to 9 percent of assets, a step that would require an increase in the banking industry's capital base of almost 50 percent, or roughly $50 billion.[37] An interesting feature of the FDIC proposal is that it would also allow up to one-third of the required capital to be uninsured subordinated debt. Unlike depositors, holders of subordinated debt cannot withdraw their investments at will. They thus have strong incentives to discipline depository institutions either by

---

34. One recent study found that banks responded to the capital guidelines that federal banking agencies imposed in 1981 (discussed in the text above) by significantly increasing their shareholders' equity. Larry D. Wall and David R. Peterson, "Capital Changes at Large Affiliated Banks," Working Paper 86-4 (Federal Reserve Bank of Atlanta, 1986). This point was also discussed in chapter 3.

35. Black, Miller, and Posner, "Approach to the Regulation of Bank Holding Companies," p. 402.

36. The initial standard adopted in 1981 applied only to regional and community banks. Multinational banks were covered in 1984. See Reid Nagle and Bruce Peterson, "Capitalization Problems in Perspective," in Richard C. Aspinwall and Robert A. Eisenbeis, eds., Handbook for Banking Strategy (Wiley, 1985).

37. Panos Konstas, "Additional Bank Capital Required under FDIC's Proposed 9% Standard," FDIC, Economic Outlook, vol. 3 (June 1985), p. 4. In August 1986 the Federal Home Loan Bank Board adopted new rules requiring thrift institutions gradually to increase their "regulatory" capital to 6 percent of assets over a period of six to twelve years.

demanding higher interest premiums or by refusing to purchase subordinated debt issues.

A major argument against imposing a penalty capital requirement on banking organizations that also engage extensively in nonbanking activities is that the penalty would fail to discriminate between those organizations for which activity diversification would reduce risk and those that would use added product-line authority to expose their banks to greater risk. Accordingly, a higher capital standard for diversified depository organizations would hamper efficient activity diversification.

The subordinated debt feature of the FDIC proposal has a different drawback: the market for subordinated debt is currently quite thin.[38] Many small banks could find it difficult, perhaps impossible, to market their subordinated debt issues.[39] In addition, requiring troubled banks and thrifts to sell new issues of unsecured and uninsured debt would be unrealistic.[40]

A second model for modifying capital standards would be to tie the bank's required capital to its own risk, as in risk-based deposit insurance pricing. This approach has been recently in favor. In 1986 the Federal Reserve proposed a new set of capital standards designed both to increase the aggregate capital of the banking industry and to tie the required standard for each bank to the proportions of its investments in four asset classes, ranging from zero-risk cash and marketable securities to ordinary consumer and commercial loans. Significantly, the Fed's proposal would require for the first time that capital be set aside against off-balance sheet financial guarantees (such as standby letters of credit and

38. At the end of 1985, subordinated debt for the banking system totaled $14.6 billion, as compared with $167.6 billion in equity capital. U.S. General Accounting Office, *Deposit Insurance: Analysis of Reform Proposals,* Staff Study, GAO/GGD-86-32A (GAO, 1986), p. 104.

39. Most small banks, however, would not need to issue subordinated debt because they already have capital exceeding 9 percent of assets. American Enterprise Institute, *Proposals for Reform of the Deposit Insurance System,* Legislative Analyses (Washington, D.C.: AEI, 1985), p. 27. In addition, it might be possible to combine the subordinated debt issues of various small banks into pools and then to issue securities backed by those pools, as is currently done with automobile and mortgage loans. This activity would permit investors to diversify their risks and thus the small banks to lower the interest cost on their subordinated debt issues.

40. Some commentators have argued that higher capital requirements can *increase* the likelihood that weak banks will fail by pushing their managements to take greater risks in the hope of increasing earnings. See Michael Koehn and Anthony M. Santomero, "Regulation of Bank Capital and Portfolio Risk," *Journal of Finance,* vol. 35 (December 1980), pp. 1235–44.

other guarantees). The Fed's new system, however, makes no attempt to assess the *ex ante* risks of different loans or securities *within* each risk-asset class, nor to assess the risk relationships between asset classes (covariances). The Comptroller proposed in the same year a similar risk-based capital scheme, but one whose effect would be to lower aggregate capital in the banking industry.[41]

Although the risk classification mechanisms proposed by federal regulators may improve upon the earlier uniform standards, these devices would encounter the same difficulties as any risk-based deposit insurance system. Again, portfolio theory suggests that, as a general proposition, banking organizations that increase the range of their product or service offerings should be held to a lower capital requirement than less diversified banking organizations. But lowering existing capital requirements for diversified institutions would only give a green light to organizations inclined to take advantage of their enhanced product-line freedom to assume greater risks.

Summary. Several techniques are available for limiting the safety-related risks of enhanced financial product diversification. However, none are magic solutions. Some would be difficult, perhaps impossible, to implement. Others have serious drawbacks and may even be potentially counterproductive.

Minimizing Aggregations of Social and Political Power

The threat that financial conglomerates would become too big and powerful can be contained in several ways. But each of these techniques could also have serious costs.

Merger Restrictions. Deregulation could lead large banking organizations to merge with large nonbanking corporations. The result, it is feared, would be the emergence of the American equivalent of Japanese "zaibatsu" corporations, or huge conglomerates with bank and nonbank subsidiaries or affiliates.

One straightforward technique for preventing rapid asset growth by conglomerate merger may be borrowed from antitrust doctrines. This

41. The new capital requirements adopted by the FHLBB require thrifts to maintain additional capital against certain assets thought to be especially risky, including direct investments, land loans, and construction loans. Significantly, the Comptroller, the Federal Reserve, and the FDIC coordinated the announcement of their capital proposals with banking regulators in the United Kingdom.

device would allow banks and thrifts above a certain asset threshold to diversify into other activities only by establishing a new entity (*de novo* entry) or by acquiring small nonbanking firms (foothold acquisition).[42] Parallel restrictions would be imposed on large nonbanking organizations seeking to enter banking or thrift activities.[43]

The financial deregulation bill proposed by Senator Garn in 1983 (S. 2181) contained similar restrictions. Specifically, the Garn bill would have prohibited large holding companies—those with consolidated U.S. deposits of at least 0.3 percent of all domestic deposits—from acquiring any firm outside the bank or thrift industries if as a result of the acquisition the holding company would have investment in any single nonbank activity exceeding 25 percent of consolidated capital. The senator estimated that this restriction would have applied only to the twenty-five largest bank holding companies.[44]

Paradoxically, however, the approach to limiting concentration suggested in S. 2181 could be counterproductive because it would encourage nonbanking firms interested in banking to merge with the largest bank possible to meet the 25 percent nonbanking diversification test. Thus, for example, if holding companies were limited to investing no more than 25 percent of their consolidated assets in nonbank activities, a financial organization not engaged in banking would be required to acquire a bank so large that the bank's assets represented at least 75 percent of the combined organization's total assets after the acquisition. In contrast, existing bank holding companies would be free to enter nonbank activities up to the aggregate 25 percent of asset limitation.

A more evenhanded manner of restricting mergers between banking and nonbanking firms would apply the *de novo* entry or foothold acquisition requirements to all cross-industry mergers involving a depository with assets or deposits above a minimum amount. Aside from its effects in limiting concentration of resources, a policy of restricting

42. Under the "potential competition doctrine," courts may declare unlawful a conglomerate merger when the acquired firm belongs to a concentrated industry if the acquiring firm is a most likely entrant into that industry *de novo* or could have entered through foothold acquisition. This doctrine has been deemphasized in recent years by antitrust enforcement officials, however.

43. Given the narrowing distinctions between banks and thrifts, the merger restrictions could be written to apply to all federally insured depositories (and their holding companies).

44. *Congressional Record,* daily edition, November 18, 1983, pp. S17031-32 (statement of Senator Jake Garn).

bank-nonbank mergers would also be procompetitive. Otherwise, financial giants like Chase Manhattan, Aetna Life and Casualty, and Merrill Lynch could merge without increasing the strength of competition in the banking, insurance, and securities industries in which each of these firms competes.

At the same time, however, merger restrictions would prevent large organizations from realizing the full benefits of economies of scope and portfolio diversification, which the analysis in chapter 3 suggests would be collectively more important than the benefits of added competition. Moreover, for the largest firms, merging with another major organization in a different line of business may be the only feasible way of acquiring the expertise and experience required to compete effectively (and safely) in the new activities.

In sum, merger restrictions implemented to constrain the asset growth of financial conglomerates may be effective in preventing dramatic increases in concentrations of economic resources but could impose some significant inefficiencies.

Capital Requirements. Government-imposed minimum capital standards for banks can be effective not only in enhancing bank safety and soundness but also in restricting the growth of banks and their holding companies. With a minimum capital requirement of 5 percent of assets, for example, a banking organization can lever each one dollar of additional capital, whether obtained through earnings or raised in the open market, into twenty dollars of assets. If the capital standard is doubled, this leverage factor correspondingly falls in half.

As already discussed, the Federal Reserve Board sets minimum capital standards for bank holding companies. It does so pursuant to its statutory obligation to safeguard the safety and soundness of the banking system. If the activity authority of BHCs were widened, the Board could also be specifically directed to consider the potential for undue concentration of resources in setting capital standards for BHCs. Thus, under one approach, the Board could adopt a "progressive" capital requirement, much like the progressive marginal tax rates in the federal income tax law. That is, the marginal capital requirement on added assets would rise as total assets in the organization increased.[45]

But larger capital requirements may also penalize the ability of

45. This concept was suggested to the author by Jane D'Arista, formerly chief economist of the Subcommittee on Telecommunications, Consumer Protection, and Finance of the House Energy and Commerce Committee.

American financial organizations to compete in worldwide capital markets. As noted in chapter 4, only two of the world's ten largest banking organizations are headquartered in the United States. By increasing the cost of doing business, a progressive capital requirement (or limitation on bank asset size) could make it more difficult for the largest American banks to regain the world leadership they once enjoyed.

Preventing Conflicts of Interest

Finally, a range of alternatives is available for preventing or minimizing conflicts of interest within diversified financial organizations. In designing these remedies, however, it is important to distinguish between three types of conflicts: bank favoritism of nonbank affiliates; bank discrimination against independent competitors of their nonbank affiliates; and bank favoritism of customers of their affiliates.

Bank Favoritism of Nonbank Affiliates. As indicated in chapter 4, existing law tightly restricts the ability of banks and thrifts to favor or channel funds to their affiliates. Banks are subject to the restrictions on interaffiliate transactions of section 23A of the Federal Reserve Act; thrifts belonging to holding companies are prohibited from transacting with affiliates. Nevertheless, gaps in the legal structure remain. In extreme circumstances, a depository may be tempted to find ways to rescue an ailing affiliate, perhaps endangering the depository itself or, at a minimum, compromising the neutrality of credit allocation.

One solution is to bar diversified depository organizations from engaging in *any* interaffiliate transactions, as now occurs under the Savings and Loan Holding Company Act Amendments.[46] This solution would also limit the dangers of product diversification to the payment system by preventing banks from aiding troubled affiliates. However, just as unscrupulous bankers might violate the interaffiliate transaction limitations of section 23A, they might not comply with a flat prohibition.

---

46. This approach is strongly advocated by Clark, "Regulation of Financial Holding Companies." However, Clark would permit bank subsidiaries to pay dividends to their parents and, in turn, parent companies to make capital contributions to their subsidiaries. Shared services among affiliates would also be permitted when the organization could demonstrate the benefits to the regulators by a "preponderance of the evidence."

The Federal Reserve Board has also prohibited nonbank bank subsidiaries from entering into any transactions with bank holding company affiliates other than payments of dividends to and receipts of capital infusions from their parent holding companies without the Board's approval.

The obvious drawback of prohibiting interaffiliate transactions is the sacrifice of economies of scope, a major benefit of activity diversification. A ban on all interaffiliate transactions also appears unnecessarily broad, given the evidence reviewed in chapter 4 indicating that transactions between banks and their holding company affiliates have been insignificant.

Less extreme, but more justified, measures appear in both the Reagan administration's proposed financial product deregulation bill and the deregulation bill that the Senate passed in 1984. Each proposal would have added a new section to the Federal Reserve Act requiring member banks to engage in any transactions with affiliates only at arm's length, so as not to disadvantage nonaffiliated companies. This section would also permit banks to purchase securities that are underwritten by an affiliate only if a majority of the bank's outside directors approved in advance. Furthermore, a bank could not purchase in its fiduciary capacity any securities from an affiliate unless such a purchase was permitted by the instrument establishing the fiduciary relationship, by court order, or by the law under which the trust is administered. All these measures appear to be designed to prevent "worst case" abuses without imposing excessive costs on diversified organizations.

Bank Discrimination against Competitors of Nonbank Affiliates. There are no easy ways to prevent banks from discriminating against competitors of their nonbank affiliates. The best protection against this practice, as explained in chapter 4, is competition in lending and nonbanking markets. Such competition makes this type of discrimination pointless. Admittedly, competition in these markets could be imperfect in less populated geographic areas. But even in these regions, potential economies of scope realized through financial activity diversification may more than offset any efficiency losses from the diminished competition and discrimination of this kind.

Bank Favoritism of Customers of Nonbank Affiliates. One of the dangers that neither the administration deregulation proposal nor the 1984 Senate bill addresses is potential favoritism by banks toward customers of their affiliates. Under both bills, for example, banks could still extend risky loans to customers of their security underwriting affiliates in the hope that liberal lending policies would persuade these customers to call upon the affiliate to underwrite new securities. Similarly, ownership of real estate brokerage or development affiliates by depository institutions might provide strong incentives for these organizations to extend credit for transactions in which the affiliates are involved. In both cases, the consequences of the added risk may not show up for years, while fee income generated on all parts of such transactions would immediately be realized.

Several preventive steps could be taken. At a minimum, requiring depository institutions and their affiliates to have different managements and directors would make the preferential channeling of loans to customers of nonbank affiliates more difficult. Another suggestion aimed at bank affiliations with securities underwriters is contained in the FDIC's recent securities underwriting rule. Specifically, the FDIC prohibits state-chartered nonmember banks from extending credit to current customers of the affiliate whose securities are being underwritten by the affiliate unless these securities are of "investment grade quality." This approach could be toughened by dropping the exception.

A more extreme technique would apply quantitative restrictions to bank loans made to customers or partners of affiliates, both on total lending to any single customer or partner and on such lending in the aggregate. This approach, however, would require the Federal Reserve Board to exercise vigilance in monitoring the activities of nonbank affiliates rather than to deemphasize its scrutiny of the nonbanking activities of bank holding companies, as the administration's deregulation proposal suggests.[47]

A Comprehensive Approach to Financial Product Diversification

There is an alternative approach for addressing all the major concerns that have been voiced about further financial product-line diversification. Instead of various tools to guard against specific risks, a single technique would comprehensively and simultaneously deal with all the risks involved.

Under this comprehensive approach, highly diversified financial

47. The administration proposal would have reaffirmed the Federal Reserve Board's authority to examine bank holding companies and each of their subsidiaries, although it would have directed the Board to minimize the scope and frequency of examinations of the nonbank subsidiaries. This last limitation was designed to minimize any competitive disadvantages that a diversified bank holding company might face relative to financial service firms that are not affiliated with banks and therefore not regulated by the Federal Reserve.

conglomerates that choose to offer banking services would be required to organize their banks in a fundamentally different way: by separating deposit-taking from lending activities. Specifically, this approach would authorize the creation of new "financial holding companies" (FHCs), which would be free to engage through separate subsidiaries in *any* activity, financial or nonfinancial, subject to the following restrictions.[48]

—The "banks" in FHCs would be required to operate as (insured) money market mutual funds, accepting deposits and investing only in highly liquid safe securities, or in practice, obligations of the United States Treasury or other federally guaranteed instruments. Under one version of the proposal, FHC depositories would serve only as transactions processors, accepting only demand deposits; under a broader version, the depositories could accept deposits across a broad range of maturities.

—Financial holding companies could extend loans, but only through separately incorporated lending subsidiaries wholly funded by uninsured liabilities (such as commercial paper or debentures) and equity, issued directly or by the parent FHC itself.

—To ensure a level playing field, financial conglomerates that now own insured nonbank banks or savings and loans would be required to restructure themselves to conform to this model, as would all nonbanking firms seeking to open or acquire insured depositories in the future.

—To address the payments system concerns discussed in the Corrigan plan, the proposed regime would allow only the narrow banks (as well as their conventional bank competitors), but not their parent holding companies or nonbank affiliates, access to the payments system. As a result, nonbank corporations could not hold deposit accounts at their affiliated narrow banks. This restriction would not detract from the proposal's attractiveness because financial organizations that want to own banks do so not because of the payments services the banks may provide but because diversification would allow the organizations to market and deliver a wide-ranging package of financial services anchored by the services of the insured depository.

48. A special organizational structure could be created for mutual insurance companies that want to affiliate with a bank. Because mutual insurers are owned by their policyholders, they cannot operate in the holding company format. Moreover, mutual insurers are chartered under state rather than under federal law. Accordingly, mutual insurance companies could be permitted to engage in banking activities through separate deposit-taking and lending subsidiaries, provided state laws were amended to permit such operations.

—Finally, given the full securitization of the assets of narrow bank depositories, no restrictions would be placed on the cross-selling of services by diversified parents of narrow banks or on names and places of business of both the narrow banks and their affiliates.

The notion that deposit-taking and lending activities should be separated is not a new one. Several decades ago, Professors Henry Simons and Milton Friedman of the University of Chicago urged that *all* banks be prohibited from making loans and instead be allowed to hold reserves equal to 100 percent of their deposits.[49] The "100 percent reserve banking" proposal was advanced both to enhance the safety of the banking system and to help control monetary policy. With private deposit-taking banks out of the lending business and therefore unable to create money, the Federal Reserve would have absolute control over the money supply (if "money" consists of currency and demand deposits).

The proposal advanced here borrows from the 100 percent reserve banking concept and applies a variation of it solely to *highly diversified* firms that seek to offer both deposit and lending services.[50] This selective feature is a critical element of the proposal. No existing bank or its holding company would be required to alter its mode of operation as

49. Henry C. Simons, *Economic Policy for a Free Society* (University of Chicago Press, 1948); and Milton Friedman, *A Program for Monetary Stability* (Fordham University Press, 1959), pp. 65–76.

50. An earlier version of the proposal discussed here was presented in Robert E. Litan, "Taking the Dangers Out of Bank Deregulation," *Brookings Review,* vol. 4 (Fall 1986), pp. 3–12. As discussed in that article, a number of others have offered similar but less detailed proposals. See Henry C. Wallich, "A Broad View of Deregulation," speech at the Conference on Pacific Basin Financial Reform, sponsored by the Federal Reserve Bank of San Francisco, December 2, 1984; Hans H. Angermueller, "The Emerging Shape of the Banking Business," speech delivered at the Deutsche Bank Seminar in Frankfurt, West Germany, June 27, 1985; Carter H. Golembe and John J. Mingo, "Can Supervision and Regulation Ensure Financial Stability," in *The Search for Financial Stability: The Past Fifty Years,* a conference sponsored by the Federal Reserve Bank of San Francisco, June 23–25, 1985 (San Francisco, 1985), pp. 125–46; Alice Haemmerli, "Quarantine: An Approach to the Deposit Insurance Dilemma," *Banking Expansion Reporter,* vol. 4 (September 1985), pp. 7–10; Robert J. Lawrence, "Minimizing Regulation of the Financial Services Industry," *Issues in Bank Regulation,* vol. 9 (Summer 1985), pp. 22–31; James Tobin, "Financial Innovation and Deregulation in Perspective," *Bank of Japan Monetary and Economic Studies,* vol. 3 (September 1985), pp. 19–29; John H. Kareken, "Federal Bank Regulatory Policy: A Description and Some Observations," *Journal of Business,* vol. 59 (January 1986), pp. 3–48; and R. Alton Gilbert, "Banks Owned by Nonbanks: What Is the Problem and What Can Be Done about It?" *Business and Society,* vol. 26 (Spring 1986), pp. 9–17.

long as it chooses to offer only those services currently authorized by the Bank Holding Company Act (BHCA). However, for those firms that wish to diversify further, the proposal would go a long way toward meeting each of the concerns that opponents of broader bank powers have raised.

First, the proposed separation requirements would prevent financial holding companies from using the resources of their depositories to bail out "risky" nonbank affiliates. In the structure just outlined, deposit-taking subsidiaries would be limited to investing in high-quality, marketable instruments; they could not legally channel funds to support affiliated corporations or their customers. The separation requirement would eliminate the threat that through "contagion" effects, failure of a nonbanking enterprise would trigger a deposit run on its related bank and thus require federal intervention to prevent runs on other depository institutions as well.

In extreme versions of this proposal, FHC-owned depositories would also not be permitted to channel any dividends to the parent holding company.[51] In less restrictive versions, earnings generated by an FHC depository subsidiary could be flowed upstream to the FHC parent and from there to the ailing nonbank affiliates. However, the size of such transfers could be limited by existing or supplemental restrictions on dividend payments by the depository to its parent.[52]

Second, the proposed structure should ease qualms that highly diversified financial organizations would hold excessive concentrations of economic power. These fears stem mainly from the fact that deposit insurance allows banks to gather large pools of funds and thereby to exercise significant control over the allocation of credit. If the banks in FHCs could not fund loans with insured deposits, there would be much less reason to be concerned about the size of the holding company. Any remaining concern could be addressed by allowing bank holding companies to enter other activities only through newly created firms (*de novo* entry) or through foothold acquisition, as discussed earlier in this chapter.

Third, the proposal to separate deposit-taking from lending activities within diversified financial conglomerates should ease concerns about conflicts of interest and tie-ins. Both these potential abuses also arise

51. See Haemmerli, "Quarantine," p. 8.
52. Under current law, in any single year a bank may pay to its parent holding company dividends no greater than twice its earnings.

from the fear that in a fully deregulated environment banks could channel government-insured funds collected from depositors to favored borrowers within the same organization or to customers of nonbank affiliates or could tie loans to the purchase of other services offered by sister nonbank corporations. Since deposits collected by FHC depositories could not be used to fund loans, these specific abuses could not arise.

The proposed separation requirements would even prove advantageous to those organizations and interests that do not believe that financial product diversification otherwise poses significant risks. As suggested in chapter 2, although continuing advances in technology and competition between regulatory authorities make financial product deregulation inevitable in the long run, comprehensive reform is unlikely to come soon, at least at the federal level. Given the powerful interests on both sides of the financial product deregulation debate—banks on one side and the securities, insurance, and real estate industries on the other—Congress will probably loosen the activity restrictions in the BHCA, if at all, only on a piecemeal basis.

The comprehensive reform approach, in contrast, offers Congress a way out of the current and projected stalemates by addressing all the fears about financial product diversification that opponents have voiced. It lets banking and nonbanking organizations diversify their service offerings, but only under rigorous conditions. Thus it sets the ground rules for diversification generally without choosing which services that corporations owning banks may offer and thereafter lets the market decide how and in what combination financial services will be delivered. Furthermore, the comprehensive approach outlined here has the virtue of simplicity. It does not require each of the relevant actors—Congress and the various bank regulatory agencies—to do its part to minimize the risks of financial product deregulation.

In short, the proposed separation requirements could speed the process of financial product diversification while at the same time safeguarding the financial system against the risks that diversification may entail. Such an outcome should prove attractive to interests on both sides of the financial product deregulation debate.

Mechanics

Like any comprehensive reform suggestion, however, the foregoing proposal cannot be implemented without addressing numerous practical issues. Six of the most important issues are discussed below.

Deposit Insurance and the Class of Permissible Investments. The first obvious question is whether the deposits collected by narrow banks should be eligible for federal deposit insurance.

The answer primarily depends on which assets narrow banks would be allowed to hold. Certainly, if the permissible asset list included only short-term Treasury obligations (for example, with maturities less than one year), the current form of deposit insurance would not be needed. Treasury securities carry no default risk. And interest rate risk, which arises once the maturities of bank investments differ from those of bank liabilities, can virtually be eliminated by permitting narrow banks to invest only in short-term government obligations. Depositors would remain subject to the risk of fraud or theft, but this possibility exists now with uninsured money market mutual funds. Some level of deposit insurance at reduced premium assessments could nevertheless be made available to protect smaller deposits and to maintain public confidence in narrow banks.

In all likelihood, however, the proposed separation requirements could not be implemented if the permissible asset powers of narrow banks were restricted to Treasury bills. The reason is that the total supply of privately held short-term Treasury securities (with maturities up to one year) is limited—roughly $390 billion at the end of 1985.[53] By comparison, the thirty-five leading banks in the United States collectively hold more than $700 billion in loans. If all the parent companies of these banks suddenly elected to establish FHCs by transferring all loans currently held by their bank subsidiaries to newly formed lending subsidiaries, the new narrow banks would have to purchase up to $700 billion in securities to replace these loans, an amount clearly greater than the volume of short-term government instruments available.

To be sure, the likelihood that the depository subsidiaries of newly formed financial organizations would retain the same volume of deposits as they currently have is small. Some bank customers would be more than willing to exchange at least some portion of their insured bank deposits for the higher yielding, albeit uninsured, securities issued by the new lending affiliates. In addition, the volume of required securities would depend on the range of deposits narrow banks would be allowed to accept. Restricting narrow banks to accepting only transaction accounts would place far less pressure on the securities markets than permitting them to accept deposits across a broad spectrum of maturities.

53. Outstanding Treasury securities with maturity up to one year at the end of 1985 totaled $490 billion, of which $99 billion were held by Federal Reserve Banks.

What other instruments could narrow banks be safely permitted to hold? One obvious candidate would be longer term Treasury obligations. At the end of 1985, $424 billion in Treasury bonds with one-to-five year maturities were outstanding; another $324 billion were available in longer maturities. Subtracting the $70 billion in Treasury notes that the Federal Reserve banks held, roughly $680 billion in Treasury notes and bonds were privately held at the end of 1985. Other candidates would be securities guaranteed by the federal government or federal agencies, such as securities backed by mortgages insured by the Federal Housing Administration or the Federal National Mortgage Association, or securities backed by packages of federally insured student loans. These federally guaranteed instruments, which totaled $410 billion at the end of 1985, are equivalent to Treasury notes and bonds; narrow banks that invest in them could remain insulated from the economic health of other financial intermediaries. In combination, all Treasury obligations and federally insured securities that are privately held total close to $1.5 trillion, or twice the volume of loans issued by all thirty-five of the largest bank holding companies combined.

As the maturities of permissible government obligations are lengthened, however, narrow banks would be exposed to increasing interest rate risk, which in turn would increase the need for deposit insurance. The depositories could avoid this risk if, like mutual bond funds, they constantly repriced each deposit account at market value. Nevertheless, most depositors place their funds with banks precisely because the banks do *not* operate like mutual funds, but instead denominate accounts in their nominal values plus accrued interest (if applicable).

If narrow banks were permitted to invest across a broad spectrum of government obligations, the deposit insurance premiums they pay could be tied to the interest rate risk posed by their asset and liability structures. Unlike the assets of conventional banks, the assets of depositories invested only in Treasury securities would carry no default risk, thus eliminating the central obstacle to implementing risk-related deposit insurance premiums.[54] Indeed, there is no reason why regulators could not require FHC depositories to abide by market value accounting since all of their assets would be readily marketable. Deposit insurance

---

54. For illustrations of techniques used to measure interest rate risk, see J. Huston McCulloch, "Interest-Risk Sensitive Deposit Insurance Premia: Stable ACH Estimates," *Journal of Banking and Finance,* vol. 9 (March 1985), pp. 137–56.

premiums could then be tied to capital, measured as the difference between the market value of assets and total liabilities.

A more controversial—and much more problematic—class of potential investments for narrow banks would be highly rated commercial paper. Although the stock of commercial paper outstanding is smaller than all Treasury debt, by the end of 1985 it had reached significant and rapidly growing proportions—$301 billion, of which $87 billion consisted of issues by nonfinancial corporations. Deposit insurance would strongly be recommended if narrow banks were allowed to invest in commercial paper, which like ordinary bank lending carries a risk of default. In addition, it would be desirable to prohibit narrow banks from purchasing commercial paper issued by customers of their lending affiliates, in order to prevent the exploitation of conflicts of interest.

Allowing narrow banks to invest in commercial paper, however, would undermine the case for separating deposit-taking and lending activities in diversified FHCs. Because commercial paper issues are unsecured borrowings, many corporate issuers can only market them at reasonable interest rates if they have obtained standby or backup letters of credit (LCs) from banks or other financial institutions promising to pay if the borrowers themselves cannot. At a minimum, therefore, permitting narrow banks to hold commercial paper would make their financial health ultimately dependent on the health of the other firms that stand as backup guarantors. This consequence would be inconsistent with one of the fundamental objectives of separation—to create virtually risk-free depository institutions, invulnerable to credit risk. The inconsistency would especially be apparent if narrow banks were permitted to invest in commercial paper issued by the new lending subsidiaries of other FHCs. For then, narrow banks would in effect be extending loans indirectly—by funding the uninsured lending affiliates of competitor FHCs.

To be sure, if narrow banks were *not* permitted to invest in commercial paper or, perhaps more importantly, not allowed to issue standby LCs, then the market for commercial paper itself could be expected to change. The banking organizations most likely to take advantage of the FHC proposal advanced here—the largest banks—are also the major issuers of standby LCs.[55] If, therefore, many of these banks were to convert to

---

55. The twenty-five largest banks are responsible for issuing roughly three-quarters of the volume of standby LCs. See Barbara Bennett, "Off Balance Sheet Risk in

FHC status, many corporations that now rely on the commercial paper market for funds would conceivably not be able to issue their paper, but instead would return to borrowing from conventional banks or would seek funds from the new FHC lenders. The resulting void in the commercial paper market would be filled at least partly, perhaps completely, by the new issues of the most creditworthy FHCs (or their lending subsidiaries) with the ability to issue commercial paper without backup guarantees.

The same objections to including commercial paper on the list of permissible investments by narrow banks also apply to non-federally guaranteed mortgage-backed securities or the newer securities backed by packages of auto loans and other receivables. None of these securities can be marketed without some type of credit enhancement or financial guarantee. Clearly, where the guarantor is another private bank or insurance company, the financial health of the narrow bank cannot be insulated from that of the other guaranteeing entities. Nevertheless, expanding the list of permissible investments to include securitized mortgages or consumer loans would permit narrow banks to realize higher returns (by assuming greater risks). Such activity would reduce the incentives of diversified FHCs to create uninsured short-term liabilities outside narrow banks, which may pose risks similar to deposit runs, as discussed in greater detail below.

A final class of potential investments by narrow banks—which would even more clearly require the expansion of deposit insurance—is non-securitized consumer loans. Broadening the list of permissible investments to include this class of loan would make the FHC proposal equivalent to the so-called consumer banking concept that the Treasury Department endorsed in 1986 and that such financial conglomerates as Sears have strongly urged. The consumer banking concept may have the political advantage of appearing less radical than requiring FHCs to separate *all* their lending operations from their deposit-taking activities. However, because it would be less far reaching, the consumer bank variation of the FHC model could also fall short of meeting the concerns that have been raised about broader bank powers.

For example, although a consumer bank could be totally insulated

Banking: The Case of Standby Letters of Credit," *Federal Reserve Bank of San Francisco Economic Review*, no. 1 (Winter 1986), pp. 19–29; and James Chessen, "Standby Letters of Credit," in *Recent Legislative and Other Developments Impacting Depository Institutions* (FDIC, 1985), pp. 1–13.

from any nonbanking affiliates, it could still indirectly prop them up by extending loans to their customers. Banks affiliated with retailers could also favor customers of those retailers by extending loans. A depository restricted to investing in high-quality marketable instruments could not exploit this potential conflict of interest. Moreover, given their ability to fund consumer loans with insured deposits, FHCs that owned consumer banks could grow larger than those that owned lending affiliates that had to rely on uninsured sources of capital. For those concerned about the effects of deregulation on the concentration of assets, therefore, the consumer bank proposal should be less attractive than completely separating lending from deposit-taking services.

Choosing the assets in which depositories would be permitted to invest requires a balancing of competing economic and political objectives. On the one hand, the wider the class of permissible assets, the easier it would be to implement the FHC model. On the other hand, the risks that separation is designed to address grow as the list of allowable asset investments is expanded.

Competing political forces parallel this spectrum of economic considerations. Clearly, bank and thrift organizations would prefer to keep as much of their existing asset authority as possible. At the same time, the broader the list of permissible investments, the more likely the FHC model will be opposed by those nonbanking interests that have fought the expansion of bank powers. One possible way of resolving this controversy is to delegate the authority to define the permissible assets of narrow banks to a bank regulator—most logically the FDIC, since that agency is the one most concerned with the moral hazard problem created by deposit insurance. Congress could limit the regulator's discretion by requiring that the permissible assets be securities that are safe and liquid. As the range of securities meeting this criterion expands, so too could the permissible narrow bank asset list.

However broad the permissible asset list may be, the requirement that narrow banks invest only in securities also implies that they be required to report their financial condition on a market value basis. This kind of reporting would enable bank regulators not only to know more about the current financial status of narrow banks than that of conventional banks (much of whose assets are illiquid) but also to be in a position to close or force the merger of narrow banks if their market value equity approaches or dips below zero.

Capital and Reserve Requirements. Given their inherently safe structure, narrow banks would require much lower levels of capital than conventional banks. Under one approach, all such depositories could be subject to a uniform but lower capital requirement. Alternatively, required capital could be tied to interest rate risk, as with the risk-based capital standards that the Federal Reserve has proposed for all conventional banks. More simply, as already discussed, regulators could require narrow banks to abide by market value accounting and then to maintain minimum levels of capital measured on that basis.

Narrow banks should also be subject to the same reserve requirement as conventional banks. As discussed further below, the bank reserve requirement determines the amount by which any increase in bank reserves can be "multiplied" throughout the economy as a whole to increase the money supply. If different reserve requirements were applied to deposits at conventional and narrow banks, the level of the multiplier would fluctuate if depositors switched funds between the different institutions. These fluctuations, in turn, would complicate the Federal Reserve's task of controlling the money supply. Requiring both types of depositories to adhere to the same rules would eliminate this potential concern.

Addressing Payments Systems Risks. As indicated in chapter 4, the risk always exists that as financial product diversification proceeds, banking organizations would find ways—lawful or unlawful—of channeling funds to rescue ailing affiliates. Although the FHC proposal would bar narrow banks from such transfers, what is to prevent officers of these organizations from attempting them anyway? When such breaches of the law are serious enough to threaten the solvency of the bank, they could expose the Federal Reserve to the risk of loss in its role as guarantor of the integrity of the payments system.[56]

At a minimum, the Federal Reserve could reduce concerns about intraday transfers of bank credit to nonbank affiliates by supplementing section 23A restrictions on interaffiliate transactions with a requirement that all intraday transfers be fully collaterized.[57] An alternative (but related) option is to require narrow banks to carry securities with market

---

56. In December 1986, the Federal Reserve Board solicited public comment on various proposals to limit daylight overdrafts in an effort to reduce risks of bank overdrafts to the payments system.

57. This suggestion is endorsed in the Statement of Hans H. Angermueller before the Commerce, Consumer, and Monetary Affairs Subcommittee of the House Committee on Government Operations, December 17, 1986.

values slightly exceeding total deposits—that is, to provide the Federal Reserve with a "margin of safety." This "excess collateralization" requirement would force FHCs to subsidize their narrow banks, a price that should be worth paying if it provides organizations with opportunities to engage in banking and nonbanking activities simultaneously. With a sufficient commitment of funds by the Federal Reserve, regulators should soon be able to maintain on-line monitoring of securities held by all depositories. Such monitoring would enable the Federal Reserve to satisfy itself that narrow banks have more than sufficient collateral to cover any payments shortfalls that might materialize because of unauthorized transfers of funds to affiliates.[58]

Yet another approach to limiting payments system risk is reflected in the deregulation proposal recently advanced by E. Gerald Corrigan. Under the Corrigan plan, only those institutions restricted to offering financial services would have access to the payments system.[59] Corrigan's suggestion that bank product diversification be limited only to financial activities could easily be incorporated in the proposed FHC structure. If, as suggested here, however, narrow banks belonging to FHCs are prohibited from extending credit—to nonbank affiliates as well as to the general public—then the case for restricting FHCs only to financial activities is considerably weakened.

The final option for containing risks to the payments system is simply to prohibit nonbank affiliates from maintaining deposit accounts with their narrow banks.[60] Coupled with the prohibition on narrow bank lending, this prohibition would eliminate the ability of diversified organizations to threaten the integrity of the payments system by running large intraday overdrafts on their narrow banks. Barring nonbank corporations from holding deposits at affiliated narrow banks would be straightforward, simple, and effective. It is the recommended approach

58. The excess collaterization concept was suggested to the author by Robert Eisenmenger and Richard Kopcke of the Federal Reserve Bank of Boston.

59. Specifically, the Corrigan proposal would create three classes of firms offering financial services: (1) "commercial-financial conglomerates," which would be allowed to offer any financial service except banking, but would not be allowed to have access to the payments system; (2) "financial holding companies," which would be allowed to engage solely in financial activities exclusive of banking and to have access to the "large-dollar" payments system; and (3) "bank and thrift holding companies," which would be allowed to engage in any financial activity including bank and thrift activities and to have unrestricted access to the payments system.

60. See Hal S. Scott, "Deregulation and Access to the Payment System," *Harvard Journal on Legislation*, vol. 23 (Summer 1986), pp. 331–56.

for removing payments system risk in a more broadly regulated environment.

Coverage. A fourth issue concerns the coverage of the FHC proposal. Clearly, because of the risks to the deposit insurance agencies and to the financial system as a whole posed by the failures of large banks, the FHC model would apply to all organizations owning large depositories. Indeed, the proposed FHC model may be both feasible and attractive only for the largest firms or those with the highest credit ratings, or both.[61] Any organization that sought to engage in both deposit taking and lending within the FHC structure must be able to market the commercial paper of either the parent FHC or the FHC lending subsidiary. Large banking organizations or diversified financial conglomerates without excellent credit ratings would be unable to establish FHC lending affiliates because the market would not accept their commercial paper issued without a backup guarantee, and few conventional banks or insurance companies would have both the interest and the size to provide such credit enhancement. As a result, only those firms with credit ratings high enough to issue commercial paper not backed by standby LCs would be able to convert to FHC status. Through market forces, financial activity diversification would be limited to those firms perceived to be in the strongest financial health.

Nevertheless, the separation requirements could be prohibitively costly for smaller but financially sound banking organizations with limited abilities to market the commercial paper of their new lending affiliates (or of their parent FHCs). Accordingly, exempting banks and thrifts below a certain size threshold may be desirable. An exemption feature would fail to allow market forces to screen out riskier enterprises from diversifying, much as they would for the larger institutions. But society need not be as concerned with the failures of small banks as it is with the failures of large banks.[62]

Regardless of whether an exemption is provided, any federal law creating the FHC option would have to preempt state bank and thrift

---

61. The largest bank holding companies (those with assets over $10 billion) have thus far had the greatest success in diversifying their activities. See Larry D. Wall, "Nonbank Activities and Risk," *Federal Reserve Bank of Atlanta Economic Review*, vol. 71 (October 1986), p. 27.

62. As one former FDIC chairman and director has recently observed, "Disruptive as it may be to the local community and individuals, the truth is the failure of most of the banks in the United States would have no discernible impact on the FDIC fund or on the economy." Sprague, *Bailout*, p. 252.

activity authority.[63] Without preemption, depository organizations could avoid the federal separation requirements by converting to state bank or thrift charters with more liberal activity powers.

Timing. A fifth important implementation issue relates to timing. The banking organizations most likely to be interested in forming FHCs— the largest banks—could find it difficult, if not impossible, immediately to refinance all their loans with uninsured securities. Citibank alone, for example, has over $100 billion in outstanding loans. If banking organizations could not expand their activities until their loan portfolios were *completely* transferred to separate lending affiliates, the likelihood that many would undertake the restructuring is small.

A sensible transition rule, therefore, would be to free existing bank holding companies from the activity restrictions so long as their subsidiary banks adhere to a schedule in transferring their loan portfolios to new lending affiliates. Thus if the transition period were ten years, a bank organization that has $20 billion in loans would have to transfer at least $2 billion in loans out of its subsidiary bank the first year it chose to convert to FHC status, $2 billion more the second year, and so on. If at any time the banking organization fell behind the statutory schedule and failed to correct the situation within a short period (for example, sixty days), it would be required to divest those subsidiaries involved in activities not authorized by the Bank Holding Company Act.

This transition rule would also have two salutary (and perhaps indispensable) side effects. First, it would minimize any disruption in the monetary control functions of the Federal Reserve, a subject discussed in greater detail below. Second, a transition period would reduce the pressure on the markets in Treasury securities and commercial paper that would arise if many large financial corporations simultaneously attempted to separate their deposit-taking from their lending activities.

Regulation. A final design issue that must be addressed is which, if any, federal bank regulatory agency should regulate and supervise FHCs? Clearly, narrow banks should be members of the Federal Reserve System, if only to have access to the discount window in emergencies. Given its role in administering the deposit insurance fund, the FDIC is the logical agency to define the permissible assets narrow banks may invest in.[64] As already discussed, the assets on the permissible list must pass both a "safety" and a "liquidity" test.

63. If a small depository exemption were included, the preemption would apply only to the larger depositories above the small institution threshold.
64. There would be no separate "bank" and "thrift" FHC depositories and thus no

Whether a separate system of regulating and supervising FHCs should be established at the holding company level is more controversial. A strong case can be made that if the chartering authority is properly ensuring that narrow banks are not making loans and are abiding by any limitations or prohibitions on the payment of dividends to their corporate parents, holding company regulation is not needed. The Federal Reserve, however, has a legitimate interest in maintaining the integrity of the payments system. Accordingly, as discussed above, it is recommended that nonbank corporations not be allowed to hold depository accounts at the narrow banks with which they are affiliated. Finally, given the increase in lending that would take place through uninsured FHC lenders, it may be necessary for the Securities and Exchange Commission to buttress its enforcement staff to insure that FHC lenders (like other finance companies) are complying with the requisite disclosure requirements.

Possible Objections

Given their potentially radical effects, the proposed separation requirements for diversified financial organizations could encounter strong resistance. Certain of the most important potential objections are discussed below. Several raise fundamental questions that cannot be answered without implementing the FHC proposal and then observing how both market participants and regulators react. However, if the analysis in chapter 2 is correct—that financial activity diversification by both banking and nonbanking firms is inevitable—then the critical question is whether these objections raise problems more severe than would occur under alternative frameworks, including the expansion of bank powers within the framework of the existing Bank Holding Company Act or through increasingly liberal state banking charters. In this author's view, they would not.

Increased Interest Rates. The first concern is that separating deposit-taking activities from lending activities would require FHC lenders to charge higher interest rates than conventional banks and thrifts because the FHC lending affiliates would be forced to rely on uninsured debt and equity rather than on less expensive federally insured deposits. In fact,

---

need for the FSLIC to ensure narrow banks separately. Instead, all narrow banks would be insured by the FDIC.

a substantial differential has existed between the average cost of funds for the banking system and the commercial paper rate, which would roughly measure the average cost of funds for FHC lenders. This differential stood at approximately 250 basis points at the end of 1985.

The differential between the average cost of funds for banks and the commercial paper rate has been declining in recent years, however, and it should continue to decline. Interest rate deregulation has had the effect of raising the average cost of funds for the banking system as a whole relative to other market interest rates. Moreover, banks face additional increases in their funds costs as depositors continue to move out of low-interest bearing accounts and into higher yielding investments.

More importantly, differentials based on the *average* cost of funds provide a poor guide to the differences one would expect to exist between lending rates charged by FHC lenders and those charged by conventional banks and thrifts. The reason is that lending rates are determined in competitive markets by the *marginal* costs of attracting funds. If these rates were determined differently, banks with relatively large proportions of low-interest bearing deposits—and thus with a low average cost of funds—could charge lower interest rates on loans. In fact, however, in competitive lending markets, as in competitive markets for other goods and services, lending rates for borrowing projects of equivalent risks across banks generally are quite uniform. This indicates that lending rates are based on the marginal costs of attracting funds.[65]

For banks, the interest rate on large certificates of deposit (CDs) is a good measure of the marginal cost of funds, since any bank that aggressively wants additional funds to lend has little choice but to "purchase" funds by offering jumbo CDs at competitive rates. Lending affiliates of FHCs, in contrast, face a short-run marginal cost of funds determined by the commercial paper interest rate.

Figure 5-1 reveals that the difference between these two measures of marginal cost in recent years has been less than 1 percentage point, or less than 100 basis points. Specifically, rates on commercial paper with six-month maturity have been higher by an average of 89 basis points over the 1980–85 period than interest rates on six-month CDs. Significantly, this differential narrowed to just 53 basis points between 1983 and 1985.

---

65. See Thomas A. Pugel and Lawrence J. White, "An Analysis of the Competitive Effects of Allowing Commercial Bank Affiliates to Underwrite Corporate Securities," in Ingo Walter, ed., *Deregulating Wall Street* (Wiley, 1985), p. 130.

Figure 5-1. *Differentials between Commercial Paper and CD Interest Rates*

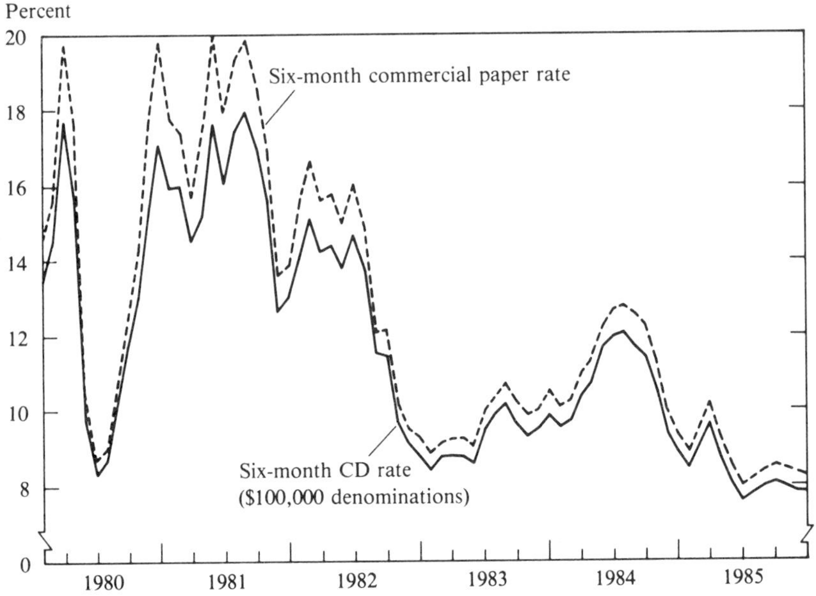

Percent

Sources: *Federal Reserve Bulletin* (monthly), various issues, table 1.35.

Admittedly, commercial paper–CD rate differentials might widen if banking organizations began to convert to FHC status and thus to turn increasingly toward commercial paper to replace deposits as sources of funds. The commercial paper–CD interest rate differential by itself ignores the marginal costs of other funding sources, including both unsecured longer term debt and equity. Because their liabilities are uninsured, FHC lenders would have to maintain higher ratios of capital to assets than conventional banks to secure prime ratings for their commercial paper issues.[66] In addition, FHC lenders would bid up commercial paper rates to attract funds, particularly from holders of large deposit accounts at commercial banks and thrifts.

Several factors, however, would work in the opposite direction. FHC lending affiliates would not be subject to various regulatory costs that either raise the cost of funds for conventional banks or lower the rates

66. Significantly, large finance companies currently have capital-to-asset ratios in the 13 percent range. See Richard H. Mead and Kathleen A. O'Neil, "The Performance of the Banks' Competitors," in Federal Reserve Bank of New York, *Recent Trends in Commercial Bank Profitability,* p. 315. In contrast, the largest bank holding companies have capital-to-asset ratios of between 6 and 7 percent.

of return on their asset investments. Conventional banks, for example, must set aside noninterest bearing reserves equal to 3 percent of their short-term large CDs that corporate depositors hold, thus raising the marginal cost of funds by roughly 3 percent. At interest rates of 7 percent, the reserve requirement adds approximately 20 basis points to the cost of funds. In addition, conventional banks must pay deposit insurance on domestic deposits, currently equivalent to roughly 8 basis points, and must comply with various restrictions on their lending portfolios. And many banks, including smaller institutions exempted from the separation requirements, would choose to remain as they are, funding their lending activities by insured deposits. These conventional banks would constrain the abilities of FHC lending subsidiaries to charge significantly higher interest rates.

Credit Availability for Small Business. Another concern raised by the FHC proposal is that it might facilitate the diversion of credit from smaller to larger businesses. Larger organizations, such as Citibank or American Express, it may be argued, may choose to engage only in deposit taking in various regions across the country without offering lending services in all of the same locations through affiliated FHC subsidiaries. If diversified firms were to attract deposits away from locally based nondiversified banks and thrifts, smaller businesses that now rely on local institutions for their financing needs may find less credit available.

This concern, however, runs counter to market trends in the banking industry over the last several decades. The largest banking organizations already collect greater deposit sums than they can lend to customers in the states in which they are chartered. For this reason, many of the largest banks have opened loan production offices across the country in search of profitable lending opportunities. The FHC proposal would do nothing to disturb this trend and, indeed, could accelerate it by enhancing competition across all phases of the financial services industry, thus intensifying the search by banks for portfolio lending opportunities.

Moreover, by allowing banking organizations that choose to split their deposit-taking and lending activities to underwrite corporate securities, the FHC proposal should widen financing options for medium-sized companies in particular. Entry of new firms in the corporate securities underwriting business, especially by regional bank holding companies with customer bases of medium-sized companies, should both lower the costs of and increase the opportunities for taking these companies public.

More generally, three features of the FHC proposal advanced here should ameliorate concern about financing opportunities for the smallest of businesses. First, as already discussed, the FHC option would be *voluntary*. Many locally based banking organizations would prefer to stick with what they know best—banking and activities closely related to banking—and thus would continue to service the credit needs of their existing business clientele. Second, the small bank exemption feature of the FHC proposal would permit the smaller depository institutions that may currently pay special attention to the credit needs of small business to compete effectively with the larger diversified financial service firms without being required to operate their depositories as narrow banks. Finally, the proposed transition period for implementing the separation requirements would cushion any disruption in credit flows that might otherwise occur.

Federal Rescues and Financial Instability. Critics of the proposed separation requirements may concede that the requirements would be effective in limiting, perhaps removing, the risk that troubled nonbank enterprises would detract from the safety of their affiliated depositories. In this respect, the proposed FHC structure not only would minimize the safety-related risks of financial product diversification, but it could enhance the safety and soundness of the entire financial system.

Nevertheless, the separation provisions may have potentially important offsetting effects. The essence of the FHC model is to shift lending or credit risks out of insured depositories belonging to highly diversified organizations and into lending affiliates funded by non-insured instruments. If existing banking organizations convert to FHC status, therefore, lending institutions now implicitly (perhaps explicitly) protected by the deposit insurance system would be losing that protection. In particular, if the largest banking organizations that are thought to be "too large to fail" take advantage of the FHC option, their lending operations would no longer be eligible for rescue by the FDIC or the Federal Reserve. Would this ineligibility not increase the risks of financial instability? Perhaps equally important, would federal policymakers so fear the adverse consequences of a failure by a large FHC lender that they would engineer a rescue either through Federal Reserve lending or a congressionally approved bailout plan, as occurred with the federal rescue of Chrysler Corporation in 1980?[67] And if federal bailouts of large

67. The Federal Reserve has the legal authority to advance credit to nonbanking firms and individuals, although such authority has typically not been used since the 1930s.

FHC lenders are inevitable, then what would the proposed separation requirements accomplish?

These are fundamental questions. Answering them requires first a recognition that, for reasons already discussed, financing limitations would allow only the most highly rated banking organizations to convert to FHC status. Bank holding companies with poor credit ratings that seek to separate deposit taking and lending in order to take advantage of the broader activity authority under the FHC structure would find it difficult, if not impossible, to fund their loan portfolios with commercial paper. Market discipline alone, therefore, should minimize the likelihood of failure by FHC lending affiliates. Indeed, the continuing discipline that the commercial paper market exerts against imprudent lending or insufficient loan diversification would give FHC lenders stronger incentives than conventional banks have now, given the presence of deposit insurance, to avoid excessive risk taking in lending activities. Thus large FHC lenders should face a *lower* probability of failure—both at the time of conversion to FHC status and in continuing operations thereafter—than the current probability that federal regulators will need to rescue a large conventional bank.

But how confident can policymakers be that the financial system would be better able to withstand the collapse of a major FHC lender than that of a large conventional bank? Put another way, would the potential ripple effects from the failure of a major FHC lending institution be significantly smaller than those from the failure of a conventional bank of equivalent size?

The answer is complicated because two types of ripple effects are involved. One important risk posed by the failure of any large deposit-based lending institution is the threat of contagion effects—the danger that depositors at *other* banks will run to convert their deposits to currency. Deposit insurance and the Federal Reserve's lender-of-last resort facilities are designed to eliminate the contagion effect. Nevertheless, gaps in the federal safety net may still remain, particularly for large banks. Major depository institutions tend to rely heavily on large uninsured deposit accounts, which the 1984 crisis with Continental Illinois Bank demonstrated can be quickly withdrawn. In addition, the failure of one or more large money center banks could so shatter confidence in the American banking system that even small insured depositors could run, albeit to other banks. The institutions in question may be too large to be absorbed by other banks (which may also be

constrained from undertaking a rescue by state banking laws restricting
or prohibiting interstate takeovers). Depositors wanting quick access to
their funds may thus have incentives to withdraw their accounts immediately rather than to wait for the FDIC to fulfill its insurance obligations.
If confidence in large banks generally were weakened—as federal
regulators who engineered the rescue of Continental Illinois Bank in
1984 feared—then the deposit insurance system could be severely
pressured.[68]

The FHC structure, however, should eliminate risks to the money
supply from contagion effects arising from the failure of nonbank
affiliates. Since FHC lenders would not rely on deposits, they would not
be subject to their creditors' demands for an immediate return of their
funds (with or without penalty). In short, FHC lenders would conceptually be no different from other nondepository firms that can fail without
generating a run on the banking system. When Chrysler was threatened
with failure, for example, there was no suggestion that bank depositors
would run. There is no reason to expect the reaction to be any different
if a major FHC lender were to fail.

To be sure, the threatened failure of a major FHC lender could send
tremors through the commercial paper market—such as occurred when
Penn Central and Chrysler were on the edge of bankruptcy—producing
temporary "spikes" in commercial paper interest rates and, at worst,
temporary interruptions in availability of funds through the commercial
paper market. But these disruptions pale in significance to the heavy
social costs of a generalized bank run. Moreover, those investors who
temporarily move from commercial paper back to insured deposit
accounts at conventional banks would increase the available supply of
loanable funds at those institutions.

The failure of a large FHC lender could also lead to a contraction of
economic activity. If holders of commercial paper or other liabilities
issued by FHC lenders are not able to collect their funds when these
instruments are due, they may be unable to pay suppliers and other third
parties, who in turn may be unable to satisfy other parties, and so on.
The larger the ailing FHC lender in question is, the more significant these
domino effects can be and thus the more likely the Federal Reserve will
be tempted to engineer a rescue.

68. At the time the Continental Illinois Bank was in financial difficulty, federal
regulators were concerned that rumors about the health of Manufacturers Hanover
Bank could have also brought down that bank if Continental were not rescued.

Predicting how the Federal Reserve would react if any specific FHC lender were threatened with failure is impossible. Nevertheless, given the absence of potential contagion effects in the FHC structure, the temptation for monetary authorities to rescue large FHC lenders would be lower than it is to rescue conventional banks of equal size. Recognizing this added uncertainty, FHC lenders would be less tempted than conventional banks now are to take large risks in the hope of large rewards. As already indicated, such action should lower the susceptibility of the financial system as a whole to the kind of crisis that can be precipitated by the threatened failure of a large financial institution.

The "End-Run" Problem. Given the restrictions on asset powers of narrow banks, diversified FHCs may seek to attract short-term funds by issuing uninsured liabilities through their lending subsidiaries. In the limit, these liabilities could be viewed by their holders as the equivalent of demand deposits. As a result, markets in these instruments as well as the institutions that issued them would be susceptible to the equivalent of deposit runs if one of the larger uninsured lenders were threatened with failure.

This susceptibility is a valid concern but one that should not be overstated. Lending affiliates of narrow banks would constantly be required to turn to the securities markets for funds and thus to convince potential purchasers of their uninsured liabilities of the soundness of their institutions. Lenders that relied on high proportions of potentially "hot" short-term instruments would be required by the market to pay higher rates and thus to suffer a funding disadvantage relative to competing (insured) conventional banks. Of course, those lenders with strong capital positions would have greater freedom to issue short-term liabilities, but then their higher capital ratios would provide an extra cushion against loss. As already noted, finance companies that today rely on uninsured sources of funds have significantly higher capital ratios than insured banks. The same would be true of lending affiliates of narrow banks.

Equally important, many individuals and firms would continue to prefer having their transactions balances safely invested with an insured bank (narrow or conventional) rather than in higher yielding short-term uninsured paper. And for those investors who prefer the higher yields, there are safer uninsured alternatives, such as money market mutual funds, than the short-term liabilities that the more illiquid FHC lenders could issue.

Frustration of Monetary Policy. Another important question raised by the proposed FHC structure centers on the effect it would have on the Federal Reserve's conduct of monetary policy. The answer is best illustrated by quickly reviewing the process of money creation.

The money supply, as conventionally measured, consists of both currency and deposits.[69] The Federal Reserve largely controls money creation through its reserve requirement—the fraction of deposits that banks must hold as non-interest bearing reserve in the Federal Reserve banking system—and the level of purchases of securities on the open market. The reserve requirement determines the amount by which any given amount of bank reserves can be multiplied by the private banking system. For example, with a 10 percent reserve requirement, a dollar of bank reserves can be multiplied through the conventional banking system by a process of lending and relending to a maximum of ten dollars.[70] This process can be demonstrated by assuming that banks loan out all excess reserves and that the monetary authorities wish to increase bank reserves by purchasing $1,000 of Treasury securities. For simplicity, further assume that only one private "conventional" bank exists. If the seller of Treasury securities deposits his $1,000 in the conventional bank, that bank will initially hold $100 in reserves and will loan out the remaining $900. The borrower in turn will deposit the $900 in the conventional bank, which after holding $90 in reserves will loan out the remaining $810. As this process continues, total deposits will ultimately expand to $10,000.[71]

Now, suppose that the only bank is a depository within an FHC and that all depositors continue to prefer insured bank deposits to commercial paper issued by the new FHC lending affiliates. Thus with the initial $1,000 deposit by the original seller of the Treasury securities, that bank holds aside $100 and purchases $900 of Treasury securities. The seller of those securities deposits the $900 in the FHC depository, which after holding $90 in reserves purchases $810 of Treasury instruments with the

69. The most commonly used measure of the money supply, "M1," includes currency and all demand deposit equivalents. Other variations of "M" include progressively broader categories of deposits.

70. Since 1983 the reserve requirement applicable to large transactions accounts has been 12 percent; for smaller transactions accounts, time deposits and certificates of deposit held by corporate customers, it has been 3 percent.

71. Formally, the money supply will, at a maximum, be equal to total bank reserves divided by the average reserve requirement.

remaining funds. In the limit, the effect on the money supply is exactly the same as with a conventional bank.[72]

The Federal Reserve's ability to create money may be limited by the total available Treasury securities outstanding not held by narrow banks. If all existing banks and thrifts converted to FHC status, this limitation might be a significant constraint. It would be less significant if smaller depositories were exempted from the separation requirements. Nevertheless, if policymakers observed bank and thrift conversions running at a significant pace, strong consideration could be given to expanding the investment authority of the Federal Reserve.[73]

It is highly unlikely, however, that this last option would be necessary. As already suggested, the market would allow only the most creditworthy existing banks and thrifts to consider adopting the FHC structure. And of those institutions eligible, not all would diversify their activities. Many would prefer to remain as they are, specialists in conventional banking and a few other related activities. Most important, given a ten-year transition period, the markets would have time to absorb the increased demands that new narrow banks would place on the Treasury security markets. Indeed, with current and projected federal budget deficits in the range of $150 billion to $200 billion per year, the supply of available Treasury instruments is expanding far more rapidly than the money supply.

In short, the life of Federal Reserve policymakers could become more complicated with the FHC option in effect. In particular, the Federal Reserve might have less control over the monetary aggregates than it has now. However, considering the recent deemphasis on the aggregates as monetary policy targets, it is doubtful that this reduction in control poses much of a concern.

Insufficient Interest in the FHC Option. Some may fear that conversions to FHC status would be numerous enough to impair the Federal

72. The effects on monetary policy would not be identical if narrow banks were required to hold 100 percent of their deposits as interest bearing reserves with the Federal Reserve System, as Milton Friedman previously proposed in his *Program for Monetary Stability*, p. 69. In that event, the monetary multiplier applicable to narrow banks would fall to one. The economy-wide monetary multiplier would then be computed as the weighted average of the multipliers applicable to conventional banks and to narrow banks, with the weights representing the proportions of the economy's deposits held in the two types of institutions.

73. Milton Friedman offered this last suggestion in his *Program for Monetary Stability*, p. 71.

Reserve's ability to control the economy. Others may claim that the separation requirements would be restrictive enough to keep financial organizations from adopting the FHC option. To be concrete, why would an existing bank currently funding its lending operations with federally insured deposits abandon that advantage for the more expensive FHC lending structure, which permits loans to be funded only with the proceeds of uninsured security issues?

To be sure, many banks—particularly those with limited access to commercial paper or with subpar credit ratings—would not make this choice. For this reason, the FHC proposal would not produce the kind of wholesale conversions that many might fear.

Still, there are good reasons why at least a significant number of existing banking and thrift organizations with the capability to adopt the FHC structure would seriously consider the idea. The FHC option would allow those organizations that take advantage of it to obtain the benefits of portfolio diversification and to cross-sell each of the bank and nonbank services and products that the FHCs could offer. These are the major reasons why banks have sought greater financial product-line freedom. Indeed, a major reason for FHCs to remain in the deposit-taking business is to develop a potential customer base for delivering other financial services. Moreover, while FHC lending affiliates would face higher funding costs than conventional commercial banks, the credit markets have ample room to accommodate the affiliates. The strong success of GE Credit, currently one of the ten largest commercial lenders in the United States, proves that access to insured deposits is not a necessary condition for competing in the commercial lending business. Various consumer finance companies, which also do not rely on insured deposits, have enjoyed similar success.

If the advantages of financial product diversification are potentially significant, then why have not any major banks dropped their commercial bank charters and chosen to operate as nonbank banks (engaged solely in deposit taking or consumer lending or both) or as money market funds? While potentially attractive, the option of downgrading to non-bank bank status has been shrouded in considerable legal uncertainty. As noted in chapter 2, a federal district court in Florida has enjoined the Comptroller of the Currency from issuing new national bank charters to applicants desiring to operate nonbank banks.[74] Most significant, Con-

74. *Independent Bankers Association of America* v. *Comptroller of the Currency,*

gress may soon enact legislation closing the door on the formation of new nonbank banks.

Finally, as the continuing lobbying efforts of the banking industry attest, many bankers apparently hope that Congress will soon relax financial product-line restrictions by amending the Bank Holding Company Act without requiring a separation of deposit-taking and lending activities. As long as separation requirements are not part of the financial product deregulation process, banking and thrift organizations have little incentive to undertake what would be for many a radical, perhaps impossible, restructuring—shedding in a short time tens of billions of dollars of loans to gain additional activity authority.

Conclusion

Although it may take time, liberalization of the current restrictions on financial product-line diversification is inevitable. The invasion into traditional banking activities by other types of organizations will eventually grow to the point where the states and then Congress will attempt to level the playing field. As long as the existing restrictions are properly removed, society will benefit. Financial services should be delivered more cheaply and in a manner more convenient to their users.

The critical policy question, which this book has addressed, is whether policymakers will at the same time act to limit the risks that financial product deregulation could pose. This chapter has outlined two broad and potentially effective approaches for meeting this challenge. The sooner either of these safeguard approaches is in place, the more rapidly the United States can move toward the efficient financial system the nation deserves.

---

no. 84-1404 (D. Fla., February 15, 1985), unpublished opinion. Because many state banking statutes are modeled at least to some degree on the National Bank Act, a decision by the federal courts on the lawfulness of nonbank banks would set an important precedent for determining the legal status of nonbank banks under state banking law.

Distinguishing Benefits of Added Competition from Economies of Scope

THIS APPENDIX briefly distinguishes in graphic form the social gains that may accrue from added competition in the financial services industries from the resource savings that new entrants should be able to realize or produce by offering banking and nonbanking services jointly.

Figure A-1 illustrates the distinction by depicting a market for any financial service where demand declines as price increases (represented by demand curve DD) and where, for simplicity, all existing competitors have constant marginal costs, represented by the line MC_E. If this market were perfectly competitive, prices would equal MC_E, and output OB would be produced or delivered. The market would be imperfectly competitive, however, if suppliers could charge a price P_E exceeding marginal costs without attracting entry and thus limit total output to OA. Under these circumstances, society would gain in two ways from additional competition.

First, if new entrants forced existing competitors to lower their price to MC_E, society would benefit from the additional output AB, valued at the price consumers would pay for it minus the marginal cost of producing it, or the so-called shaded Harberger triangle KNL.[1] To be sure, consumers would benefit from the drop in price that the added competition would make possible. At the imperfectly competitive level of output OA, the price decline, $P_E - MC_E$, would be valued at a sum measured by the rectangle $JMNK$. The added competition would cause these "monopoly rents" previously earned by producers to be trans-

1. The triangle concept is often attributed to Arnold Harberger, who published a comprehensive estimate of the economywide welfare cost of imperfect competition in the 1950s. See Arnold C. Harberger, "Monopoly and Resource Allocation," *American Economic Review*, vol. 44 (May 1954, *Papers and Proceedings, 1953*), pp. 77–78.

Figure A-1. *Benefits of Additional Competition and Lower Cost Entry in an Imperfectly Competitive Market*

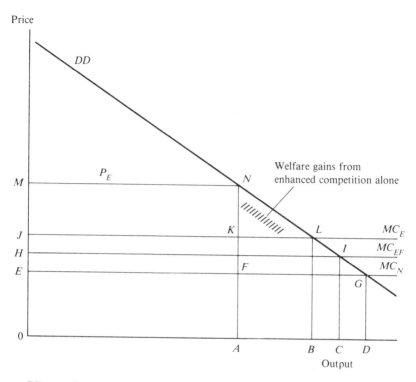

DD = demand curve
MC_E = marginal costs for existing competitors
MC_{EF} = marginal costs for existing competitiors in the absence of X-inefficiency
MC_N = marginal costs for new entrants
P_E = prices charged by existing competition

ferred to consumers, but it would not generate additional resources. Only the *new* output generated by the drop in price would represent a net gain in economic welfare.[2]

2. Some portion of the monopoly rents, however, may be devoted to socially wasteful activities, including lobbying and litigation designed to maintain the imperfect competition that exists and, in particular, to prevent new entrants from competing away those rents. If lower prices associated with larger output reduce or eliminate spending on these wasteful activities, society will benefit. See Richard A. Posner, "The Social Costs of Monopoly and Regulation," *Journal of Political Economy*, vol. 83 (August 1975), pp. 807–28.

Second, new entry could stimulate all market suppliers to be more efficient, lowering marginal costs and prices to MC_{EF} and thereby increasing output and demand to OC. The lower costs would reduce resources required to produce all units demanded and thus would generate additional gains measured by the trapezoidal area $HJLI$.

Finally, new entry may make it possible for firms to realize economies of scope through jointly producing and delivering multiple services or goods. In figure A-1, these potential gains may be illustrated by assuming that producing and delivering a new financial service lowers the marginal costs of providing the original service even further, to MC_N. Lowering marginal costs would stimulate additional demand and output out to OD. The total resource gains—over and above those produced by additional competition alone—can be represented by the trapezoidal area $EHIG$, or the cost reduction per unit (HE) multiplied by the total volume of new output (OD).

Estimating the Reduction in Risk from Financial Product Diversification

CHAPTER 3 presented estimates of reduction in risk that a typical banking orgnization could achieve by diversifying into financial activities that banks or their holding companies are currently prohibited from entering under federal or state law. These estimates were based on profit data reported in the Corporate Source Book of Statistics of Income published annually by the Internal Revenue Service (IRS) and were derived by comparing the mean-variance combination of earnings in commercial banking with an estimated efficient frontier of diversified financial organizations.

This appendix technically describes the computational procedure that was used to estimate the efficient frontier. It also discusses the conditions under which a diversified banking organization may lower its risk of failure but nevertheless move to a higher risk-return position than the one occupied by commercial banking alone. In this connection, it also demonstrates the inverse relationship between the variation in the earnings of an institution and its probability of failure.

Estimating the Efficient Frontier

The computational procedure for estimating the efficient frontier was drawn from Eugene Fama.[1] As outlined by Fama, the efficient frontier represents the set of portfolios that for any given level of earnings minimizes the variance of earnings. Mathematically the minimum variance portfolios can be determined by solving the following constrained minimization problem:

1. *Foundations of Finance: Portfolio Decisions and Securities Prices* (Basic Books, 1976), pp. 260–70.

193

Minimize $\sigma^2 (r_p)$ subject to the constraints:

(1) $$\sum_{i=1}^{n} x_{ip} E(r_i) = E(r_e)$$

(2) $$\sum_{i=1}^{n} x_{ip} = 1.0$$

(3) $$x_{ip} \geq 0,$$

where

r_p = return of the portfolio
r_i = return on the ith security or activity
r_e = target level of earnings
x_{ip} = proportion the ith security or activity represents of the entire portfolio.

Equation 1 states that the weighted sum of the returns on each activity or security must equal the target level of earnings. Equation 2 requires that the proportions of the various securities or activities sum to 1.0. Equation 3 requires that the proportion of the portfolio represented by any security or activity be not less than 0; in practice, this constraint rules out short-selling, which cannot be accomplished by firms desiring to diversify their activities.

The problem just outlined can be solved by forming the following Lagrangian expression:

(4) $$L = \sigma^2 (r_p) + 2\lambda_1 \left[E(r_e) - \sum_{i=1}^{n} x_{ip} E(r_e) \right]$$
$$+ 2\lambda_2 \left[1 - \sum_{i=1}^{n} x_{ip} \right].$$

This expression is minimized by differentiating it for each Lagrangian multiplier ($2\lambda_1$ and $2\lambda_2$) and x_{ip}, $i = 1_1 \ldots u$, and setting each of the resulting partial derivatives equal to 0. For the Lagrangian multipliers, this computation yields constraints 1 and 2 above. But for the x_{ip}, Fama demonstrates that the differentiation yields

(5) $$\sum_{j=1}^{n} x_{je} \sigma_{ij} - a E(r_i) - b = 0, i = 1, \ldots . n,$$

where σ_{ij} is the variance-covariance matrix of the returns of the various securities or activities and $x_{je}, j = i, \ldots u$ are the specific proportions invested in individual securities or activities in the minimum variance portfolio with the target level of return.

In short, the minimization problem reduces to three equations, condition 5 and constraints 1 and 2, which can simultaneously be solved for the proportions of assets in the portfolio invested in each security or activity at each target level of return. Collectively, these equations are as follows:

$$\sum_{j=1}^{n} x_{je}\,\sigma_{ij} - a\,E(r_i) - b = 0$$

$$\sum_{i=1}^{n} x_{ip} = 1$$

$$\Sigma\, x_{ip}\,E(r_i) = E(r_e).$$

Or, in matrix form,

$$\begin{bmatrix} \sigma_{ij} & -E(r_i) & -1 \\ 1 & 0 & 0 \\ E(r_i) & 0 & 0 \end{bmatrix} \times \begin{bmatrix} x_{je} \\ a \\ b \end{bmatrix} = \begin{bmatrix} 0 \\ 1 \\ E(r_e) \end{bmatrix}.$$

This set of equations can be solved simultaneously by using the average returns for the financial activities reported by the IRS [the $E(r_i)$] and the variance-covariance matrix generated by these returns (σ_i). The solutions yield, for different levels of target portfolio earnings [$E(r_e)$], the proportions of the efficient portfolio invested in each financial activity (the x_{je}). The constraint against short positions in activity (equation 3) was satisfied by successively eliminating from the variance-covariance matrix any activities that yielded negative proportions until the final portfolio contained only activities with positive fractions of the portfolio. The variances of the optimal portfolios along the efficient frontier [$\sigma^2(r_e)$] were separately computed, using the investment proportions that emerged from the minimization calculations. As explained in the text, the computer program used to solve the system of simultaneous equations limited the optimization exercise to eleven bank and nonbanking activities reported in the IRS data.

Portfolio Diversification and the Risk of Failure

The discussion of the estimated benefits of diversification in chapter 3 narrowly focused on two extreme measures of the reduction in risk

Figure B-1. *Hypothetical Diversification Opportunities Open to Bank Holding Companies in a Deregulated Environment*

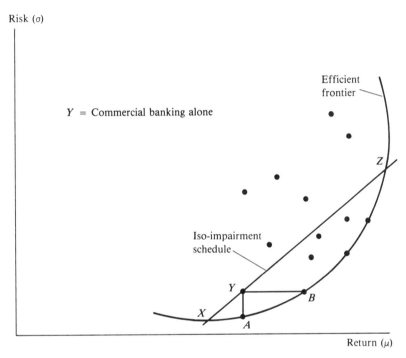

that a banking organization could accomplish by diversifying into non-banking activities. At one extreme, the reduced risk was represented as the lower variance in earnings of the diversified portfolio at the same mean level of earnings in commercial banking alone, or the distance *YA* in figure B-1. At the other extreme, the gains from diversification were stated as the increase in average earnings generated by the portfolio at the same variance of earnings for commercial banking, or the distance *YB* in figure B-1. The figure also highlights that a banking organization that moved to any point between these two extremes, that is, within the area *AYB*, by diversifying its activities would be reducing its risk.

The range of outcomes represented by the area *AYB* in figure B-1 is too restrictive, however. As noted in the text, a banking organization could diversify in a way that increased the variance of its future earnings path *but nevertheless reduced its risk of failure.* This situation could occur if the beneficial effect of the increase in earnings generated by diversification outweighs the adverse effect of the added variance.

Larry Wall and John Boyd and collaborators have outlined a framework that can be adapted to identify where this upper limit of additional variance may lie.[2] In this framework, efficient diversification occurs when a banking organization reduces the probability that it will fail, that is, will have earnings that exhaust stockholders' equity.

In formal terms, the probability that return on equity (ROE) will fall below -1.0, or $P(ROE) < -1$) will equal

$$(6) \qquad P(ROE < -1) = 1 - f[(1 + \mu)/\sigma],$$

where f is the cumulative distribution of a standard normal variable. Wall has shown that the normality assumption can be relaxed so that the expression $(1 + \mu)/\sigma$ represents a distribution-free measure of risk of insolvency.

More simply, Wall's distribution-free risk expression can be stated as μ/σ, or K, the inverse of the coefficient of variation. In essence, K measures the number of standard deviations average earnings stand away from 0 (or -1.0). Clearly, the larger the value of K, the less likely an institution is to fail—under any distribution of failure. Moreover, since any single K corresponds to a specific probability of failure, then each value of K defines an "iso-impairment" schedule of mean-variance points. This schedule may be represented by rearranging the terms of the identity, $K = \mu/\sigma$, as follows:

$$(7) \qquad \sigma = \mu/K$$

Since $1/K$ is the slope of equation 7, a higher level of K (which represents a lower probability of capital impairment) translates into a flatter iso-impairment schedule.

The federal deposit insurance agencies are interested exclusively in the iso-impairment schedule on which the typical bank (Y) lies. The critical question, however, is what level of $1/K$, or risk of failure, the insurance agencies are willing to tolerate. For example, if the agencies wanted banks to have no risk of failure, then K would be infinite, and

---

2. Larry D. Wall, "Has Bank Holding Companies' Diversification Affected Their Risk of Failure?" *Journal of Economics and Business* (forthcoming); and John H. Boyd, Gerald A. Hanweck and Pipat Pithyachariyakul, "Bank Holding Company Diversification," in *Proceedings of a Conference on Bank Structure and Competition* (Federal Reserve Bank of Chicago, 1980), pp. 105–21. See also David R. Meinster and Rodney D. Johnson, "Bank Holding Company Diversification and the Risk of Capital Impairment," *Bell Journal of Economics*, vol. 10 (Autumn 1979), pp. 683–94.

the slope of the iso-impairment schedule would be 0. The schedule itself in that event would be represented in part by the line *YB*.

However, the insurance agencies cannot want banks to have zero risk of failure, since eliminating the risk of failure requires all banks to invest only in short-term Treasury bills. The iso-impairment schedule running through point *Y*, therefore, has some positive slope, as depicted by line *XZ* in figure B-1. Since mean-variance combinations below this line represent higher values of *K*, then any diversification that yields portfolio returns and risks below *XZ* lowers the probability of capital impairment, or equivalently, the probability of failure.

This result is important because it implies that diversified banking organizations that move to points on the efficient frontier above *B* (but below *Z*), or positions with higher earnings variance than displayed by banks alone, can nevertheless reduce their susceptibility to failure. At points on the frontier above *Z*, the diversified organization has moved to a lower level of *K*, and hence a higher risk of failure. These outcomes could arise if banks choose to diversify in ways that increase their risk exposure or because banking organizations may through inexperience produce subaverage returns in the nonbanking activities they enter. Both of these possibilities were explored in chapter 4.

As explained in chapter 3, the estimated efficient frontier calculations used return on asset (ROA) rather than return on equity (ROE) data. The reason was that bank holding companies tend to capitalize their nonbanking subsidiaries differently from independently operated firms. However, prior studies of activity diversification by banking organizations have shown little difference in results between calculations based on returns on assets and those based on returns on equity. Hence, in the financial services context, efficient frontiers estimated on ROA data can be as useful as, if not more useful than, those based on ROE data.

Index

Aetna Life and Casualty Company, 46, 80n, 161
Alaska, 37
Aldrich, Winthrop W., 28
Aluminum Corporation of America, 119
American banks: in colonial times, 10–11; during Depression, 129; federal and state, 19; first banks, 13; and foreign competitors, 56, 125; and foreign markets, 28, 54–55; investment banking, 17n, 56; largest, 162; and market value capitalization, 126. *See also* Banks; Commercial banks; Financial system of the United States; National banks; State banks; Thrifts
American City Bank Trust Co. of Milwaukee, 137n
American Council of Life Insurance (ACLI), 133n
American Express, 79n, 126, 181
Angermueller, Hans H., 166n, 174n
Antitrust regulations, for banks and nonbank combinations, 119, 132, 159–60
Arizona, 57
Armstrong investigation of *1905–06*, 24
Aspinwall, Richard C., 157n
Auerbach, Ronald Paul, 22n, 24n
Avery, Robert B., 156n

Baer, Herbert, 37n, 104n, 128n
Bain, Joe S., 62n
Bank and nonbank activity: restricting mergers, 161; stronger enforcement of, 152–54. *See also* Narrow banks; Nonbank banks
Bankers Trust, 54, 67
Bank failure rate, 17; by chartered banks, 20n; and congressional reluctance to raise FDIC-FSLIC rates, 100; inversely related to bank size, 40–41; and nonbank affiliates, 137
Bank favoritism: to customers of nonbank affiliates, 140–43, 162–64; toward nonbank affiliates, 135–36, 138

Bank holding companies (BHCs): activity diversification by, 60, 103–09; assets of top *10*, 120; challenges to tying regulations, 134; decline in, 29; and diversification, 31–33; financial transactions, 136; freezing of powers, 50; legislation to restrict, 29–30; lending to customers of affiliates, 143; nonbanking activities, 13, 31; power, 2, 159–62
Bank Holding Company Act (BHCA) of *1956*, 30–31, 35, 38, 45, 119, 148n, 167, 178; Congress to loosen restrictions piecemeal, 168; Douglas amendment to, 30; and full service banking offices, 37; and hopes of bankers, 189; interstate banking grandfathered, 36; and nonbank bank loophole, 39; progressive capital requirement as assets increase, 162; and regional banking statutes, 37; tie-ins of services, 131–33
Bank holiday, 11, 25
Banking: combined with nonbanking reduces risk, 89–91; conflicts of interest in, 135–38; and lending operations with federally insured deposits, 140; by nonbanking organizations, 5, 41–49, 74, 89; reform of, 25; regulations, 147; relaxed financial-product restrictions, 104; safety of system, 11, 131; Senate deregulation bill of *1984*, 163; separation from commerce, 4; separation of deposit taking from lending, 6, 20, 68, 166–81. *See also* Banks; Bank holding companies
Banking Act of *1933*, 26, 30
Banking Act of *1982*, 40n
Banking chains, 24–25
Bank of America, 25, 125–26
Bank of England, 13–14
Bank of North America, 14
Bank regulation: bank examiners, 153; circumvention of, 32–33; crumbling of, 33–59; motivation for, 11, 12; nonpublished enforcement actions, 151; secrecy, 151

Banks: acquisition by nonbanks, 113; affiliated with industries, 119; affiliated with retailers, 173; benefits of separation from other financial institutions, 60; board underwriters, 23; capital guidelines by federal agencies, 157; chartering and regulation at federal and state levels, 2, 19, 58, 118–19; clearinghouse function, 11; concentration and economic growth, 125–29; constraints on, 25–33; and development of financial services, 12–25; discount brokerage services, 51; in foreign countries, 56; geographic limits, 1, 38; lending behavior of large banks, 127–28; as life insurance sellers, 72; loans, 89; managers of payment and intermediation, 11; original limited activities, 12; overview, 8–12; production and marketing by, 76; profitability, 48–49; purpose, 1; risks to payments system, 113–18; scale of economies in, 40n; and securities underwriting, 88–89; in service markets, 61n; and share of mortgage and business credit, 41; as special intermediaries, 10. *See also* American banks; Commercial banks; Financial system of the United States; Narrow banks; National banks; Nonbank banks; State banks; Thrifts
Banks and thrifts: asset authority, 173; expansion, 49–59; failures, 2, 5; futures market transactions, 81–82; during high-inflation periods, 33; and IRAs, 43–44; secondary consumer loan market, 82; secondary mortgage market, 82; supervision of, 153
Bank size, 162; economic and political power, 12; and loan production offices, 181; reason for growth of interstate banks, 40
Barnard, Doug, 145
Barney, Chas. D., and Co., 22
Barth, James R., 57n, 102n, 111n, 153n
Baumol, William J., 63n, 147n
Belongia, Michael T., 81n
Beneficial Corporation, 80n
Bennett, Barbara, 171–72n
Bennett, Paul, 155n
Bennett, Veronica, 78n
Benston, George J., 26n, 75n, 104n, 110, 153n
Berger, Allen, 75
Berry, John M., 102n
Beverly Hills Bancorp, 137n
BHCs. *See* Bank Holding Companies

Biddle, Nicholas, 17
Bisenius, Donald J., 102n
Black, Fischer, 146n, 157n
Blanden, Michael, 71n
Blyn, Martin R., 14n, 16n, 19n, 20n
Board of Governors of the Federal Reserve System v. Dimension Financial Corporation et al., 39n
Bogen, Jules I., 17n
Bovenzi, John, 41n, 49n, 153n
Boyd, John H., 40n, 96, 109, 197
Bradburd, Ralph M., 62n
Brenner, Lynn, 72n
Brozen, Yale, 63n
Brumbaugh, R. Dan, Jr., 57n, 102n, 111n
Bryan, Lowell L., 82n
Building and loan associations, 16

Cacace, Michael, 122
California: banking centers, 38; FHLBB rules against investments in, 110; liberal intrastate branching provisions in, 123–24; and regional banking statutes, 37; thrifts invest in real estate, 57
Call reports, 150–51
CAMEL, 152–53
Campbell, Tim S., 10n
Canada: banks in Depression, 129; dropped financial product-line barriers, 55; no limit on geographic range of banks, 129
Capital requirements: for banks, 161–62; for narrow banks, 173–74; and regulatory supervision, 157; tied to interest rate risk, 174
Capital standard: for diversified depository organizations, 157; strengthened or modified, 156–59
Capital value risks, 81
Carosso, Vincent P., 17n
Carron, Andrew S., 47n, 83n
Cash management account, 35
Caves, Richard E., 130n
Certificates of deposit (CDs), 32, 179
Chartering national banks, 2, 20, 188–89.
   See also State banks
Chase Manhattan Bank, 28, 59n, 72, 161
Chase, Salmon P., 21
Chase, Sam, 146n
Checking accounts, 11, 21. *See also* NOW accounts; Super-NOWs
Chessen, James, 172n
Chrysler Corporation, 182, 184
Citibank, 25n, 177, 181
Citicorp, 1, 54, 58n, 71–72, 126, 137

Civil War banking legislation, 20
Clark, Robert Charles, 146n, 149n, 162n
Clayton Act, 119, 132
Cleveland, Harold Van B., 25n
Cobos, Dean, 104n
Comanor, William S., 62n
Commercial banks: assets, 29n, 45; decline as financial intermediary, 45; deposits used for loans, 10; divorced from investment banking, 13, 17–18, 27, 55; dominant financial intermediary in nineteenth century, 18–19; economies in, 75; failure of, 25; history, 13; and loan defaults, 89; portfolios versus nonbanking activities, 95; specialization, 15; and thrift holding companies, 46; as underwriters of municipal bonds, 143n; after World War II, 32
Commercial paper: CD rate of differentials, 179–80; and narrow banks, 171–72
Comptroller of the Currency, 22n; "call reports," 150; capital bank standard, 157, 159; chartered national banks, 20; 1987 ruling on underwriting securities, 54
Computers, 34–35, 70, 77
Congress: and banking industry, 2; and interstate banking, 12; stalemate on expanded bank powers, 50. See also Interstate banking
Consumer banking concept, 172–73
Consumer Federation of America, 72–73n
Contagion effects, 167, 183–84
Continental Illinois Bank, 83, 107, 137, 155n, 183, 184
Continental Illinois holding company, 137
Control Data Corp., 46
Cornyn, Anthony G., 136–37n
Corporate securities, 22n, 68, 69; in Glass-Steagall Act, 76, 89, 150
Corporate separateness: provisions, 149–50; reasons for, 144–48
Corrigan, E. Gerald, 145, 175
Corrigan proposal, 165, 175n
Coulson, Edmund, 151n
Credit allocation: by bank, 12; in banking system, 131; and deposit insurance of banks, 6
Credit availability for small business, 181–82
Credit card: insurance available through, 133n; marketing and interstate banking, 36–37; receivables, 54
Credit unions, 13, 16
Czechoslovakia, 26n

Dai-Ichi Kangyo Bank of Japan, 126
D'Arista, Jane, 161n
Danker, Deborah J., 48n
Data storage and retrieval, 2. See also Computers
Dayton plan, 16
de Jong, H.W., 63n
Demsetz, Harold, 63n
Deposit insurance: and banks gathering large pool of funds, 6; and credit allocation, 6; flat-rate system, 142; moral hazards, 111, 142; and narrow banks, 169–73; premium paid by banks, 100; premium tied to loan risks, 5, 155–57, 170–71; reform, 2; risk-based, 154–56, 158, 159; on state level, 26n
Deposit interest rate, 1, 33, 35, 47
Depository institutions: asset growth in, 82; curbing abuses of affiliates of, 164; development affiliates, 163–64; during high inflation, 33; reducing risk through diversification, 84; soundness, 1, 111–12
Depository Institutions Deregulation and Monetary Control Act, 47n
Depository Institutions Deregulation Committee (DIDC), 35
Deposit taking and lending, as separate operations, 6, 20, 68, 166–81
Depression, The, 1–2, 11, 25–29, 33, 129
Diamond, Douglas W., 11n
"Discover" Card, 47
Diversification of benefits, pair-wise risk comparisons, 84–89
Diversified financial organizations, 80–81; advertising and mailings, 77; and conflicts of interest, 136–37, 162–64; conglomerates, 4, 47; economies of marketing, 77; and favored bank customers, 141
Drexel Burnham Lambert, 46, 70
Dreyfus Corp., 46
Drucker, Peter F., 127n
Dual bank, 20–22
Duffy, John J., 55n
Duschenau, Thomas E., 62n
Dybvig, Philip, 11n

Edge Act corporations, 35
Eisemann, Peter C., 85n, 95, 108–09
Eisenbeis, Robert A., 47n, 87n, 104n, 112, 128n, 133n, 157n
Eisenmenger, Robert, 175n
Estey, Daniel C., 130n
Eurobond market, 55, 67, 143n
Europe, first banks in, 13

Fama, Eugene F., 82n, 193
FDIC. *See* Federal Deposit Insurance
    Corporation
Federal Communications Commission
    (FCC), and AT&T breakup, 146n
Federal deposit insurance, 11–12, 26n, 146
Federal Deposit Insurance Corporation
    (FDIC), 5, 26, 83; capital bank standard,
    157–58; and deposits by narrow banks,
    169; define assets of narrow bank, 173;
    prohibition on state-chartered nonmem-
    ber banks, 164; proposal on enforce-
    ment orders against insured banks, 152;
    rebates by, 100n; regulate narrow
    banks, 152, 177–78; report on risk-based
    insurance, 154; and quick withdrawal
    from failing banks, 183–84; separation
    requirements, on state nonmember
    banks, 149–50; subordinated debt,
    157–58; tying arrangement rulemaking,
    134n
Federal Home Loan Bank Board
    (FHLBB), 38–39, 58; examine thrift in-
    stitutions, 152, 153; regulatory capital of
    thrift institutions, 157n, 159n; risk-based
    insurance, 154; special assessment,
    100n; supervisory approval for direct in-
    vestments, 110; and thrifts, 58n, 159n
Federal Home Loan Bank system, 26n
Federal Housing Administration (FHA),
    170
Federal National Mortgage Association
    (FNMA), 170
Federal rescues of banks, 100-01, 182–85
Federal Reserve, 148; absolute control
    over money supply, 166; bank holding
    companies register with, 29n; broaden
    list of nonbank activities of BHCs,
    50–51; capital bank standard, 157–59,
    162; capital tied to interest rate risk,
    174; and financial holding company op-
    tion, 184–85, 187; investment authority,
    187; membership requirements, 27; and
    monetary policy frustration, 186–87; on-
    line monitoring of securities held by all
    depositories, 175; stands behind FDIC
    and FSLIC, 83; and suit on brokerage
    firm owned by bank, 51; *10* percent mar-
    gin requirement, 33n, 68
Federal Reserve Act of *1913*, 22n, 27;
    amendments to, 163; bank examination
    by, 152; constrains amount lent by
    banks to affiliates, 113, 118; controls
    transactions between banks, 136; cre-
ated Federal Reserve System, 22n; sec-
    tion *23*A, 162
Federal Reserve Bank: of Atlanta, 78; of
    New York, 49n, 77n, 80
Federal Reserve Board: and bank holding
    company legislation, 30; and Glass-
    Steagall barriers, 53–54; 68; monetary
    policy frustration, 186–87; monitors
    nonbank affiliates, 164; monitors inter-
    affiliate transactions, 135; and prohibi-
    tion on nonbank-bank subsidiaries, 162;
    and rescue of FHCs, 184–85; and timing
    of transition of FHCs, 177–78
Federal Savings and Loan Insurance Cor-
    poration (FSLIC), 26, 50, 58, 83, 102,
    111, 136
Federal thrift associations, 47n
Federal Trade Commission (FTC) Act, tie-
    ins of services, 132
FHA. *See* Federal Housing Administra-
    tion
FHCs. *See* Financial holding companies
FHLBB. *See* Federal Home Loan Bank
    Board
Fidelity National Bank of Concord, 39n
Financial assets, aggregate concentration
    of, 124–31
Financial holding companies (FHCs), 165;
    benefits of portfolio diversification, 188;
    depositories, and deposits, 165, 167;
    failure, 183; and Federal Reserve transi-
    tion, 177–78; and investments of deposi-
    tory subsidiaries, 5–6; lenders, 179,
    182–84; and loan extensions, 165; non-
    funding of loans with insured deposits,
    167; options, 176–77, 182, 187–89; regu-
    lation, 177–78; separation requirements,
    166–67
Financial intermediaries, 4; assumption of
    risk by, 9–10, 81; and diversification im-
    portance, 81–84; growth, 19n; interlock-
    ing relationships among, 24
Financial panics, 11
Financial product deregulation, 3; history,
    8–59; and holding company structure, 5;
    legislation, 4, 145, 149n; policy issues,
    2; risks, 99–143; and safety of banking
    system, 4; and size limits, 5
Financial product diversification: advan-
    tages, 188–89; and aggregate concentra-
    tion, 120–25; benefits from, 7, 60–98;
    benefits from competition, 61–74,
    190–92; comprehensive approach to,
    164–89; and economies of scope, 120;

and independent decisionmaking, 129; legislation, 145; and rescuing ailing affiliates, 174; risks and risk reduction, 3, 7, 148–64, 182, 193–98; and unwanted tie-ins, 131–35

Financial product-line barriers: erosion of, 3, 41, 46, 188; restrictions, 6, 133

Financial services firms: attractions to states, 58; diversification and savings in, 76; economies of scope, 6; and GNP, 3; market statistics of, 64; and middle-class growth, 19; and new economic realities, 2; regulatory framework, 4; supermarkets, 60–61, 76–78

Financial system of United States: history, 8–59; risks, 99–118

Fireman's Fund, 79n

First Bank of the United States, 14, 19, 20n, 119

Fischer, Thomas G., 28n, 34n

Fisher, Franklin M., 65–66n

Flannery, Mark J., 12n, 23n, 28n, 29n, 74n, 104n

Florida, 39, 57, 188

FNMA. See Federal National Mortgage Association

Ford Motor Co., 44, 46

Fortner Enterprises, 133n

Franklin National Bank of New York, 83

Free banking act, first, 19, 19–20n

Frieder, Larry A., 37n

Friedman, Milton, 12n, 166, 187n

Friedman, Stephen J., 51n

Friend, Irwin, 22n

Friesen, Connie M., 51n

FSLIC. See Federal Savings and Loan Insurance Corporation

Futures market transactions, of banks and thrifts, 81–82

Galbraith, John Kenneth, 11n, 12n, 20n

Garn, Senator Jake, 50, 160

Garn–St Germain Act of 1982, 35, 38–39, 154

General Accounting Office (GAO), problems of thrift institutions, 102

General Electric (GE) Credit, 44, 188

General Motors, 44

Georgia, 37n

Giddy, Ian H., 89

Gilbert, Gary G., 150n

Gilbert, R. Alton, 34n, 166n

Gilligan, Thomas W., 75n

Glass, Carter, 27

Glass-Steagall Act, 13, 27–29, 51–54, 67n; and advisory service of banks, 70; and corporate securities underwriting, 76, 89, 150; effect on American banks underwriting foreign debt, 55–57; prohibits favoritism, 140; repeal, 60, 68, 70–71

Glassman, Cynthia A., 130n

Goldman Sachs and Co., 22n, 56–57n

Goldsmith, Raymond W., 19n

Golembe, Carter H., 166n

Goodman, Laurie S., 156n

Goudreau, Robert E., 47n

Graham, Stanley L. 40n, 109

Gray, Edwin J., 111n

Greenwood Trust Company of Delaware, 47–48

Gregorash, Sue F., 37n, 128n

Gulf and Western, 46

Gurley, John G., 19n

Haemmerli, Alice, 166n, 167n

Halpert, Stephen, 30n, 119n

Hamilton, Alexander, 119, 130n

Hamilton National Bank of Chattanooga, 137n

Hammond, Bray, 11n, 13n, 14n, 15n

Hanley, Thomas H., 67n, 107n, 121n

Hand, Learned, 119

Hanweck, Gerald A., 75, 96n, 156n, 197n

Harberger, Arnold C., 190n

Heffindahl-Herschman index, 62–63n

Heggestad, Arnold, 85n

Herstatt Bank (Germany), 83

Hester, Donald D., 33n

Holding companies: double leverage of, 87; legislation on, 29–31. See also Financial holding companies; Financial product diversification; Thrift holding companies

Horvitz, Paul M., 77–78n

Household International, 80n

Huertas, Thomas F., 25n, 29n

Humphrey, David, 75

Hutton, E. F., 80n

Independent Bankers Association of America v. Comptroller of the Currency, 39n, 188n

Individual retirement accounts (IRAs), 43–44

Industrial organization economics, 62–63

Insurance: agency system inefficiency, 77; brokers' functions, 9–10; companies, 1–2, 16n, 24, 91; as computer data base,

77; and economy, 78; life insurance sellers, 72; marketing as financial diversification proceeds, 139–40; profitability similar to commercial banking, 72, 74n, 91; regulations, 147; versus state regulation of, 118; underwriters, 5, 16, 74n. *See also* Life Insurance; Mutual insurance companies

Interest: prohibited on demand deposits, 26; rate controls demise, 33–34, 34n; rate risks, 81. *See also* Moral hazards.

International Banking Act of *1978*, 36n

Internal Revenue Service (IRS): corporate income statistics, 85, 193; profit data, 95; study on banks earnings variability, 6–7

International Telephone and Telegraph (ITT), 46

Interstate banking: and bank concentration, 123; barriers to, 2, 12, 50; and credit card marketing, 36–37; eases burden of bank and thrift failures, 38; evolution, 35–41; expansion prohibition, 30; law on, 37; movement, 38; regulation removal, 33–34, 74n

Interstate branching restriction, 23–24

Investment banking: added competition benefits, 68; advisory fees source of in, 70; bankers' compensation, 66; and broader bank participation in, 65–72; imperfect competition in, 65, 66–67; pre–Civil War, 18

Investment: funding by individuals, 8–12; syndicates, 17

IRAs. *See* Individual retirement accounts

James, Bessie R., 25n
James, Marquis, 25n
Japan: banks, 40n, 126–27, 159, competition for Eurobonds, 55; securities business in, 56n; U.S. loses jobs to, 71
Japanese Finance Ministry, 55–56n
Jay, John, 130n
Jefferson, Thomas, 119
Johnson, Rodney D., 87n, 95, 197n
Jones, Rosamund, 126n
Junk bonds, 70

Kane, Edward J., 76n, 152n, 153n
Kaneko, Takashi, 40n
Kareken, John H., 166n
Kelly, Edward J., III, 28n, 140n
Kennedy, Susan, 25n
Kentucky, bank reciprocity law in, 37n
Kidder Peabody and Co., 22n, 44

King, B. Frank, 40n, 124n
Klebaner, Benjamin J., 17n, 22n
Kling, Arnold, 49n
Koehn, Michael, 158n
Konstas, Panos, 157n
Kopcke, Richard, 175n
Krooss, Herman E., 14n, 16n, 19n, 20n
Kuhn, Loeb and Co., 22n
Kuroda, Masahiro, 40n
Kwast, Myron, 156n

Langevoort, Donald C., 70n
Langley, Monica, 153n
Lawrence, Colin, 40n, 75n, 78n
Lawrence, Robert J., 166n
Lehman Brothers, 22n
Leibenstein, Harvey, 62n
Lending: of large banks, 127–28; by nonbanks, 41; rates determined by marginal costs of attracting funds, 179; syndicates, 40n. *See also* Thrifts
Levich, Richard M., 142–43n
Liberty Bonds, 23
Life insurance: industry versus commercial banking, 72; premiums of, 72, 78; in United States, 17
Litan, Robert E., 41n, 85n, 130n, 166n
Loan production offices (LPOs), and interstate banking, 35–36
Loans: as bank's principal assets, 11; extension of, 1; of five-leading lending banks in U.S., 169; through separate corporate affiliates, 6

McCarthy, Ian S., 26n
McCulloch, J. Huston, 170n
McFadden Act of *1927*, 23, 24, 26–27, 30, 35, 38
McFadden, Frank E., 153n
McGowan, John J., 65–66n
McKinsey and Company, 124
McLaughlin, Mary M., 48n
Madison, James, 130n
Maine, 37
Mandell, Lewis, 128n
Manufacturers Hanover Bank, 184n
Marino, James A., 153n
Market value accounting, of banks, 151–52
Markowitz, Harry, 82n
Marr, M. Wayne, 69n
Marshall, William, 75n
Maryland reciprocity law, 37n
Massachusetts: life insurance premiums of state-chartered banks, 78; thrifts and NOW accounts, 34

Mayer, Martin, 118n
Mayne, Lucille S., 104n, 137n
Mead, Richard H., 43n, 51n, 69n, 70n, 72n, 73n, 80n, 103n, 180n
Meehan, James W., 62n
Meinster, David R., 87n, 95, 197n
Mendelsohn, M. S., 55n
Merchants: clubs of, 13; as early insurers, 16
Merger and acquisition: business links prohibited by banks, 70–71, 159–61; financial and nonfinancial, 112–13, 124. *See also* Antitrust regulations for banks, and nonbank combinations
Merrick, John J., 83n
Merrill Lynch, 34, 46, 79, 80n, 161
Michigan, 19, 19–20n
Miller, Ervin, 22n
Miller, Geoffrey P., 37n
Miller, Merton H., 146n, 157n
Mingo, John J., 166n
Money market deposit accounts (MMDAs), 35
Money market funds (MMFs), 34–35, 47
Money market mutual funds (MMMFs), 1, 165
Money supply, 186
Moral hazard: of deposit insurance, 173; of deposit insurance premiums, 84
Morgan, J. P., 54
Morgan Stanley and Co., 22n
Mortgage banking, 41, 103; secondary market, 82
Mortgage-backed securities, 54, 172
Multibank holding companies, prohibition on, 30
Municipal bonds, 28, 54, 68, 89. *See also* Revenue bonds
Mutual funds: and removal of Regulation Q, 38; securities and IRAs, 44
Mutual insurance companies, 16, 147, 165n
Mutual savings banks, origin of, 15–16

Nagle, Reid, 157n
Narrow banks, 6: capital and reserve requirements, 173–74; lending affiliates, 185; as members of the Federal Reserve System, 177, 178; and monetary policy, 186–87; and payments systems risks, 174–75; permissible assets, 169–73
National Bank Act, 20, 31; challenge to nonbank banks, 39; created dual banking system, 21; by Saxon interpretation, 31

National banks, barred from commercial activities, 22n; and corporate underwriting, 22n, 33; examination of, 152; purchased federal securities for investment, 22; restricted to deposit and loan activities, 31
National City Bank, 25
National Conference of State Legislatures, 57
National Currency Act of *1863*, 20
National Steel Corp., 46
Negotiable order of withdrawal. *See* NOW accounts
Nejezchleb, Lynn, 49n
New Jersey, 37n
New York: bank charter in, 14; banking centers in, 38; bank laws restrict banks from securities, 17; capital requirements for bank charters, 19; liberal interstate branching provisions in, 123–23; and life insurance premiums of state-chartered banks, 78; and regional banking statutes, 37; and underwriting permission, 54n
New York City banks, loans and discounts of, 23n
Nonbank banks, 39, 50, 188–89
Nonbanking organizations, entry into banking, 33, 41–49, 74, 89, 112–13, 114–17
Nordhaus, William D., 130n
North Carolina, 37n
North, Douglass C., 24n
Northeast Bancorp, Inc. v. *Board of Governors of the Federal Reserve System*, 37n, 120n
NOW accounts, 34, 35, 47. *See also* Super-NOWs

O'Connell, Joan M., 124n
Ohio, 16, 57
One-bank holding companies, 30–31
O'Neil, Kathleen A., 43n, 51n, 69n, 70n, 72n, 73n, 80n, 103n, 180n
Osborn, Neil, 126n
Over, A. Mead, Jr., 62n

Palmer First National Bank Trust Co. of Sarasota, 137n
Panzar, John C., 63n
Parker Pen Co., 46
Pavel, Christine, 41n, 82n
Peach, W. Nelson, 23n
Pecora, Ferdinand, 27
Pecora hearings, 28, 140–41n
Penn Central, and bankruptcy effect on commercial paper market, 184

Penney Company, J. C., 46
Pennsylvania, bank charter in, 14
Peterson, Bruce, 157n
Peterson, David R., 91, 157n
Pithyachariyakul, Pipat, 96n, 197n
Porter, Michael E., 124n
Portfolio theory, 89–98; 95, 159
Posner, Richard A., 146n, 157n, 191n
Property-casualty insurance underwriting, 73
Proxmire, William, 50
Prudential-Bache Securities, 46, 79–80
Public corporations, borrowing by, 42–43
Pugel, Thomas A., 68n, 69n, 179n
Pujo committee "money trust investigation," 24

Railroad: bonds, 17; financing, 22; influence on banking, 24; property leasing, 87
Ravenscraft, David J., 124n
Reagan administration, 147n; financial institutions deregulation, 145, 146; and financial product deregulation, 4; financial product deregulation bill, 134, 163, 164; and focus of competition in individual markets, 119n; sympathetic to broadened banking powers, 49–50
Real bills doctrine, 14–15
Real estate brokerage affiliates, of depository institutions, 163–64
Real estate investment trusts (REITs), 137
Redlich, Fritz, 17n
Regional banking organizations, 122–24
Regional banking statutes, 37, 39, 57, 110
Regional "super-banks," 38
Regulation Q, 26, 31, 33; and CDs, 32; ceilings on interest rates, 32; and disintermediation of funds, 32; effects of elimination, 34, 48–49; innovation around, 34; removal and competition stimulation, 38
Rehnquist, William, 120n
Revenue bonds, 31, 68. See also Municipal bonds
Rhoades, Stephen A., 74n, 103n, 104n, 124n, 130n
Roosevelt, Franklin D., 11, 25
Rose, John T., 130n, 136n
Rosenblum, Harvey, 41n
Rutz, Roger D., 130n

St Germain, Fernand J., 102n. See also Garn–St Germain Act of 1982
Santomero, Anthony M., 158

Santoni, G. J., 81n
Sauerhaft, Daniel, 57n, 102n, 111n
Saulsbury, Victor L., 37n, 57n, 58n
Saunders, Anthony, 27–28n, 83n, 89
Savage, Donald T., 29n, 124n
Savings and investing, as separate activities, 8–12
Savings and loan associations (S&Ls), 16
Savings and Loan Holding Company Act, 31, 45–46, 58, 79; Amendments, 136, 148n, 162–63
Saxon, James J., 31
Scheld, Karl A., 128n
Scherer, Frederic M., 62n, 63n, 124n
Schmitt, Richard B., 152n
Schwartz, Anna Jacobson, 12n
Schweiker, Richard S., 133n
Schweitzer, Paul R., 133n
Scott, Hal S., 175n
Scott, Kenneth E., 20n, 31n, 148n
Sears, Roebuck and Co., 44, 46, 80n; consumer banking concept of, 172–73; diversified credit card sales, 47
Second Bank of the United States, 14n, 15n, 17, 19, 119
Securities: backed by consumer installment debt, 54; backed by receivables, 170, 172; guaranteed by federal government, 170; regulations on, 147; subsidiary defined, 54; technological changes in market, 69; underwriters, 19, 23–24, 67, 70
Securities Act of 1934, 29, 143
Securities and Exchange Commission: and FHC compliance with disclosures, 178; information about underwriters, 143n; reports, 151; rule 415, 69
Securities brokers: American firms lose jobs to Japan, 71; dealing and trading distinction eliminated, 55; functions, 9; match buyers and sellers, 77
Securities firms: and financial instruments, 2; and removal of Regulation Q, 38
Securities Industries Association, 54
Securities Industries Association v. The Board, 52n
Securities underwriting: banks, 88–89; concentration, 66; placement of federal and state government bonds, 17; prohibition on, 164; state banks, 22–23; versus deposit banking, 27
Security Pacific, 72
Seidman, William, 156
Senate Banking Committee, 50
Shaffer, Sherrill, 40n, 156n

Shaw, Edward S., 19n
Shay, Robert P., 40n, 75n, 78n
Shepherd, William G., 63n
Sherman Antitrust Act of *1890*, 119, 132
Shull, Bernard, 14n, 127–28n
Silber, William L., 68
Silver, Andrew, 48–49n
Simons, Henry C., 166
Small business, 128, 139
Small Business Administration, 127n
Smirlock, Michael L., 75n
Smith, Adam, 14n
Smith, Barney and Co., 22n
South Carolina, 37n
Specialized financial institutions, rise of, 13–19
Spellman, Lewis J., 15n
Sprague, Irvine H., 155n
State banks: advantages, 21; banking statutes in, 21, 189n; bank powers, 34, 57–58; bank regulators, 152; charters, 19, 21, 31, 34, 57–58, 178; depository banks, 2, 23n; extend mortgages or loans secured by real estate, 21; under Federal supervision, 26; liberalization of powers, 57–58; reciprocity among, 37n; and removal of banks' product-line expansion, 34; and rural farmers, 21; and securities underwriting, 22–23; usury ceilings for, 16. *See also individual states*
Stover, Roger D., 85n, 95
Struck, Peter L., 128n
Sumitomo Bank, 56n
Super-NOWs, 35
Supreme Court, U.S., 38
Swartz, Steve, 80n
Symons, Edward L., Jr., 14n, 15n, 17n, 20n, 23n

Talley, Samuel H., 40n, 103n, 136–37n
Tax-exempt securities, 97
Tax reform legislation in *1986*, 130
Technological advances, 3, 8, 24, 33, 34n. *See also* Computers
Texas, and regional banking statutes, 37, 39, 57, 110
Thompson, G. Rodney, 69n
Thrift holding companies (THCs), 45–46, 58, 109–11
Thrifts: affiliate trading prohibition, 162; asset diversification risk moderating, 110; chartering, 2; deposits used for loans in, 10; direct investments, 110; examination, 152; expansion authority, 39;

failures and direct investment losses 111; and holding companies, 45–46; and industry problems, 102; institutions of, 1; interstate expansion authority for, 39; lending practices, 41, 47; and risk shifting, 81; and thrift holding companies, 109–11
Times-Picayune Publishing Co. v. United States, 132
Tobin, James, 166n
Toumey, Donald J., 57n
Transamerica, 25, 30, 46, 80n
Transfers of bank credit to nonbank affiliates, 174–75
Treasury, Department of the, 83, 165, 187; securities, 169, 177
Trust companies, 22
Tucker, George, 14n
Tying arrangements. *See* Bank holding companies; Financial product diversification

U.S. Steel Corporation, 133n
U.S. Steel Corp. v. Fortner Enterprises, Inc., 132n
United Kingdom, 55, 71, 159n
United States Bank of Pennsylvania, 17
United States v. Aluminum Co. of America, 119n

Volcker, Paul A., 51n, 124n

Waage, Donn, 146n
Walker, Charls E., 119n
Wall, Larry D., 48n, 87n, 91n, 105n, 108, 112n, 136n, 157n, 176n, 197
Wallich, Henry C., 166n
Wallison, Peter J., 57n, 146n
Walter, Ingo, 23n, 28n, 68n, 89n, 140n, 179n
Weatherstone, Dennis, 42n
Weiner, Steve, 80n
White, James J., 14n, 17n, 20n, 23n
White, Lawrence J., 68n, 69n, 179n
Whitehead, David D., 35–36n
Willig, Robert D., 63n, 147n
Willis, H. Parker, 17n
Witcher, S. Karene, 152n
Wojnilower, Albert M., 26n, 82n
Wriston, Walter B., 1, 137

Yingling, Edward, 73n

"Zaibatsu" arrangements between banks and industry, 119
Zweig, Phillip, 67n, 68n